Flash Boys

Flash Boys

Cracking the Money Code

MICHAEL LEWIS

ALLEN LANE
an imprint of
PENGUIN BOOKS

ALLEN LANE

Published by the Penguin Group
Penguin Books Ltd, 80 Strand, London WC2R 0RL, England
Penguin Group (USA) Inc., 375 Hudson Street, New York, New York 10014, USA
Penguin Group (Canada), 90 Eglinton Avenue East, Suite 700, Toronto, Ontario, Canada M4P 2Y3
(a division of Pearson Penguin Canada Inc.)
Penguin Ireland, 25 St Stephen's Green, Dublin 2, Ireland (a division of Penguin Books Ltd)
Penguin Group (Australia), 707 Collins Street, Melbourne, Victoria 3008, Australia
(a division of Pearson Australia Group Pty Ltd)
Penguin Books India Pvt Ltd, 11 Community Centre, Panchsheel Park, New Delhi – 110 017, India
Penguin Group (NZ), 67 Apollo Drive, Rosedale, Auckland 0632, New Zealand
(a division of Pearson New Zealand Ltd)
Penguin Books (South Africa) (Pty) Ltd, Block D, Rosebank Office Park,
181 Jan Smuts Avenue, Parktown North, Gauteng 2193, South Africa

Penguin Books Ltd, Registered Offices: 80 Strand, London WC2R 0RL, England

www.penguin.com

First published in the United States of America by W. W. Norton & Company 2014
First published in Great Britain by Allen Lane 2014
005

Copyright © Michael Lewis, 2014

The moral right of the author has been asserted

Printed in Great Britain by Clays Ltd, St Ives plc

A CIP catalogue record for this book is available from the British Library

Hardback ISBN: 978–0–241–00363–3

www.greenpenguin.co.uk

FOR JIM PASTORIZA

WHO HAS NEVER MISSED AN ADVENTURE

A man got to have a code.

—*Omar Little*

CONTENTS

FLASH
BOYS

WINDOWS
ON THE WORLD

I suppose this book started when I first heard the story of Sergey Aleynikov, the Russian computer programmer who had worked for Goldman Sachs and then, in the summer of 2009, after he'd quit his job, was arrested by the FBI and charged by the United States government with stealing Goldman Sachs's computer code. I'd thought it strange, after the financial crisis, in which Goldman had played such an important role, that the only Goldman Sachs employee who had been charged with any sort of crime was the employee who had taken something from Goldman Sachs. I'd thought it even stranger that government prosecutors had argued that the Russian shouldn't be freed on bail because the Goldman Sachs computer code, in the wrong hands, could be used to "manipulate markets in unfair ways." (Goldman's were the right hands? If Goldman Sachs was able to manipulate markets, could other banks do it, too?) But maybe the strangest aspect of the case was how difficult it appeared to be—for the few who attempted—to explain what the Russian had done. I don't mean only what he had done wrong: I mean what he had done. His job. He was usually described as a "high-frequency trading programmer," but that wasn't an explanation. That was a term of art that, in the summer of 2009, most people, even on Wall Street, had never before heard. What was high-frequency trading? Why was the code that enabled Goldman Sachs to do it so important that, when it was discovered to have been copied by some employee, Goldman Sachs needed to call the FBI? If this code was at once so incredibly valuable and so dangerous to financial markets, how did a Russian who had worked for Goldman Sachs for a mere two years get his hands on it?

At some point I went looking for someone who might answer those questions. My search ended in a room looking out at the World Trade Center site, at One Liberty Plaza. In this room were gathered a small army of shockingly well-informed people from every corner of Wall Street—big banks, the major stock exchanges, and high-frequency trading firms. Many of them had left high-paying jobs to declare war on Wall Street, which meant, among other things, attacking the very problem that the Russian computer programmer had been hired by Goldman Sachs to create. In the bargain they'd become experts on the questions I sought answers to, along with a lot of other questions I hadn't thought to ask. These, it turned out, were far more interesting than I expected them to be.

I didn't start out with much interest in the stock market—though, like most people, I enjoy watching it go boom and crash. When it crashed on October 19, 1987, I happened to be hovering around the fortieth floor of One New York Plaza, the stock market trading and sales department of my then employer, Salomon Brothers. *That* was interesting. If you ever needed proof that even

Wall Street insiders have no idea what's going to happen next on Wall Street, there it was. One moment all is well; the next, the value of the entire U.S. stock market has fallen 22.61 percent, and no one knows why. During the crash, some Wall Street brokers, to avoid the orders their customers wanted to place to sell stocks, simply declined to pick up their phones. It wasn't the first time that Wall Street people had discredited themselves, but this time the authorities responded by changing the rules—making it easier for computers to do the jobs done by those imperfect people. The 1987 stock market crash set in motion a process—weak at first, stronger over the years—that has ended with computers entirely replacing the people.

Over the past decade, the financial markets have changed too rapidly for our mental picture of them to remain true to life. The picture I'll bet most people have of the markets is still a picture a human being might have taken. In it, a ticker tape runs across the bottom of some cable TV screen, and alpha males in color-coded jackets stand in trading pits, hollering at each other. That picture is dated; the world it depicts is dead. Since about 2007, there have been no thick-necked guys in color-coded jackets standing in trading pits; or, if they are, they're pointless. There are still some human beings working on the floor of the New York Stock Exchange and the various Chicago exchanges, but they no longer preside over any financial market or have a privileged view inside those markets. The U.S. stock market now trades inside black boxes, in heavily guarded buildings in New Jersey and Chicago. What goes on inside those black boxes is hard to say—the ticker tape that runs across the bottom of cable TV screens captures only the tiniest fraction of what occurs in the stock markets. The public reports of what happens inside the black boxes are fuzzy and unreliable—even an expert cannot say what exactly happens

inside them, or when it happens, or why. The average investor has
no hope of knowing, of course, even the little he needs to know.
He logs onto his TD Ameritrade or E★Trade or Schwab account,
enters a ticker symbol of some stock, and clicks an icon that says
"Buy": Then what? He may think he knows what happens after
he presses the key on his computer keyboard, but, trust me, he
does not. If he did, he'd think twice before he pressed it.

The world clings to its old mental picture of the stock market
because it's comforting; because it's so hard to draw a picture of
what has replaced it; and because the few people able to draw it
for you have no interest in doing so. This book is an attempt to
draw that picture. The picture is built up from a bunch of smaller
pictures—of post-crisis Wall Street; of new kinds of financial
cleverness; of computers, programmed to behave impersonally in
ways that the programmer himself would never do personally; of
people, coming to Wall Street with one idea of what makes the
place tick only to find that it ticks rather differently than they had
supposed. One of these people—a Canadian, of all things—stands
at the picture's center, organizing the many smaller pictures into
a coherent whole. His willingness to throw open a window on
the American financial world, and to show people what it has
become, still takes my breath away.

As does the Goldman high-frequency trading programmer
arrested for stealing Goldman's computer code. When he worked
for Goldman Sachs, Sergey Aleynikov had a desk on the forty-
second floor of One New York Plaza, the site of the old Salomon
Brothers trading floor, two floors above the place I'd once watched
the stock market crash. He hadn't been any more interested in
staying in that building than I had been and, in the summer of
2009, had left to seek his fortune elsewhere. On July 3, 2009, he
was on a flight from Chicago to Newark, New Jersey, blissfully

unaware of his place in the world. He had no way of knowing what was about to happen to him when he landed. Then again, he had no idea how high the stakes had become in the financial game he'd been helping Goldman Sachs to play. Oddly enough, to see the magnitude of those stakes, he had only to look out the window of his airplane, down on the American landscape below.

CHAPTER ONE

HIDDEN IN PLAIN SIGHT

B y the summer of 2009 the line had a life of its own, and two thousand men were digging and boring the strange home it needed to survive. Two hundred and five crews of eight men each, plus assorted advisors and inspectors, were now rising early to figure out how to blast a hole through some innocent mountain, or tunnel under some riverbed, or dig a trench beside a country road that lacked a roadside—all without ever answering the obvious question: *Why?* The line was just a one-and-a-half-inch-wide hard black plastic tube designed to shelter four hundred hair-thin strands of glass, but it already had the feeling of a living creature, a subterranean reptile, with its peculiar needs and wants. It needed its burrow to be straight, maybe the most insistently straight path ever dug into the earth. It needed to connect a data center on the South Side of Chicago* to a stock exchange in northern New Jersey. Above all, apparently, it needed to be a secret.

---

* The principal data center was later moved to Aurora, Illinois, outside Chicago.

The workers were told only what they needed to know. They tunneled in small groups apart from each other, with only a local sense of where the line was coming from or where it was going to. They were specifically not told of the line's purpose— to make sure they didn't reveal that purpose to others. "All the time, people are asking us, 'Is this top secret? Is it the government?' I just said, 'Yeah,'" said one worker. The workers might not have known what the line was for, but they knew that it had enemies: They all knew to be alert to potential threats. If they saw anyone digging near the line, for instance, or noticed anyone asking a lot of questions about it, they were to report what they'd seen immediately to the head office. Otherwise they were to say as little as possible. If people asked them what they were doing, they were to say, "Just laying fiber." That usually ended the conversation, but if it didn't, it didn't really matter. The construction crews were as bewildered as anyone. They were used to digging tunnels that connected cities to other cities, and people to other people. This line didn't connect anyone to anyone else. Its sole purpose, as far as they could see, was to be as straight as possible, even if that meant they had to rocksaw through a mountain rather than take the obvious way around it. *Why?*

Right up until the end, most workers didn't even ask the question. The country was flirting with another depression and they were just happy for the work. As Dan Spivey said, "No one knew why. People began to make their reasons up."

Spivey was the closest thing the workers had to an explanation for the line, or the bed they were digging for it. And Spivey was by nature tight-lipped, one of those circumspect southerners with more thoughts than he cared to share. He'd been born and raised in Jackson, Mississippi, and, on those rare occasions he spoke, he sounded as if he'd never left. He'd just turned forty but was still as lean as a teenager, with the face of a Walker Evans tenant farmer. After some unsatisfying years working as a stockbroker in Jackson he'd quit, as he put it, "to do something more sporting." That turned out to be renting a seat on the Chicago Board Options Exchange and making markets for his own account. Like every other trader on the Chicago exchanges, he saw how much money could be made trading futures contracts in Chicago against the present prices of the individual stocks trading in New York and New Jersey. Every day there were thousands of moments when the prices were out of whack—when, for instance you could sell the futures contract for more than the price of the stocks that comprised it. To capture the profits, you had to be fast to both markets at once. What was meant by "fast" was changing rapidly. In the old days—before, say, 2007—the speed with which a trader could execute had human limits. Human beings worked on the floors of the exchanges, and if you wanted to buy or sell anything you had to pass through them. The exchanges, by 2007, were simply stacks of computers in data centers. The speed with which trades occurred on them was no longer constrained by people. The only constraint was how fast an electronic signal could travel between Chicago and New York—or, more precisely, between the data center in Chicago that housed the Chicago Mercantile Exchange and a data center beside the Nasdaq's stock exchange in Carteret, New Jersey.

What Spivey had realized, by 2008, was that there was a big difference between the trading speed that was available between these exchanges and the trading speed that was theoretically possible. Given the speed of light in fiber, it should have been possible for a trader who needed to trade in both places at once to send his order from Chicago to New York and back in roughly 12 milliseconds, or roughly a tenth of the time it takes you to blink your eyes, if you blink as fast as you can. (A millisecond is one thousandth of a second.) The routes offered by the various telecom carriers—Verizon, AT&T, Level 3, and so on—were slower than that, and inconsistent. One day it took them 17 milliseconds to send an order to both data centers; the next, it took them 16 milliseconds. By accident, some traders had stumbled across a route controlled by Verizon that took 14.65 milliseconds. "The Gold Route," the traders called it, because on the occasions you happened to find yourself on it you were the first to exploit the discrepancies between prices in Chicago and prices in New York. Incredibly to Spivey, the telecom carriers were not set up to understand the new demand for speed. Not only did Verizon fail to see that it could sell its special route to traders for a fortune; Verizon didn't even seem aware it owned anything of special value. "You would have to order up several lines and hope that you got it," says Spivey. "They didn't know what they had." As late as 2008, major telecom carriers were unaware that the financial markets had changed, radically, the value of a millisecond.

Upon closer investigation, Spivey saw why. He went to Washington, DC, and got his hands on the maps of the existing fiber cable routes running from Chicago to New York. They mostly followed the railroads and traveled from big city to big city. Leaving New York and Chicago, they ran fairly straight toward each other, but when they reached Pennsylvania they began to wiggle and bend. Spivey studied a map of Pennsylvania and saw the main problem: the Allegheny Mountains. The only straight line running through the Alleghenies was the interstate highway, and there was a law against laying fiber along the interstate highway. The other roads and railroads zigzagged across the state as the landscape permitted. Spivey found a more detailed map of Pennsylvania and drew his own line across it. "The straightest path allowed by law," he liked to call it. By using small paved roads and dirt roads and bridges and railroads, along with the occasional private parking lot or front yard or cornfield, he could cut more than a hundred miles off the distance traveled by the telecom carriers. What was to become Spivey's plan, then his obsession, began with an innocent thought: I'd like to see how much faster someone would be if they did this.

In late 2008, with the global financial system in turmoil, Spivey traveled to Pennsylvania and found a construction guy to drive him the length of his idealized route. For two days they rose together at five in the morning and drove until seven at night. "What you see when you do this," says Spivey, "is very small towns, and very tiny roads with cliffs on one side and a sheer rock wall on the other." The railroads traveling east to west tended to tack north and south to avoid the mountains: They were of limited use. "Anything that wasn't absolutely east-west that had any kind of curve in it I didn't like," Spivey said. Small country roads were better for his purposes, but so tightly squeezed into the rough terrain that there was no place to lay the fiber but under the road. "You'd have to close the road to dig up the road," he said.

The construction guy with him clearly suspected he might be out of his mind. Yet when Spivey pressed him, even he couldn't come up with a reason why the plan wasn't at least theoretically possible. That's what Spivey had been after: a reason not to do it. "I was just trying to find the reason no [telecom] carrier had done it," he says. "I was thinking: Surely I'll see some road-block." Aside from the construction engineer's opinion that no one in his right mind wanted to cut through the hard Allegheny rock, he couldn't find one.

That's when, as he puts it, "I decided to cross the line." The line separated Wall Street guys who traded options on Chicago exchanges from people who worked in the county agencies and Department of Transportation offices that controlled public rights-of-way through which a private citizen might dig a secret tunnel. He sought answers to questions: What were the rules about laying fiber-optic cable? Whose permission did you need? The line also separated Wall Street people from people who knew how to dig holes and lay fiber. How long would it take? How many yards a day might a crew with the right equipment tunnel through rock? What kind of equipment was required? What might it cost?

Soon a construction engineer named Steve Williams, who lived in Austin, Texas, received an unexpected call. As Williams recalls, "It was from a friend of mine. He said, 'I have an old friend whose cousin is in trouble, and he has some construction questions he needs answers to.'" Spivey himself then called. "This guy gets on the phone," recalls Williams, "and is asking questions about case sizes, and what kind of fiber you use, and how would you dig in this ground and under this river." A few months later Spivey called him again—to ask him if he would supervise the laying of a fifty-mile stretch of fiber, starting in Cleveland. "I didn't know what I was getting into," said Williams. Spivey told him nothing more about the project than what he needed to know to lay a single fifty-mile stretch of cable. In between, Spivey had persuaded Jim Barskdale, the former CEO of Netscape Communications and a fellow native of Jackson, to fund what Spivey estimated to be a $300 million tunnel. They named the company Spread Networks, though they disguised the construction behind shell companies with dull names like Northeastern ITS and Job 8. Jim Barksdale's son, David Barksdale, came on board—to cut, as quietly as possible, the four hundred or so deals they needed to cut with townships and counties in order to be able to tunnel through them. Williams then proved so adept at getting the line into the ground that Spivey and Barksdale called and asked him to take over the entire project. "That's when they said, 'Hey, this is going all the way to New Jersey,'" Williams said.

Leaving Chicago, the crews had raced across Indiana and Ohio. On a good day they were able to lay two to three miles of the line in the ground. When they arrived in western Pennsylvania they hit the rock and the pace slowed, sometimes to a few hundred feet a day. "They call it blue rock," says Williams. "It's hard limestone. And it's a challenge to get through." He found himself having the same conversation, over and over again, with Pennsylvania construction crews. "I'd explain to them that we need to go through some mountain, and one after another they would say, 'That's crazy.' And I would say, 'I know that's crazy, but that's how we're doing it.' And they would ask, 'Why?' And I'd say, 'It's more of a customized route to the owner's wishes.'" To which they really didn't have much to say except, "Oh." His other problem was Spivey, who was all over him about the slightest detours. For instance, every so often the right-of-way crossed over from one side of the road to the other, and the line needed to cross the road within its boundaries. These constant road crossings irritated Spivey—Williams was making sharp right and left turns. "Steve, you're costing me a hundred nanoseconds," he'd say. (A nanosecond is one billionth of one second.) And: "Can you at least cross it *diagonally*?"

Spivey was a worrier. He thought that when a person took risks, the thing that went wrong was usually a thing the person hadn't thought about, and so he tried to think about the things he wouldn't naturally think about. The Chicago Mercantile Exchange might close and move to New Jersey. The Calumet River might prove impassable. Some company with deep pockets—a big Wall Street bank, a telecom carrier—might discover what he was doing and do it themselves. That last fear—that someone else was already out there, digging his own straight tunnel—consumed him. Every construction person he talked to thought he was out of his mind, and yet he was sure the Alleghenies were crawling with people who shared his obsession. "When something becomes obvious to you," he said, "you immediately think surely someone else is doing this."

What never crossed his mind was that, once his line was finished, Wall Street would not want to buy the line. Just the reverse: He assumed that the line would be the site of a gold rush. Maybe for that reason, he and his backers hadn't thought much about how to sell the line until the time came to do it. It was complicated. What they were selling—speed—was only valuable to the extent that it was scarce. What they did not know was the degree of scarcity that would maximize the line's market value. How much was it worth to a single player in the U.S. stock market to have an advantage in speed over everyone else? How much to twenty-five different players—to share the same advantage over the rest of the market? To answer these sorts of questions, it helps to know how much money traders can make purely from speed in the U.S. stock market, and how, exactly, they make it. "No one knew this market," says Spivey. "It was opaque."

They considered holding a Dutch auction—that is, start at some high reserve price and lower it until the line was bought by a single Wall Street firm, which would then enjoy a monopoly. They weren't confident that any one bank or hedge fund would fork over the many billions of dollars they assumed the monopoly was worth, and they didn't like the sound of the inevitable headlines in the newspapers: Barksdale Makes Billions Selling Out Ordinary American Investor. They hired an industry consultant named Larry Tabb, who had caught Jim Barksdale's attention with a paper he'd written called "The Value of a Millisecond." One way to price access to the line, Tabb thought, was to figure out how much money might be made from it, from the so-called spread trade between New York and Chicago—the simple arbitrage between cash and futures. Tabb estimated that if a single Wall Street bank were to exploit the countless minuscule discrepancies in price between Thing A in Chicago and Thing A in New York, they'd make profits of $20 billion a year. He further estimated that there were as many as four hundred firms then vying to capture the $20 billion. All of them would need to be on the fastest line between the two cities—and there were only places for two hundred of them on the line.

Both estimates happily coincided with Spivey's sense of the market, and he took to saying, with obvious pleasure, "We have two hundred shovels for four hundred ditch diggers." But what to charge for each shovel? "It was really a total wet finger in the air," says Brennan Carley, who had worked closely with a lot of high-speed traders, and who had been hired by Spivey to sell his network to them. "All of us were just guessing." The number they came up with was $300,000 a month, roughly ten times the price of the existing telecom lines. The first two hundred stock market players willing to pay in advance and sign a five-year lease would get a deal: $10.6 million for five years. The traders who leased Spread's line would also need to buy and maintain their own signal amplifiers, housed in thirteen amp sites along Spread's route. All-in, the up-front cost to each of the two hundred traders would come to about $14 million, or a grand total of $2.8 billion.

By early 2010 Spread Networks still hadn't informed a single prospective customer of their existence. A year after the workers had started digging, the line was, incredibly, still a secret. To maximize the line's shock value and minimize the chance that someone else would seek to replicate what they had done, or even announce their intention to do so, they decided to wait until March 2010, three months before the line was due to be completed, before they tried to sell it. How to approach the rich and powerful men whose businesses they were about to disrupt? "The general modus operandi was to find someone at one of these firms one of us knew," says Brennan Carley. "We'd say, 'You know me. You know of Jim Barksdale. We have something we want to come over and talk to you about. We can't tell you what it is until we get there. And, by the way, we want you to sign an NDA [non-disclosure agreement] before we come in.'"

That's how they went to Wall Street—in stealth. "There were CEOs at every meeting," says Spivey. The men with whom they met were among the most highly paid people in the financial markets. The first reaction of most of them was total disbelief. "People told me later that they thought, Surely not, but let's talk to him anyway," says Spivey. Anticipating their skepticism, he carried with him a map, four feet by eight feet. He finger-walked them through his cross-country tunnel. Even then people still demanded proof. You couldn't actually see a fiber-optic line buried three feet under the ground, but the amp sites were highly visible thousand-square-foot concrete bunkers. Light fades as it travels; the fainter it becomes, the less capable it is of transmitting data. The signals transmitted from Chicago to New Jersey needed to be amplified every fifty to seventy-five miles, and for the amplifiers that did the work, Spread had built these maximum-security bunkers along the route. "I know you guys are straight shooters," one trader said to them. "But I never heard of you before. I want to see a *picture* of this place." Every day for the next three months, Spivey emailed this man a photograph of the most recent amp site under construction to show him that it was actually being built.

Once their disbelief faded, most of the Wall Street guys were just in awe. Of course they all still asked the usual questions. *What do I get for my $14 million in assorted fees and expenses?* (Two glass fibers, one for each direction.) *What happens if the line's cut by a backhoe?* (We have people on the line who will have it up and running in eight hours.) *Where is the backup if your line goes down?* (Sorry, there isn't one.) *When can you supply us with the five years of audited financial statements that we require before we do business with any firm?* (Um, in five years.) But even as they asked their questions and ticked their boxes, they failed to disguise their wonder. Spivey's favorite meeting was with a trader who sat stone-faced listening to him for fifteen minutes on the other side of a long conference table, then leapt to his feet and shouted, "SHIT, THIS IS COOL!"

In these meetings what didn't get said was often as interesting as what did. The financial markets were changing in ways even professionals did not fully understand. Their new ability to move at computer, rather than human, speed had given rise to a new class of Wall Street traders, engaged in new kinds of trading. People and firms no one had ever heard of were getting very rich very quickly without having to explain who they were or how they were making their money: These people were Spread Networks' target audience. Spivey actually didn't care to pry into their warring trading strategies. "We never wanted to come across as if we knew how they were making money on this," he said. He didn't ask, they didn't say. But the response of many of them suggested that their entire commercial existence depended on being faster than the rest of the stock market—and that whatever they were doing wasn't as simple as the age-old cash to futures arbitrage. Some of them, as Brennan Carley put it, "would sell their grandmothers for a microsecond." (A microsecond is one millionth of a second.) Exactly why speed was so important to them was not clear; what was clear was that they felt threatened by this faster new line. "Somebody would say, 'Wait a second,'" recalls Carley. "'If we want to continue with the strategies we are currently running, we have to be on this line. We have no choice but to pay whatever you're asking. And you're going to go from my office to talk to all of my competitors.'"

"I'll tell you my reaction to them," says Darren Mulholland, a principal at a high-speed trading firm called Hudson River Trading. "It was, 'Get out of my office.' The thing I couldn't believe was that when they came to my office they were going to go live in a month. And they didn't even know who the clients were! They only discovered us from reading a letter we'd written to the SEC. . . .Who takes those kinds of business risks?"

For $300,000 a month plus a few million more in up-front expenses, the people on Wall Street then making perhaps more money than people have ever made on Wall Street would enjoy the right to continue doing what they were already doing. "At that point they'd get kind of pissed off," says Carley. After one sales meeting, David Barksdale turned to Spivey and said, *Those people hate us.* Oddly enough, Spivey loved these hostile encounters. "It was good to have twelve guys on the other side of the table, and they are all mad at you," he said. "A dozen people told us only four guys would buy it, and they all bought it." (Hudson River Trading bought the line.) Brennan Carley said, "We used to say, 'We can't take Dan to this meeting, because even if they have no choice, people do not want to do business with people they're angry with.'"

When the salesmen from Spread Networks moved from the smaller, lesser-known Wall Street firms to the big banks, the view inside the post-crisis financial world became even more intriguing. Citigroup, weirdly, insisted that Spread reroute the line from the building next to the Nasdaq in Carteret to their offices in lower Manhattan, the twists and turns of which added several milliseconds and defeated the line's entire purpose. The other banks all grasped the point of the line but were given pause by the contract Spread required them to sign. This contract prohibited anyone who leased the line from allowing others to use it. Any big bank that leased a place on the line could use it for its own proprietary trading but was forbidden from sharing it with its brokerage customers. To Spread this seemed an obvious restriction: The line was more valuable the fewer people that had access to it. The whole point of the line was to create inside the public markets a private space, accessible only to those willing to pay the tens of millions of dollars in entry fees. "Credit Suisse was outraged," says a Spread employee who negotiated with the big Wall Street banks. "They said, 'You're enabling people to screw their customers.'" The employee tried to argue that this was not true—that it was more complicated than that—but in the end Credit Suisse refused to sign the contract. Morgan Stanley, on the other hand, came back to Spread and said, *We need you to change the language.* "We say, 'But you're okay with the restrictions?' And they say, 'Absolutely, this is totally about optics.' We had to wordsmith it so they had plausible deniability." Morgan Stanley wanted to be able to trade for itself in a way it could not trade for its customers; it just didn't want to seem as if it wanted to. Of all the big Wall Street banks, Goldman Sachs was the easiest to deal with. "Goldman had no problem signing it," the Spread employee said.

It was at just this moment—as the biggest Wall Street banks were leaping onto the line—that the line stopped in its tracks.

There'd been challenges all along the route. After leaving Chicago they had tried and failed six times to tunnel 120 feet under the Calumet River. They were about to give up and find a slower way around when they stumbled upon a century-old tunnel that hadn't been used in forty years. The first amp site after leaving Carteret was supposed to be near a mall in Alpha, New Jersey. The guy who owned the land said no. "He said he knew it was going to be some kind of terrorist target and he didn't want it in the neighborhood," said Spivey. "There's always little gotchas out there that you have to be careful of."

Pennsylvania had proved even more difficult than Spivey had imagined. Coming from the east, the line ran to a small forest in Sunbury, just off the east bank of the Susquehanna River, where it stopped and waited for its western twin. The line coming from the west needed to cross the Susquehanna. That stretch of river was breathtakingly wide. There was one drill in the world—it would cost them $2 million to rent—capable of boring a tunnel under the river. In June 2010, the drill was in Brazil. "*We need a drill that is in Brazil*," says Spivey. "That idea is quite alarming. Obviously someone is using the drill. When do we get to use it?" At the last minute they overcame some objections from Pennsylvania bridge authorities and were permitted to cross the river on the bridge—by boring holes through its concrete pylons and running the cable on the underside of the bridge.

At which point the technical problems gave way to social problems. Leaving the bridge, the road split; one branch went north; the other, south. If you attempted to travel due east, you hit a dead end. The road just stopped, near a sign beside a levee that said, Welcome to Sunbury. Blocking the line's path were two big parking lots. One belonged to a company that manufactured wire rope, the cable used on ski lifts; the other was owned by a century-old grocery store named Weis Markets. To reach its twin in the Sunbury forest, the line needed to pass through one of these parking lots or travel around the entire city. The owners of both Weis Markets and the Wirerope Works were hostile or suspicious, or both; they weren't returning calls. "The whole state has been abused by coal companies," Steve Williams explained. "When you say you want to dig, everyone gets suspicious."

Going around rather than through the town, Spivey calculated, would cost several months and a lot of money and would add four microseconds to his route. It would also prevent Spread Networks from delivering the cable on time to the Wall Street banks and traders ready to write checks for $10.6 million for it. But the guy who ran the wire rope factory was for some reason so angry with Spread's local contractor that he wouldn't speak to them. The guy who ran the Weis Markets was even harder to reach. His secretary told Spread that he was at a golf tournament, and unavailable. He'd already decided—without informing Spread Networks—to reject the somewhat strange offer of low six figures plus free high-speed Internet access they had offered him in exchange for a ten-foot easement under his parking lot. The line passed too close to his ice cream–making plant. The chairman had no interest in signing over a permanent easement that would make it difficult to expand the ice cream plant.

In July 2010 the line dropped back underground beneath the bridge in Sunbury and just stopped. "We had all this fiber out there and we needed it to talk to each other and it couldn't," said Spivey. Then, for some reason he never fully understood, the wire rope people softened. They sold him the easement he needed. The day after Spread Networks acquired lifetime rights to a ten-foot-wide path under the wire rope factory's parking lot, it sent out its first press release: "Round-trip travel time from Chicago to New Jersey has been cut to 13 milliseconds." They'd set a goal of coming in at under 840 miles and beaten it; the line was 827 miles long. "It was the biggest what-the-fuck moment the industry had had in some time," said Spivey.

Even then, none of the line's creators knew for sure how the line would be used. The biggest question about the line—*Why?*—remained imperfectly explored. All its creators knew was that the Wall Street people who wanted it wanted it very badly—and also wanted to find ways for others not to have it. In one of his first meetings with a big Wall Street firm, Spivey had told the firm's boss the price of his line: $10.6 million plus costs if he paid up front, $20 million or so if he paid in installments. The boss said he'd like to go away and think about it. He returned with a single question: "Can you double the price?"

CHAPTER TWO

BRAD'S PROBLEM

Up till the moment of the collapse of the U.S. financial system, Brad Katsuyama could tell himself that he bore no responsibility for that system. He worked for the Royal Bank of Canada, for a start. RBC might be the ninth biggest bank in the world, but it was on no one's mental map of Wall Street. It was stable and relatively virtuous, and soon to be known for having resisted the temptation to make bad subprime loans to Americans or peddle them to ignorant investors. But its management didn't understand just what an afterthought their bank was—on the rare occasions American financiers thought about them at all. Brad's bosses had sent him from Toronto to New York back in 2002, when he was twenty-four years old, as part of a "big push" to become a player on Wall Street. The sad truth about the big push was that hardly anyone noticed it. As a trader who moved to RBC from Morgan Stanley put it, "When I got there, it was like, 'Holy shit, welcome to the small time!'" Brad himself said, "The people in Canada are always saying,

'We're paying too much for people in the United States.' What they don't realize is that the reason you have to pay them too much is that no one wants to work for RBC. RBC is a nobody." It was as if the Canadians had summoned the nerve to audition for a role in the school play, then turned up for it wearing a carrot costume.

Before they sent him there to be part of the big push, Brad had never laid eyes on Wall Street or New York City. It was his first immersive course in the American way of life, and he was instantly struck by how different it was from the Canadian version. "Everything was to excess," he said. "I met more offensive people in a year than I had in my entire life. People lived beyond their means, and the way they did it was by going into debt. That's what shocked me the most. Debt was a foreign concept in Canada. Debt was evil. I'd never been in debt in my life, ever. I got here and a real estate broker said, 'Based on what you make, you can afford a $2.5 million apartment.' I was like, *What the fuck are you talking about?*" In America, even the homeless were profligate. Back in Toronto, after a big bank dinner, Brad would gather the leftovers into covered tin trays and carry them out to a homeless guy he saw every day on his way to work. The guy was always appreciative. When the bank moved him to New York, he saw more homeless people in a day than he saw back home in a year. When no one was watching, he'd pack up the king's banquet of untouched leftovers after the New York lunches and walk it down to the people on the streets. "They just looked at me like, 'What the fuck is this guy doing?'" he said. "I stopped doing it because I didn't feel like anyone gave a shit."

In the United States, Brad also noticed, he was expected to accept distinctions between himself and others that he'd simply ignored in Canada. Growing up, he'd been one of the very few

Asian kids in a white suburb of Toronto. During World War II, his Japanese Canadian grandparents had been interned in prison camps in western Canada. Brad never mentioned this or anything else having to do with race to his friends, and they ended up thinking of him almost as a person who did not have a racial identity. His genuine lack of interest in the subject became an issue only after he arrived in New York. Worried that it needed to do more to promote diversity, RBC invited Brad along with a bunch of other nonwhite people to a meeting to discuss the issue. Going around the table, people took turns responding to a request to "talk about your experience of being a minority at RBC." When Brad's turn came he said, "To be honest, the only time I've ever felt like a minority is this exact moment. If you really want to encourage diversity you shouldn't make people feel like a minority." Then he left. The group continued to meet without him.

The episode said as much about him as it did about his new home. Ever since he was a little kid, more by instinct than conscious thought, he had resisted the forces that sought to separate him from any group to which he felt he belonged. When he was seven his mother told him he'd been identified as a gifted student, and she offered him the chance to attend special school. He told her he wanted to stay with his friends and attend the normal school. In high school the track coach thought he could be a star (he ran a 4.5-second forty-yard dash), until he told the coach that he'd rather play a team sport—he stuck with hockey and football. Upon leaving high school at the top of his class, he could have gone on scholarship to any university in the world: He was not only the best student but a college-caliber tailback and a talented pianist. Instead he chose to follow his girlfriend and his football teammates to Wilfrid Laurier University, an

hour or so from Toronto. After he graduated from Laurier, taking the prize for best student in the business program, he wound
up trading stocks at the Royal Bank of Canada—not because he
had any particular interest in the stock market but because he had
no idea what else to do for a living. Up till the moment he was
forced to, he hadn't really thought about what he wanted to be
when he grew up, or that he might end up in some radically different place than the friends he'd grown up with. What he liked
about the RBC trading floor, aside from the feeling it gave him
that it would reward his analytical abilities, was that it reminded
him of a locker room. Another group, to which he naturally
belonged.

The RBC trading floor at One Liberty Plaza looked out on
the holes once filled by the Twin Towers. When Brad arrived,
the firm was still conducting air quality studies to determine if
it was safe for its employees to breathe. In time they just sort of
forgot about what had happened in this place; the hole in the
ground became the view you looked at without ever seeing it.

For his first few years on Wall Street, Brad traded U.S. tech
and energy stocks. He had some fairly abstruse ideas about how
to create what he called "perfect markets," and they worked so
well that he was promoted to run the equity trading department, consisting of twenty or so traders. The RBC trading floor
had what the staff liked to refer to as a "no-asshole rule"; if
someone came in the door looking for a job and sounding like
a typical Wall Street asshole, they wouldn't hire him, no matter
how much money he said he could make the firm. There was
even an expression used to describe the culture: "RBC nice."
Although Brad found the expression embarrassingly Canadian,
he, too, was RBC nice. The best way to manage people, he
thought, was to convince them that you were good for their

careers. He further believed that the only way to get people to believe that you were good for their careers was actually to be good for their careers. These thoughts came naturally to him: They just seemed obvious.

If there was a contradiction between who Brad Katsuyama was and what he did for a living, he didn't see it. He assumed he could be a trader on Wall Street without its having the slightest effect on his habits, tastes, worldview, or character. And during his first few years on Wall Street he appeared to be correct. Just by being himself he became, on Wall Street, a great success. "His identity at RBC in New York was very simple," says a former colleague. "Brad was the golden child. People thought he was going to end up running the bank." For more or less his entire life, Brad Katsuyama had trusted the system; and the system, in return, trusted Brad Katsuyama. That left him especially unprepared for what the system was to do to him.

HIS TROUBLES BEGAN at the end of 2006, after RBC paid $100 million for a U.S. electronic stock market trading firm called Carlin Financial. In what appeared to Brad to be undue haste, his bosses back in Canada bought Carlin without knowing much about either it or electronic trading. In what he thought to be typical Canadian fashion, they had been slow to react to a big change in the financial markets; but once they felt compelled to act, they'd panicked. "The bank's run by these Canadian guys from Canada," a former RBC director put it. "They don't have the slightest idea of the ins and outs of Wall Street."

In buying Carlin they received a crash course. In a stroke Brad found himself working side by side with a group of American traders who could not have been less suited to RBC's culture.

The first day after the merger, Brad got a call from a worried female employee, who whispered, "There is a guy in here with suspenders walking around with a baseball bat in his hands, taking swings." That turned out to be Carlin's founder and CEO, Jeremy Frommer, who, whatever else he was, was not RBC nice. One of Frommer's signature poses was feet up on his desk, baseball bat swinging wildly over his head while some poor shoeshine guy tried to polish his shoes. Another was to find a perch on the trading floor and muse in loud tones about who might get fired next. Returning to his alma mater, the University of Albany, to tell a group of business students the secret of his success, Frommer actually said, "It's not just enough that I'm flying in first class. I have to know my friends are flying in coach." "Jeremy was emotional, erratic, and loud—everything the Canadians were not," says one former senior RBC executive. "To me, Toronto is like a foreign country," said Frommer later. "The people there are not the same culture as us. They take a very cerebral approach to Wall Street. It was just such a different world. It was a hard adjustment for me. If you were a hitter, you couldn't swing your dick around the way you could in the old days."

With each mighty swing Jeremy Frommer scored a direct hit on Canadian sensibilities. The first Christmas after the two firms merged, he took it upon himself to organize the office party. The RBC Christmas party had always been a staid affair. Frommer rented out Marquee, the Manhattan nightclub. "RBC doesn't do stuff at Marquee," says one former RBC trader. "Everyone was like, 'What the fuck is going on here?'" "I walked in and I didn't know ninety percent of the people there," says another. "It looked like we were in a Vegas hotel lobby bar. There were these girls walking around half-naked, selling cigars. I asked,

'Who are all these people?'" Into this old-fashioned Canadian bank, heretofore immune from the usual Wall Street pathologies, Frommer imported a bunch of people who were not. "The women at Carlin had a different look than the women at RBC," says another former RBC trader delicately. "You got the feeling they were hired because they were hot." With Carlin also came a boiler room full of day traders, some of whom had rap sheets with various financial police, others of whom were about to wind up in jail for financial crimes.* "Carlin was what I always imagined a bucket shop was like," says another former RBC trader. "There was a lot of the gold chains attire," said another. It was as if a tribe of 1980s Wall Street alpha males had stumbled upon a time machine and, as a prank, identified the most mild-mannered, well-behaved province in Canada and teleported themselves into it. The RBC guys were at their desks at 6:30; the Carlin guys rolled in at 8:30 or so, looking distinctly unwell. The RBC guys were understated and polite; the Carlin guys were brash and loud. "They lied or exaggerated a lot about their relationships with accounts," says a current RBC salesman. "They were like, 'Yeah, I cover [hedge fund giant John] Paulson and we're tight.' And you'd call Paulson up and they'd barely heard of the guy."

For reasons Brad did not fully grasp, RBC insisted that he move with his entire U.S. stock trading department from their offices near the World Trade Center site into Carlin's building in Midtown. This bothered him a lot. He got the distinct impression that people in Canada had decided that electronic trading was the future, even if they didn't understand why or even what

---

* In the room was, among other people, Zvi Goffer, who was later sentenced to ten years in jail for orchestrating an insider trading ring in his prior job, with the Galleon Group.

it meant. Installed in Carlin's offices, the RBC people were soon gathered to hear a state-of-the-financial-markets address given by Frommer. He stood in front of a flat panel computer monitor that hung on his wall. "He gets up and says the markets are now all about speed," says Brad. "'Trading is all about speed.' And then he says, 'I'm going to show you how fast our system is.' He had this guy next to him with a computer keyboard. He said to him, 'Enter an order!' And the guy hit Enter. And the order appeared on the screen so everyone could see it. And Frommer goes, 'See! See how fast that was!!!'" All the guy had done was type the name of a stock on a keyboard, and the name was displayed on the screen, the way a letter, once it has been typed, appears on a computer screen. "Then he goes, 'Do it again!' And the guy hits the Enter button on the keyboard again. And everyone nods. It was five in the afternoon. The market wasn't open; nothing was happening. But he was like, 'Oh my God, it's happening in real time!' And I was like, 'I don't fucking believe this.'" Brad thought: *The guy who just sold us our new electronic trading platform either does not know that his display of technical virtuosity is absurd, or, worse, he thinks we don't know.*

As it happened, at almost exactly the moment Jeremy Frommer fully entered Brad's life, the U.S. stock market began to behave oddly. Before RBC acquired this supposedly state-of-the-art electronic trading firm, his computers worked. Now, suddenly, they didn't. Until he was forced to use some of Carlin's technology, he trusted his trading screens. When his trading screens showed 10,000 shares of Intel offered at $22 a share, it meant that he could buy 10,000 shares of Intel for $22 a share. He had only to push a button. By the spring of 2007, when his screens showed 10,000 shares of Intel offered at $22 and he pushed the button, the offers vanished. In his seven years as a trader he had always been able to look at the screens on his desk and *see* the stock market. Now the market as it appeared on his screens was an illusion.

This was a big problem. Brad's main role as a trader was to sit between investors who wanted to buy and sell big amounts of stock and the public markets, where the volumes were smaller. Some investor might want to sell a 3-million-share block of IBM; the markets would only show demand for 1 million shares; Brad would buy the entire block, sell off a million shares of it instantly, and then work artfully over the next few hours to unload the other 2 million shares. If he didn't know what the markets actually were, he couldn't price the larger block. He had been supplying liquidity to the market; now, whatever was happening on his screens was reducing his willingness to do it. Unable to judge market risks, he was less happy to take them.

By June 2007 the problem had grown too big to ignore. An electronics company in Singapore called Flextronics announced its intention to buy a smaller rival, Solectron, for a bit less than $4 a share. A big investor called Brad and said he wanted to sell 5 million shares of Solectron. The public stock markets—the New York Stock Exchange (NYSE) and Nasdaq—showed the current market. Say it was 3.70–3.75, which is to say you could sell Solectron for $3.70 a share or buy it for $3.75. The problem was that, at those prices, only a million shares were bid for and offered. The big investor who wished to sell 5 million shares of Solectron called Brad because he wanted Brad to take the risk on the other 4 million shares. And so Brad bought the shares at $3.65, slightly below the price quoted in the public markets. But when he turned to the public markets—the markets on his trading screens—the share price instantly moved. Almost as if the market had read his mind. Instead of selling a million shares at

$3.70, as he'd assumed he could do, he sold a few hundred thousand and triggered a minicollapse in the price of Solectron. It was as if someone knew what he was trying to do and was reacting to his desire to sell before he had fully expressed it. By the time he was done selling all 5 million shares, at prices far below $3.70, he had lost a small fortune.

This made no sense to him. He understood how he might move the price of an infrequently traded stock simply by satisfying the demand for the highest bidder. But in the case of Solectron, the stock of a company about to be taken over at a known price by another company was trading heavily. There should be plenty of supply and demand in a very narrow price range; it just shouldn't move very much. The buyers in the market shouldn't vanish the moment he sought to sell. At that point he did what most people do when they don't understand why their computer isn't working the way it's supposed to: He called tech support. "If your keyboard didn't work, these were the guys who would come up and replace it." Like tech support everywhere, their first assumption was that Brad didn't know what he was doing. "'User error' was the thing they'd throw at you. They just thought of us traders as a bunch of dumb jocks." He explained to them that all he was doing was hitting the Enter key on his keyboard: It was hard to screw that up.

Once it was clear that the problem was more complicated than user error, the troubleshooting was bumped to a higher level. "They started to send me product people, the people who had bought and installed the systems, and they at least sort of sounded like technologists." He explained that the market on his screens used to be a fair representation of the actual stock market but that now it was not. In return he received mainly blank stares. "It wound up being me talking to someone and them looking, like, befuddled." Finally he complained so loudly that they sent him the developers, the guys who had come to RBC in the Carlin acquisition. "We would hear how they had this roomful of Indians and Chinese guys. Rarely would you see them on the trading floor. They were called "the Golden Goose." The bank did not want the Golden Goose distracted, and, when the geese arrived, they had the air of people on leave from some critical mission. They, too, explained to Brad that he, and not his machine, was the problem. "They told me it was because I was in New York and the markets were in New Jersey and my market data was slow. Then they said that it was all caused by the fact that there are thousands of people trading in the market. They'd say, 'You aren't the only one trying to do what you're trying to do. There's other events. There's news.'"

If that was the case, he asked them, why did the market in any given stock dry up *only* when he was trying to trade in it? To make his point, he asked the developers to stand behind him and watch while he traded. "I'd say, 'Watch closely. I am about to buy one hundred thousand shares of Amgen. I am willing to pay forty-eight dollars a share. There are currently one hundred thousand shares of Amgen being offered at forty-eight dollars a share—ten thousand on BATS, thirty-five thousand on the New York Stock Exchange, thirty thousand on Nasdaq, and twenty-five thousand on Direct Edge.' You could see it all on the screens. We'd all sit there and stare at the screen and I'd have my finger over the Enter button. I'd count out loud to five . . .

" 'One . . .

" 'Two. . . . See, nothing's happened.

" 'Three. . . . Offers are still there at forty-eight . . .

" 'Four. . . . Still no movement.

" 'Five.' Then I'd hit the Enter button and—boom!—all hell would break loose. The offerings would all disappear, and the stock would pop higher."

At which point he turned to the guys standing behind him and said, "You see, I'm the event. I *am* the news."

To that the developers had no response. "They were kind of like, 'Ohhh, yeah. Let me look into that.' Then they'd disappear and never come back." He called a few times, but "when I realized they really had no shot at solving the problem, I just left them alone."

Brad suspected that the culprit was the technology from Carlin that RBC had more or less bolted onto the side of his trading machines. "As the market problem got worse," he said, "I started to just assume my real problem was with how bad their technology was." A pattern was established: The moment he attempted to react to the market on his screens, the market moved. And it wasn't just him: The exact same thing was happening to all of the RBC stock market traders who worked for him. In addition, for reasons he couldn't fathom, the fees that RBC was paying to stock exchanges were suddenly skyrocketing. At the end of 2007 Brad conducted a study to compare what had happened on his trading books to what should have happened, or what used to happen, when the stock market as stated on his trading screens was the market he experienced. "The difference to us was tens of millions of dollars" in losses plus fees, he said. "We were hemorrhaging money." His bosses in Toronto called him in and told him to figure out how to reduce his rising trading costs.

Up till then, Brad had taken the stock exchanges for granted. When he'd arrived in New York, in 2002, 85 percent of all stock market trading happened on the New York Stock Exchange, and some human being processed every order. The stocks that didn't trade on the New York Stock Exchange traded on Nasdaq. No stocks traded on both exchanges. At the behest of the SEC, in turn responding to public protests about cronyism, the exchanges themselves, in 2005, went from being utilities owned by their members to public corporations run for profit. Once competition was introduced, the exchanges multiplied. By early 2008 there were thirteen different public exchanges, most of them in northern New Jersey. Virtually every stock now traded on all of these exchanges: You could still buy and sell IBM on the New York Stock Exchange, but you could also buy and sell it on BATS, Direct Edge, Nasdaq, Nasdaq BX, and so on. The idea that a human being needed to stand between investors and the market was dead. The "exchange" at Nasdaq or at the New York Stock Exchange, or at their new competitors, such as BATS and Direct Edge, was a stack of computer servers that contained the program called the "matching engine." There was no one inside the exchange to talk to. You submitted an order to the exchange by typing it into a computer and sending it into the exchange's matching engine. At the big Wall Street banks, the guys who once peddled stocks to big investors had been reprogrammed. They now sold algorithms, or encoded trading rules designed by the banks, that investors used to submit their stock market orders. The departments that created these trading algorithms were dubbed "electronic trading."

That was why the Royal Bank of Canada had panicked and bought Carlin. There was still a role for Brad and traders like Brad—to sit between buyers and sellers of giant blocks of stock and the market. But the space was shrinking.

At the same time, the exchanges were changing the way they

made money. In 2002 they charged every Wall Street broker who submitted a stock market order the same simple fixed commission per share traded. Replacing people with machines enabled the markets to become not just faster but more complicated. The exchanges rolled out an incredibly complicated system of fees and kickbacks. The system was called the "maker-taker model" and, like a lot of Wall Street creations, was understood by almost no one. Even professional investors' eyes glazed over when Brad tried to explain it to them. "It was the one thing I'd skip, because a lot of people just didn't get it," he said. Say you wanted to buy shares in Apple, and the market in Apple was 400–400.05. If you simply went in and bought the shares at $400.05, you were said to be "crossing the spread." The trader who crossed the spread was classified as the "taker." If you instead rested your order to buy Apple at $400, and someone came along and sold the shares to you at $400, you were designated a "maker." In general, the exchanges charged takers a few pennies a share, paid makers somewhat less, and pocketed the difference—on the dubious theory that whoever resisted the urge to cross the spread was performing some kind of service. But there were exceptions. For instance, the BATS exchange, in Weehawken, New Jersey, perversely paid takers and charged makers.

In early 2008 all of this came as news to Brad Katsuyama. "I thought all the exchanges just charged us a flat fee," he said. "I'm like, 'Holy shit, you mean someone will *pay* us to trade?'" Thinking he was being clever, he had all of RBC's trading algorithms direct the bank's stock market orders to whatever exchange would pay them the most for what they wanted to do—which, at that moment, happened to be the BATS exchange. "It was a total disaster," said Brad. When he tried to buy or sell stock and seize the payment from the BATS exchange, the market for that stock simply vanished, and the price of the stock moved away from him. Instead of being paid, he wound up hemorrhaging even more money.

It was not obvious to Brad why some exchanges paid you to be a taker and charged you to be a maker, while others charged you to be a taker and paid you to be a maker. No one he asked could explain it, either. "It wasn't like there was anyone saying, 'Hey, you should really be paying attention to this.' Because no one was paying attention to this." To further bewilder the Wall Street brokers who sent stock market orders to the exchanges, the amounts that were charged varied from exchange to exchange, and the exchanges often changed their pricing. To Brad this all just seemed bizarre and unnecessarily complicated—and it raised all sorts of questions. "Why would you pay anyone to be a taker? I mean, who is willing to pay to make a market? Why would anyone do that?"

He took to asking people around the bank who might know more than he did. He tried Googling, but there wasn't really anything to Google. One day he was talking to a guy who worked on the retail end in Toronto selling stocks to individual Canadians. "I said, 'I'm getting screwed, but I can't figure out who is screwing me.' And he says, 'You know, there are more players out there in the market now.' And I say, 'What do you mean *more players*?' He says, 'You know, there's this new firm that's now ten percent of the U.S. market.'" The guy mentioned the firm's name, but Brad didn't fully catch it. It sounded like Gekko. (The name was Getco.) "I'd never even heard of Getco. I didn't even know the name. I'm like, 'WHAT??' They were ten percent of the market. How can that be true? It's insane that someone could be ten percent of the U.S. stock market and I'm running a Wall Street trading desk and I've never heard of the place." And why, he wondered, would a guy from *retail* in Canada know about them first?

He was now running a stock market trading department unable to trade properly in the U.S. stock market. He was forced to watch people he cared for harassed and upset by a bunch of 1980s Wall Street throwbacks. And then, in the fall of 2008, as he sat and wondered what else might go wrong, the entire U.S. financial system went into a freefall. The way Americans handled their money had led to market chaos, and the market chaos created life chaos: The jobs and careers of everyone around him were suddenly on the line. "Every day I'd walk home and feel as if I had just got hit by a car."

He wasn't naïve. He knew that there were good guys and bad guys, and that sometimes the bad guys win; but he also believed that usually they did not. That view was now challenged. When he began to grasp, along with the rest of the world, what big American firms had done—rigged credit ratings to make bad loans seem like good loans, created subprime bonds designed to fail, sold them to their customers and then bet against them, and so on—his mind hit some kind of wall. For the first time in his career, he felt that he could only win if someone else lost, or, more likely, that someone else could only win if he lost. He was not by nature a zero-sum person, but he had somehow wound up in the middle of a zero-sum business.

His body had always tended to register stress before his mind. It was as if his mind refused to accept the possibility of conflict even as his body was engaged in that conflict. Now he bounced from one illness to another. His sinuses became infected and required surgery. His blood pressure, chronically high, skyrocketed. His doctors had him seeing a kidney specialist.

By early 2009 he'd decided to quit Wall Street. He'd just

become engaged. After work every day he'd sit down with his fiancée, Ashley Hooper—a recent Ole Miss graduate who'd grown up in Jacksonville, Florida—to decide where to live. They'd whittled the list down to San Diego, Atlanta, Toronto, Orlando, and San Francisco. He had no idea what he was going to do; he just wanted out. "I thought I could just sell pharmaceuticals or whatever." He'd never felt a need to be on Wall Street. "It was never a calling," he said. "I didn't think about money or the stock market when I was growing up. So the attachment was not strong." Maybe more oddly, he hadn't become all that wedded to money, even though RBC was now paying him almost $2 million a year. His heart had been in his job, but mainly because he really liked the people he worked for and the people who worked for him. What he liked about RBC was that it had never pressured him to be anyone but himself. The bank—or the markets, or perhaps both—was now pushing him to be someone else.

Then the bank, on its own, changed its mind. In February 2009 RBC parted ways with Jeremy Frommer and asked Brad to help find someone to replace him. Even as he had one foot out the door, Brad found himself interviewing candidates from all over Wall Street—and he saw that basically none of the people who held themselves out as knowledgeable about electronic trading understood it. "The problem was that the electronic people facing clients were just front men," he said. "They had no clue how the technology worked."

He withdrew his foot from the doorway and thought about it. Every day, the markets were driven less directly by human beings and more directly by machines. The machines were overseen by people, of course, but few of them knew how the machines worked. He knew that RBC's machines—not the computers themselves, but the instructions to run them—were third-rate, but he had assumed it was because the company's new electronic trading unit was bumbling and inept. As he interviewed people from the major banks on Wall Street, he came to realize that they had more in common with RBC than he had supposed. "I'd always been a trader," he said. "And as a trader you're kind of inside a bubble. You're just watching your screens all day. Now I stepped back and for the first time started to watch other traders." He had a good friend who traded stocks at a big-time hedge fund in Greenwich, Connecticut, called SAC Capital. SAC Capital was famous (and soon to be infamous) for being one step ahead of the U.S. stock market. If anyone was going to know something about the market that Brad didn't know, he figured, it would be them. One spring morning he took the train up to Greenwich and spent the day watching his friend trade. Right away he saw that, even though his friend was using technology given to him by Goldman Sachs and Morgan Stanley and the other big firms, he was experiencing exactly the same problem as RBC: The market on his screens was no longer the market. His friend would hit a button to buy or sell a stock and the market would move away from him. "When I see this guy trading and he was getting screwed—I now see that it isn't just me. My frustration is the market's frustration. And I was like, *Whoa, this is serious.*"

Brad's problem wasn't just Brad's problem. What people saw when they looked at the U.S. stock market—the numbers on the screens of the professional traders, the ticker tape running across the bottom of the CNBC screen—was an illusion. "That's when I realized the markets are rigged. And I knew it had to do with the technology. That the answer lay beneath the surface of the technology. I had absolutely no idea where. But that's when the lightbulb went off that the only way I'm going to find out what's going on is if I go beneath the surface."

THERE WAS NO way he, Brad Katsuyama, was going to go below the surface of the technology. People always assumed, because he was an Asian male, that he must be a computer wizard. He couldn't (or wouldn't) program his own VCR. What he had was an ability to distinguish between computer people who didn't actually know what they were talking about and those who did. The very best example of the latter, he thought, was Rob Park.

Park, a fellow Canadian, was a legend at RBC. In college in the late 1990s he'd become entranced by what was then a novel idea: to teach a machine to behave like a very smart trader. "The thing that interested me was taking a trader's thought process and replicating it," Park said. He and Brad had worked together at RBC only briefly, back in 2004, before he left to start his own business, but they had hit it off. Rob took an interest in the way Brad thought when he traded. Rob then turned those thoughts into code. The result was RBC's most popular trading algorithm. Here's how it worked: Say the trader wanted to buy 100,000 shares in General Motors. The algo scanned the market; it saw that there were only 100 shares offered. No smart trader seeking to buy 100,000 shares would tip his desire for a mere 100 shares. The market was too thin. But what was the point at which the trader should buy GM stock? The algorithm Rob built had a trigger point: It only bought stock if the amount on offer was greater than the historical average of the amount offered. That is, if the market was thick. "The decisions he makes make sense," Brad said of Rob. "He puts an incredible amount of thought into them. And since he puts so much

thought into his decisions, he's capable of explaining those decisions to others."

After Brad persuaded Rob to return to RBC, he had the perfect person to figure out what had happened to the U.S. stock
market. And in Brad, Rob saw the perfect person to grasp and
explain to others whatever he discovered. "All Brad needs is a
translator from computer language to human language," said
Park. "Once he has a translator, he completely understands it."

Brad wasn't exactly shocked when RBC finally gave up looking for someone to run its mess of an electronic trading operation and asked him if he would take it over and fix it. Everyone
else was shocked when he agreed to do it, as (a) he had a safe
and cushy $2-million-a-year job running the human traders
and (b) RBC had nothing to add to electronic trading. The market was cluttered; big investors had only so much space on their
desks for trading algorithms sold by brokers; and Goldman Sachs
and Morgan Stanley and Credit Suisse had long since overrun
that space and colonized it. All that was left of RBC's purchase
of Carlin was the Golden Goose. Thus Brad's first question to
the Golden Goose: How do we plan to make money? They had
an answer: They planned to open RBC's first "dark pool." That,
as it turned out, was what the Golden Goose had been up to all
along, writing the software for the dark pool.

Dark pools were another rogue spawn of the new financial
marketplace. Private stock exchanges, run by the big brokers,
they were not required to reveal to the public what happened
inside them. They reported any trade they executed, but they did
so with sufficient delay that it was impossible to know exactly
what was happening in the broader market at the moment the
trade occurred. Their internal rules were a mystery, and only
the broker who ran a dark pool knew for sure whose buy and sell

orders were allowed inside. The amazing idea the big Wall Street banks had sold to big investors was that *transparency was their enemy*. If, say, Fidelity wanted to sell a million shares of Microsoft Corp.—so the argument ran—they were better off putting them into a dark pool run by, say, Credit Suisse than going directly to the public exchanges. On the public exchanges, everyone would notice a big seller had entered the market, and the market price of Microsoft would plunge. Inside a dark pool, no one but the broker who ran it had any idea what was happening.

The cost of RBC's creating and running its own dark pool, Brad now learned, would be nearly $4 million a year. Thus his second question for the Golden Goose: How will we make more than $4 million from our own dark pool? The Golden Goose explained that they'd save all sorts of money in fees they paid to the public exchanges—by putting together buyers and sellers of the same stocks who came to RBC at the same time. If RBC had some investor who wanted to buy a million shares of Microsoft, and another who wanted to sell a million shares of Microsoft, they could simply pair them off in the dark pool rather than pay Nasdaq or the New York Stock Exchange to do it. In theory this made sense; in practice, not so much. "The problem," said Brad, "was RBC was two percent of the market. I asked how often we were likely to have buyers and sellers to cross. No one had done the analysis." The analysis, once finished, showed that RBC, if it opened a dark pool and routed all its clients' orders into it first, would save about $200,000 a year in exchange fees. "So I said, 'Okay, how else will we make money?'"

The answer that came back explained why no one had bothered to do any analysis on dark pools in the first place. There was a lot of free money to be made, the computer programmers explained, by selling access to the RBC dark pool to outside traders. "They said there were all these people who will *pay* to be in our dark pool," recalled Brad. "And I said, 'Who would pay to be in our dark pool?' And they said, 'High-frequency traders.'" Brad tried to think of good reasons why traders of any sort would pay RBC for access to RBC's customers' stock market orders, but he came up with none. "It just felt weird," he said. "I had a feeling of why and the feeling didn't feel good. So I said, 'Okay, none of this sounds like a good idea. Kill the dark pool.'"

That just pissed off a lot of people and fueled suspicions that Brad Katsuyama was engaged in some activity other than the search for corporate profits. Now he was in charge of a business called electronic trading—with nothing to sell. What he had, instead, was a fast-growing pile of unanswered questions. Why, between the dark pools and the public exchanges, were there nearly sixty different places, most of them in New Jersey, where you could buy any listed stock? Why did the public exchanges fiddle with their own pricing so often—and why did you get paid by one exchange to do exactly the same thing for which another exchange might charge you? How did a firm he'd never heard of—Getco—trade 10 percent of the entire volume of the stock market? How had this guy in the middle of nowhere—in *retail* in *Canada*—learned of Getco's existence before him? Why was the market displayed on Wall Street trading screens an illusion?

In May 2009, what appeared to be a scandal involving the public stock exchanges added more questions to Brad's list. New York senator Charles Schumer wrote a letter to the SEC—then issued a press release telling the world what he had done—condemning the stock exchanges for allowing "sophisticated high-frequency traders to gain access to trading information before it is sent out widely to other traders. For a fee, the exchange will 'flash' information about buy and sell orders for just a few fractions of a second before the information is made publicly available." That was the first time that Brad had heard the term "flash orders." To the growing list of mental questions, he added another: Why would stock exchanges have allowed flash trading in the first place?

HE AND ROB set out to build a team of people to investigate the U.S. stock market. "At first I was looking for guys who had worked in HFT or who had worked at large banks," said Brad. No one who had worked in high-frequency trading would return his calls. Finding people who worked for the big banks was easier: Wall Street firms were shedding people. Guys who wouldn't have given RBC a second thought were now turning up in his office begging for work. "I interviewed more than seventy-five people," he said. "We didn't hire any of them." The problem with all of these people was that even when they said they had worked in electronic trading, they clearly didn't understand how the electronics did the trading.

Instead of waiting for résumés to find him, Brad went looking for people who worked in or near the banks' technology departments. In the end his new team consisted of a former Deutsche Bank software programmer named Billy Zhao, a former manager in Bank of America's electronic trading division named John Schwall, and a twenty-two-year-old recent Stanford computer science graduate named Dan Aisen. He then set out with Rob for Princeton, New Jersey, where the Golden Goose resided, to figure out if any pieces of the Goose were worth keeping. There they found a Chinese programmer named Allen Zhang, who,

it turned out, had written the computer code for the doomed
dark pool. "I couldn't tell who was good and who was not from
just talking to them, but Rob could," said Brad. "And it became
clear that Allen was the Goose." Or, at any rate, the only part
of the Goose that might be turned to gold. Allen, Brad noticed,
had no interest in conforming to the norms of corporate life. He
preferred to work on his own, in the middle of the night, and
refused to ever take off his baseball cap, which he wore pulled
down low over his eyes, giving him the appearance of a getaway
driver badly in need of sleep. Allen was also incomprehensible:
What was just possibly English came tumbling out of him so
quickly and indistinctly that his words tended to freeze the lis-
tener in his tracks. As Brad put it, "Whenever Allen said anything, I'd turn to Rob and say, 'What the fuck did he just say?'"

Once he had a team in place, Brad persuaded his superiors
at the Royal Bank of Canada to conduct what amounted to a
series of science experiments in the U.S. stock markets. For the
next several months he and his team would trade stocks not to
make money but to test theories—to try to answer his original
question: Why was there a difference between the stock market
displayed on his trading screens and the actual market? Why,
when he went to buy 20,000 shares of IBM offered on his trading screens, did the market only sell him 2,000? To search for
an answer, RBC agreed to let his team lose up to $10,000 a day.
Brad asked Rob to come up with some theories to spend the
money on.

The obvious place to start was the public markets—the thirteen stock exchanges scattered in four different sites run by the
New York Stock Exchange, Nasdaq, BATS, and Direct Edge.
Rob invited the exchanges to send representatives to RBC to
answer a few questions. "We were asking really basic questions:

'How does your matching engine work?'" recalls Park. "'How does it handle a lot of different orders at the same price?' But they sent salespeople and they had no idea. When we kept pushing, they sent product managers, business people who knew a little about the technology—but they really didn't know much. They finally sent developers." They were the guys who actually programmed the machines. "The question we wanted to answer was, 'What happens between the time you push the button to trade and the time your order gets to the exchange?'" says Park. "People think pushing a button is as simple as pushing a button. It's not. All these things have to happen. There's a ton of stuff happening. The data we got from them about what was happening at first just seemed random. But we knew the answer was out there. It was just a question of how to find it."

Rob's first theory was that the exchanges weren't simply bundling all the orders at a given price but arranging them in some kind of sequence. You and I might both submit an order to buy 1,000 shares of IBM at $30 a share, but you might somehow obtain the right to cancel your order if my order is filled. "We started getting the idea that people were canceling orders," says Park. "That they were just phantom orders." Say the markets, together, showed 10,000 shares of Apple offered at $400 a share. Typically, that didn't represent one person who wanted to sell 10,000 shares of Apple but rather a bunch of smaller sell orders lumped together. They suspected that the orders were lined up in such a way that some people at the back of the line had the ability to jump out of the queue the moment the people in the front of the line sold their shares. "We tried calling the exchanges and asking them if that's what they did," said Park. "But we didn't even know what words to use." The further problem was that the trading reports did not separate out the exchanges: If you tried to buy 10,000 shares of Apple that seemed to be on offer and succeeded in buying only 2,000 of them, you weren't informed which exchanges the 8,000 missing shares had vanished from.

Allen wrote a new program that allowed Brad to send orders to a single exchange. Brad was fairly certain that this would prove that some, or maybe even all, of the exchanges were allowing these phantom orders. But no: When he sent an order to a single exchange, he was able to buy everything on offer. The market as it appeared on his screens was, once again, the market. "I thought, Crap, there goes that theory," said Brad. "And that's our only theory."

It made no sense: Why would the market on the screens be real if you sent your order only to one exchange but prove illusory when you sent your order to all the exchanges at once? Lacking an actual theory, Brad's team began to send orders into various combinations of exchanges. First NYSE and Nasdaq. Then NYSE and Nasdaq and BATS. Then NYSE, Nasdaq BX, Nasdaq, and BATS. And so on. What came back was a further mystery. As they increased the number of exchanges, the percentage of the order that was filled decreased; the more places they tried to buy stock from, the less stock they actually bought. "There was one exception," said Brad. "No matter how many exchanges we sent an order to, we always got one hundred percent of what was offered on BATS." Rob Park studied this and said, "I had no idea why this would be. I just thought, BATS is a great exchange!"

One morning, while taking a shower, Rob had another theory. He was picturing a bar chart Allen had created. It showed the time it took orders to travel from Brad's trading desk in the World Financial Center to the various exchanges. (To wide-

spread relief, they'd left Carlin's old offices and moved back
downtown.) "I was just visualizing that chart," he said. "It just
occurred to me that the bars are different heights. What if they
were the same height? That got me fired up immediately. I went
to work and went right to Brad's office and said, 'I think it's
because we're not arriving at the same time.'"

The increments of time involved were absurdly small: In
theory, the shortest travel time, from Brad's desk to the BATS
exchange in Weehawken, was about 2 milliseconds, and the
slowest, from Brad's desk to Carteret, was around 4 milliseconds. In practice, the times could vary much more than that,
depending on network traffic, static, and glitches in the pieces
of equipment between any two points. It took 100 milliseconds
to blink your eyes; it was hard to believe that a fraction of the
blink of an eye could have such vast market consequences. Allen
wrote a program—this one took him a couple of days—that
built delays into the orders Brad sent to exchanges that were
faster to get to, so that they arrived at exactly the same time
as they did at the exchanges that were slower to get to. "It was
counterintuitive," says Park. "Because everyone was telling us it
was all about faster. We had to go faster. And we were slowing
it down." One morning they sat down at the screen to test the
program. Ordinarily, when you hit the button to buy and failed
to get the stock, the screens lit up red; when you got only some
of the stock you were after, the screens lit up brown; and when
you got everything you asked for, the screens lit up green. Allen
hadn't taken his Series 7 exam, which meant he wasn't allowed
to press the Enter button and make a trade, so Rob actually hit
the button. Allen watched the screens light up green, and, as
he later said, "I had the thought: This is too easy." Rob did not
agree. "As soon as I pushed the button, I ran to Brad's desk,"

recalled Rob. "'It worked! It fucking worked.' I remember there was a pause and then Brad said, 'Now what do we do?'"

That question implied an understanding: Someone out there was using the fact that stock market orders arrived at different times at different exchanges to front-run orders from one market to another. Knowing that, what do you do next? That question suggested another: Do you use this knowledge to join whatever game is being played in the stock market? Or for some other purpose? It took Brad roughly six seconds to answer the question. "Brad said, 'We have to go on an educational campaign,'" recalls Park. "It would have been very easy to make money off this. He just chose not to."

THEY NOW HAD an answer to one of their questions—which, as always, raised another question. "It's 2009," said Brad. "This had been happening to me for almost three years. There's no way I'm the first guy to have figured this out. So what happened to everyone else?" They also had a tool they could sell to investors: the program Allen had written to build delays into the stock exchange orders. Before they did that, they wanted to test it on RBC's own traders. "I remember being at my desk," said Park, "and you hear people going, 'OOOOOOO!' and 'Holy shit, you can buy stock!'" The tool enabled the traders to do the job they were meant to do: take risk on behalf of the big investors who wanted to trade big chunks of stock. They could once again trust the market on their screens. The tool needed a name. Brad and his team stewed over this until one day a trader stood up at his desk and hollered, "Dude, you should just call it Thor! The hammer!" Someone was assigned to figure out what Thor might be an acronym for, and they found some words that worked, but no one remembered them. The tool was always just Thor. "I knew we were onto something when Thor became a verb," said Brad. "When I heard guys shouting, 'Thor it!'"

The other way he knew they were on to something was from conversations he had with a few of the world's biggest money managers. The first visit Brad and Rob Park made was to Mike Gitlin, who oversaw $700 billion in U.S. stock market investments for T. Rowe Price. The story they told didn't come to Gitlin as a complete shock. "You could see that something had just changed," said Gitlin. "You could see that when you were trading a stock, the market knew what you were going to do, and it was going to move against you." But what Brad described was a far more detailed picture of the market than Gitlin had ever considered—and, in that market, all the incentives were screwed up. The Wall Street brokerage firm deciding where to send T. Rowe Price's buy and sell orders had a great deal of power over how and where those orders got submitted. The firms were now paid for sending orders to some exchanges and billed for sending orders to others. Did the broker resist these incentives when they didn't align with the interests of the investors he was meant to represent? No one could say. Another wacky incentive was called "payment for order flow." As of 2010, every American stockbroker and all the online brokers effectively auctioned their customers' stock market orders. The online broker TD Ameritrade, for example, was paid hundreds of millions of dollars each year to send their orders to a high-frequency trading firm called Citadel, which executed the orders on their behalf. Why was Citadel willing to pay so much to see the flow? No one could say with certainty.

It had been hard to measure the cost of the new market structure. But now there was a tool for gauging not just how orders reached their destination but also how much money this new Wall Street intermediation machine was removing from the pockets of investors large and small: Thor. Brad explained to Mike Gitlin how his team had placed big trades to measure how much more cheaply they bought stock when they removed the ability of the machine to front-run them. For instance, they bought 10 million shares of Citigroup, then trading at roughly $4 per share, and saved $29,000—or less than a tenth of 1 percent of the total price. "That was the tax," said Rob Park. It sounded small until you realized that the average daily volume in the U.S. stock market was $225 billion. The same tax rate applied to that sum came to more than $160 million a day. "It was so insidious because you couldn't see it," said Brad. "It happens on such a granular level that even if you tried to line it up and figure it out you wouldn't be able to do it. People are getting screwed because they can't imagine a microsecond."

Thor showed you what happened when a Wall Street firm helped an investor to avoid paying the tax. The evidence was indirect but, to Gitlin's mind, damning. The mere existence of Brad Katsuyama was totally shocking. "To have RBC have the foremost electronic trading expert in the world was a little strange," said Gitlin. "You would not think that is where the world's foremost electronic expert would reside."

The discovery of Thor was not the end of a story; it was closer to a beginning. Brad and his team were building a mental picture of the financial markets after the crisis. The market was now a pure abstraction. It called to mind no obvious picture to replace the old one that people still carried around in their heads. The same old ticker tape ran across the bottom of television screens—even though it represented only a tiny fraction of the actual trading. Market experts still reported from the floor

of the New York Stock Exchange, even though trading no longer happened there. For a market expert truly to get inside
the New York Stock Exchange, he'd need to climb inside a
tall black stack of computer servers locked inside a cage locked
inside a fortress guarded by a small army of heavily armed men
and touchy German shepherds in Mahwah, New Jersey. If he
wanted an overview of the entire stock market—or even the
trading in a single company like IBM—he'd need to inspect
the computer printouts from twelve other public exchanges
scattered across northern New Jersey, plus records of the private
dealings that occurred inside the growing number of dark pools.
If he tried to do this, he'd soon learn that there actually was no
computer printout. At least no reliable one. No mental picture
existed of the new financial market. There was only this yellow-
ing photograph of a market now dead that served as a stand-in
for the living.

Brad had no idea how dark and difficult the picture he'd create
would become. All he knew for sure was that the stock market
was no longer a market. It was a collection of small markets scattered across New Jersey and lower Manhattan. When bids and
offers for shares sent to these places arrived at precisely the same
moment, the markets acted as markets should. If they arrived
even a millisecond apart, the market vanished, and all bets were
off. Brad knew that he was being front-run—that some other
trader was, in effect, noticing his demand for stock on one
exchange and buying it on others in anticipation of selling it to
him at a higher price. He'd identified a suspect: high-frequency
traders. "I had a sense that the problems are being caused by this
new participant in the market," said Brad. "I just didn't know
how they were doing it."

By late 2009 U.S. high-frequency trading firms were flying

to Toronto with offers to pay Canadian banks to expose their customers to high-frequency traders. Earlier that year, one of RBC's competitors, the Canadian Imperial Bank of Commerce (CIBC), had sublet its license on the Toronto Stock Exchange to several high-frequency trading firms and, within a few months, had seen its historically stable 6–7 percent share of Canadian stock market trading triple.* Senior managers at the Royal Bank of Canada were now arguing that the bank should create a Canadian dark pool, route their Canadian customers' stock market orders into it, and then sell to high-frequency traders the right to operate inside the dark pool. Brad thought that it made a lot more sense for RBC simply to expose the new game for what it was, and perhaps establish themselves as the only broker on Wall Street not conspiring to screw investors. "The only card left to play was honesty," as Rob Park put it.

Brad argued to his bosses that he should be permitted to launch what amounted to a public information campaign. He wanted to go out and explain, to anyone with money to invest in the United States stock markets, that they were now the prey. He wanted to tell them about this new weapon they might use to defend themselves from the predator. But the market was

---

* The rules of the Canadian stock market are different from the rules of the U.S. stock market. One rule in Canada that does not exist in the United States is "broker priority." The idea is to enable brokerage firms that have both sides of a trade to pair off buyers and sellers without the interference of other buyers and sellers. For example, imagine that CIBC (representing some investor) has a standing order to buy shares in Company X at $20 a share, but that it is not alone, and several other banks also have standing orders for Company X's shares at $20. If CIBC then enters the market with an order from another CIBC customer to sell shares in Company X at $20, the CIBC buyer has priority on the trade and is the first to have his order filled. By allowing high-frequency traders to operate with CIBC's license, CIBC was, in effect, creating lots of collisions between its own customers and the HFT firms.

already pressuring him to say nothing at all. He was in a race to win a debate in front of RBC's top management about how to respond to the newly automated stock markets. All he had going for him was his weird discovery, which proved . . . what, exactly? That the stock market now behaved strangely, except when it didn't? The RBC executives who wanted to join forces with high-frequency traders knew as little about high-frequency trading as he did. "I needed someone from the industry to verify that what I was saying was real," said Brad. He needed, specifically, someone from deep inside the world of high-frequency trading. He'd spent the better part of a year cold-calling strangers in search of an HFT strategist willing to defect. He now suspected that every human being who knew how high-frequency traders made money was making too much money doing it to stop and explain what was going on. He needed to find another way in.

CHAPTER THREE

RONAN'S PROBLEM

Part of Ronan's problem was that he didn't look like a Wall Street trader. He had pale skin and narrow, stooped shoulders, and the uneasy caution of a man who has survived one potato famine and is expecting another. He also lacked the Wall Street trader's ability to bury his self-doubt, and to seem more important and knowledgeable than he actually was. He was wiry and wary, like a mongoose. And yet from the moment he caught his first glimpse of a Wall Street trading floor, in his early twenties, Ronan Ryan badly wanted to work on Wall Street—and couldn't understand why he didn't belong. "It's hard not to get enamored of being one of these Wall Street guys who people are scared of and make all this money," he said. But it was hard to imagine anyone being scared of Ronan.

The other part of Ronan's problem was his inability or unwillingness to disguise his modest origins. Born and raised in Dublin, he'd moved to America in 1990, when he was sixteen. The Irish government had sent his father to New York to talk

American companies into moving to Ireland for the tax benefits, but few imagined that they would do so. Ireland was poor and dreary ("kind of like a shithole, to be honest"). His father, who was not made of money, had spent every last penny he had to rent a house in Greenwich, Connecticut, so that Ronan might attend the Greenwich public high school and see what life was like on the "right side of the tracks." "I couldn't believe it," says Ronan. "The kids had their own cars at sixteen! Kids would complain they had to ride on a school bus. I'd say, 'This fucking thing actually takes you to school! And it's free! I used to walk three miles.' It's hard not to love America." When Ronan was twenty-two, his father was recalled to Ireland; Ronan stayed behind. He didn't think of Ireland as a place anyone would ever go back to if given the choice, and he'd now embraced his idea of the American Dream—Greenwich, Connecticut, version. The year before, through an Irish guy his father had met, he'd landed a summer internship in the back office at Chemical Bank and had been promised a place in the management training program.

Then they canceled the training program; the Irish guy vanished. Graduating from Fairfield University in 1996, he sent letters to all the Wall Street banks but received just one false flicker of interest, from what, even to his untrained eyes, was a vaguely criminal, pump-and-dump penny stock brokerage firm. "It's not as easy as you think to get a job on Wall Street," he said. "I didn't know anyone. My family had no contacts whatsoever. We knew no one."

Eventually he gave up trying. He met another Irish guy who happened to work in the New York office of MCI Communications, the big telecom company. "He gave me a job strictly because I was Irish," said Ronan. "I guess he had a few charity cases a year. I was one of them." For no particular reason other than that no one else would hire him, he went to work in the telecom industry.

The first big job they gave him was to make sure that the eight thousand new pagers MCI had sold to a big Wall Street firm were well received. As he was told, "People are really sensitive about their pagers." Ronan traveled in the back of a repair truck in the summer heat to some office building to deliver the new pagers. He set up his little table at the back of the truck and unpacked the crates and waited for the Wall Street people to come and get their new pagers. An hour into it he was sweating and huffing inside the truck while a line of people waited for their pagers, and a crowd had formed, of guys to whom he'd already given the pagers: pager protestors. "These new pagers *suck*!" and "I hate this fucking pager!" they screamed, as he tried to pass out even more pagers. As he dealt with the revolt, one of the Wall Street firms' secretaries called him about her boss's new pager. She was so despondent about the thing that Ronan thought he could hear her crying. "She keeps saying over and over, 'It's too big! It's going to really hurt him! It's too big! It's going to really hurt him!'" Ronan was now totally confused: How could a pager inflict harm on a grown man? It was a tiny box, an inch by an inch and a half. "Then she tells me he's a midget, and it would dig into his side when he bent over," said Ronan. "And that he wasn't like a normal-sized midget. He was a *really* small dude. And I'm thinking, but I don't say it because I don't want her to think I'm a dick, *Why don't you just strap it onto his back, like a backpack?*"

At that moment, and others like it, many things crossed Ronan's mind that he did not say. Sizing pagers to little Wall Street people, and being hollered at by big Wall Street people who didn't like their new gadgets, was not what he'd imagined doing with his life. He was upset he hadn't found a path onto Wall Street. He decided to make the best of it.

That turned out to be the view that MCI offered him of the entire U.S. telecom system. Ronan had always been handy, but he'd never actually studied anything practical. He knew next to nothing about technology. Now he started to learn all about it. "It's pretty captivating, when you take the nerdiness out of it, how this shit works," he said. How a copper circuit conveyed information, compared to a glass fiber. How a switch made by Cisco compared to a switch made by Juniper. Which hardware companies made the fastest computer equipment, and which buildings in which cities contained floors that could withstand the weight of that equipment—old manufacturing buildings were best. He also learned how information actually traveled from one place to another—which was usually not in a straight line run by a single telecom carrier but in a convoluted path run by several. "When you make a call to New York from Florida, you have no idea how many pieces of equipment you have to go through for that call to happen. You probably just think it's fucking like two cans and a piece of string. But it's not." A circuit that connected New York City to Florida would have Verizon on the New York end, BellSouth on the Florida end, and MCI in the middle; it would zigzag from population center to population center; once it got there it would wind in all sorts of crazy ways through skyscrapers and city streets. To sound knowing, telecom people liked to say that the fiber routes ran through "the NFL cities."

That was another thing Ronan learned: A lot of people in and around the telecom industry were more knowing than knowledgeable. The people at MCI who sold the technology often didn't actually understand it and yet were paid far better than people, like him, who simply fixed problems. Or, as he put it, "I'm making thirty-five and they're making a buck twenty and they're fucking idiots." He got himself moved to sales and became a leading salesperson. A few years into the job, he was lured from MCI by Qwest Communications; three years later, he was lured from Qwest by another big telecom carrier, Level 3. He was now making good money—a couple of hundred grand a year. By 2005, he also couldn't help but notice, his clients were more likely than ever to be big Wall Street banks. He spent entire weeks inside Goldman Sachs and Lehman Brothers and Deutsche Bank, figuring out the best routes to run fiber and the best machines to hook that fiber up to. He hadn't lost his original ambition. At some point on every Wall Street job he had, he'd nose around for a job opening. "I'm thinking: I'm meeting so many people. Why can't I get a job at one of these places?" Actually, the big banks offered him jobs all the time, but the jobs were never finance jobs. They offered him tech jobs—working in some remote site with computer hardware and fiber-optic cable. There was a vividly clear class distinction between tech guys and finance guys. The finance guys saw the tech guys as faceless help and were unable to think of them as anything else. "They always said the same thing to me: 'You're a boxes and lines guy,'" he said.

Then, in 2006, BT Radianz called. Radianz was born of 9/11, after the attacks on the World Trade Center knocked out big pieces of Wall Street's communication system. The company promised to build for big Wall Street banks a system less vulnerable to outside attack than the existing system. Ronan's job was to sell the financial world on the idea of subcontracting their information networks to Radianz. In particular, he was meant to sell the banks on "co-locating" their computers in Radianz's data center in Nutley, New Jersey. But not long after he started his job at Radianz, Ronan had a different sort of inquiry, from a hedge fund based in Kansas City. The caller said he worked at a stock market trading firm called Bountiful Trust, and that he had heard Ronan was expert at moving financial data from one place to another. Bountiful Trust had a problem: In making trades between Kansas City and New York, it took them too long to determine what happened to their orders—that is, what stocks they had bought and sold. They also noticed that, increasingly, when they placed their orders, the market was vanishing on them, just as it was vanishing on Brad Katsuyama. "He says, 'My latency time is forty-three milliseconds,'" recalls Ronan. "And I said, 'What the hell is a millisecond?'"

Latency was simply the time between the moment a signal was sent and when it was received. There were several factors that determined the latency of a stock market trading system: the boxes, the logic, and the lines. The boxes were the machinery the signals passed through on their way from Point A to Point B: the computer servers and signal amplifiers and switches. The logic was the software, the code instructions that operated the boxes. Ronan didn't know much about software, except that, more and more, it seemed to be written by Russian guys who barely spoke English. The lines were the glass fiber-optic cables that carried the information from one box to another. The single biggest determinant of speed was the length of the fiber, or the distance the signal needed to travel to get from Point A to Point B. Ronan didn't know what a millisecond was, but he understood the problem with this Kansas City hedge fund: It was in Kansas City. Light in a vacuum traveled at 186,000 miles per second, or, put another way, 186 miles a millisecond. Light inside of fiber bounced off the walls and so traveled at only about two-thirds of its theoretical speed. But it was still fast. The biggest enemy of the speed of a signal was the distance the signal needed to travel. "Physics is physics—this is what the traders didn't understand," said Ronan.

The whole reason Bountiful Trust had set up shop in Kansas City was that its founders believed that it no longer mattered where they were physically located. That Wall Street was no longer a place. They were wrong. Wall Street was, once again, a place. It wasn't actually on Wall Street now. It was in New Jersey. Ronan moved the computers from Kansas City to Radianz's data center in Nutley and reduced the time it took them to find out what they had bought and sold from 43 milliseconds to 3.8 milliseconds.

From that moment the demand on Wall Street for Ronan's services intensified. Not just from banks and well-known high-frequency trading firms but also from prop shops (proprietary trading firms) no one had ever heard of, with just a few guys in them. All wanted to be able to trade faster than the others. To be faster they needed to find shorter routes for their signals to travel; to be faster they needed the newest hardware, stripped down to its essentials; to be faster they also needed to reduce the physical distance between their computers and the computers inside the various stock exchanges. Ronan knew how to solve all of these problems. But as all his new customers housed their computers inside the Radianz data center in Nutley, this was a tricky business. Ronan says, "One day a trader calls and asks, 'Where am I in the room?' I'm thinking, In *the room? What do you mean 'in the room'?* What the guy meant, it turned out, was *in the room.*" He was willing to pay to move his computer that sent orders into the stock market as close as possible to the pipe that exited the building in Nutley—so that he would have a slight jump on the other computers in the room. Another trader then called Ronan to say that he had noticed that his fiber-optic cable was a few yards longer than it needed to be. Instead of having it wind around the outside of the room with everyone else's cable—which helped to reduce the heat in the room—the trader wanted his cable to hew a straight line right across the middle of the room.

It was only a matter of time before the stock exchanges figured out that, if people were willing to spend hundreds of thousands of dollars to move their machines around inside some remote data center just so they might be a tiny bit closer to the stock exchange, they'd pay millions to be inside the stock exchange itself. Ronan followed them there. He came up with an idea: sell proximity to Wall Street as a service. Call it "proximity services." "We tried to trademark proximity, but you can't because it's a word," he said. What he wanted to call proximity soon became known as "co-location," and Ronan became the world's authority on the subject. When they ran out of ways to reduce the length of their cable, they began to focus on the devices on either end of the cable. Data switches, for instance. The difference between fast data switches and slow ones was measured in microseconds (millionths of a second), but microseconds were now critical. "One guy says to me, 'It doesn't matter if I'm one second slower or one microsecond; either way I come in second place.'" The switching times fell from 150 microseconds to 1.2 microseconds per trade. "And then," says Ronan, "they started to ask, 'What kind of glass are you using?'" All optical fibers were not created equal; some kinds of glass conveyed light signals more efficiently than others. And Ronan thought: Never before in human history have people gone to so much trouble and spent so much money to gain so little speed. "People were measuring the length of their cables to the foot inside the exchanges. People were buying these servers and chucking them out six months later. For microseconds."

He didn't know how much money high-frequency traders were making, but he could guess from how much they were spending. From the end of 2005 to the end of 2008, Radianz alone billed them nearly $80 million—just for setting up their computers near the stock exchange matching engines. And Radianz was hardly the only one billing them. Seeing that the fiber routes between the New Jersey exchanges were often less than ideal, Ronan prodded a company called Hudson Fiber into finding straighter ones. Hudson Fiber was now doing a land-office business digging trenches in places that would give Tony Soprano pause. Ronan could also guess how much money high-frequency traders were making by the trouble they took to conceal how they made it. One HFT firm he set up inside one of the stock exchanges insisted that he wrap their new computer servers in wire gauze—to prevent anyone from seeing their blinking lights or improvements in their hardware. Another HFT firm secured the computer cage nearest the exchange's matching engine—the computer code that, in effect, was now the stock market. Formerly owned by Toys "R" Us (the computers probably ran the toy store's website), the cage was emblazoned with store logos. The HFT firm insisted on leaving the Toys "R" Us logos in place so that no one would know they had improved their position, in relation to the matching engine, by several feet. "They were all paranoid," said Ronan. "But they were right to be. If you know how to pickpocket someone and you were the pickpocketer, you would do the same thing. You'd see someone find a new switch that was three microseconds faster, and in two weeks everyone in the data center would have the same switch."

By the end of 2007 Ronan was making hundreds of thousands of dollars a year building systems to make stock market trades faster. He was struck, over and over again, by how little the traders he helped understood of the technology they were using. "They'd say, 'Aha! I saw it—it's so fast!' And I'd say, 'Look, I'm happy you like our product. But there's no fucking way you saw anything.' And they're like, 'I saw it!' And I'm like, 'It's three milliseconds—it's fifty times faster than the blink of an eye.'" He was also keenly aware that he had only the faintest idea of the reason for this incredible new lust for speed. He heard a lot of loose talk about "arbitrage," but what, exactly, was being arbitraged, and why did it need to be done so fast? "I felt like the getaway driver," he said. "Each time, it was like, 'Drive faster! Drive faster!' Then it was like, 'Get rid of the airbags!' Then it was, 'Get rid of the fucking seats!' Towards the end I'm like, 'Excuse me, sirs, but what are you doing in the bank?'" He had a sense of the technological aptitude of the various players. The two biggest high-frequency trading firms, Citadel and Getco, were easily the smartest. Some of the prop shops were smart, too. The big banks, at least for now, were all slow.

Beyond that, he didn't even really know much about his clients. The big banks—Goldman Sachs, Credit Suisse—everyone had heard of. Others—Citadel, Getco—were famous on a small scale. He learned that some of these firms were hedge funds, which meant that they took money from outside investors. But most of them were prop shops, trading only their own founders' money. A huge number of the firms he dealt with—Hudson River Trading, Eagle Seven, Simplex Investments, Evolution Financial Technologies, Cooperfund, DRW—no one had ever heard of, and the firms obviously intended to keep it that way. The prop shops were especially strange, because they were both transient and prosperous. "They'd be just five guys in a room. All of them geeks. The leader of each five-man pack is just an arrogant version of that geek. A fucking arrogant version of that." One day a prop shop was trading; the next, it had closed, and all the people in it had moved to work for some big Wall Street bank. One group of guys Ronan saw over and over: four Russian, one Chinese. The arrogant Russian guy who was clearly their leader was named Vladimir. Vladimir and his boys ping-ponged from prop shop to big bank and back to prop shop, writing the computer code that made the actual stock market trading decisions. Ronan watched them meet with one of the most senior guys at a big Wall Street bank that hoped to employ them—and the Wall Street big shot sucked up to them. "He walks into the meeting and says, 'I'm always the most important man in the room, but in this case Vladimir is.'" Ronan knew that these roving bands of geeks felt nothing but condescension toward the less technical guys who ran the big Wall Street firms. "I was listening to them talk about some calculation they had been asked to make, and Vladimir goes, 'Ho, ho, ho. That's what Americans call math.' He said it like *moth*. That's what Americans call *moth*. I thought, I'm fucking Irish, but fuck you guys. This country gave you a shot."

By early 2008 Ronan was spending a lot of his time abroad, helping high-frequency traders exploit the Americanization of foreign stock markets. A pattern emerged: A country in which the stock market had always traded on a single exchange— Canada, Australia, the UK—would, in the name of free-market competition, permit the creation of a new exchange. The new exchange was always located at some surprising distance from the original exchange. In Toronto it was inside an old department store building across the city from the Toronto Stock Exchange. In Australia it was mysteriously located not in the Sydney financial district but across Sydney Harbor, in the middle of a residential district. The old London Stock Exchange was in central London. BATS created a British rival in the Docklands, NYSE created another, outside of London, in Basildon, and Chi-X created a third in Slough. Each new exchange gave rise to the need for high-speed routes between the exchanges. "It was almost like they picked places to set up exchanges so that the market would fragment," said Ronan.

He still didn't have a job on Wall Street, but Ronan had every reason to be pleased with himself and with his career. In 2007, the first year of the speed boom, he'd made $486,000, nearly twice as much as he'd ever made. Yet he did not feel pleased with himself or with his career. He was obviously good at what he did, but he had no idea why he was doing it, and he wanted to. At the end of 2007, on New Year's Eve, he found himself sitting in a pub in Liverpool with "Let It Be" playing dully on the radio. His wife had given him the trip as this lovely gift. Around a miniature soccer ball she'd wrapped a note that said she'd bought him a plane ticket to England and a ticket to see his favorite football team. "I'm doing something I always dreamed about doing, and it was about the most depressing moment I've ever had in my life," said Ronan. "I'm thirty-four years old. I'm thinking it's never going to get any better. I'm going to be fucking Willy Loman for the rest of my life." He felt ordinary.

In the fall of 2009, out of the blue, the Royal Bank of Canada called him and invited him to interview for a job. He was more than a little wary. He'd barely heard of RBC, and when he checked out their website it told him next to nothing. He'd grown weary of self-important Wall Street traders who wanted him to do their manual labor for them. "I said, 'I mean no disrespect, but if you're calling to offer me some tech job, I have no fucking interest.'" The RBC guy who called him— Brad Katsuyama—insisted that it wasn't a tech job but a job in finance, on a trading floor.

Ronan met Brad at seven the next morning and wondered if that was a Wall Street thing, hauling people in for interviews at seven in the morning. Brad asked him a bunch of questions and then invited him back to meet his bosses. In what seemed to Ronan like "the quickest hiring in the history of Wall Street," RBC offered him a job on the trading floor. It paid $125,000, or roughly a third of what Ronan was making peddling speed to high-frequency traders. It came with a fancy title: Head of High-Frequency Trading Strategies. For a chance to work on a Wall Street trading floor, Ronan was willing to take a big pay cut. "To be honest, I would have taken less," he said. But the title disturbed him, because, as he put it, "I didn't know any high-frequency trading strategies." He was so excited to have finally landed a job on a Wall Street trading floor that he didn't bother to ask the obvious question. His wife asked it for him. "She says to me, 'What are you going to do for them?' And I realized I didn't really fucking know. I really, honest to God, have no idea what the job is. There was no job description ever discussed. He never told me what he wanted me for."

IN THE FALL of 2009, an article in a trade magazine caught Brad Katsuyama's eye. He'd spent the better part of a year trying and failing to find anyone who actually worked in what was now regularly referred to as high-frequency trading who was willing to explain to him how he made his money. The article claimed that HFT technologists were unhappy with the widening gulf in pay between themselves and the senior trading strategists of their firms, some of whom were rumored to be taking home hundreds of millions of dollars a year. He went looking for one of these unhappy technologists. The very first call he made, to a guy at Deutsche Bank who dealt often with HFT, gave him two names. Ronan's was the first.

In his interview, Ronan described to Brad what he'd witnessed inside the exchanges: the frantic competition for nanoseconds, the Toys "R" Us cage, the wire gauze, the war for space within the exchanges, the tens of millions being spent by high-frequency traders for tiny increments of speed. As he spoke, he filled huge empty tracts on Brad's mental map of the financial markets. "What he said told me that we needed to care about microseconds and nanoseconds," said Brad. The U.S. stock market was now a class system, rooted in speed, of haves and have-nots. The haves paid for nanoseconds; the have-nots had no idea that a nanosecond had value. The haves enjoyed a perfect view of the market; the have-nots *never saw the market at all*. What had once been the world's most public, most democratic, financial market had become, in spirit, something more like a private viewing of a stolen work of art. "I learned more from talking to him in an hour than I learned from six months of reading about HFT," said Brad. "The second I met him I wanted to hire him."

He wanted to hire him without being able to fully explain, to his bosses or even to Ronan, what he wanted to hire him for. He couldn't very well call him Vice President in Charge of Explaining to My Clueless Superiors Why High-Frequency Trading Is a Travesty. So he called him Head of High-Frequency Trading Strategies. "I felt he needed a 'Head of' title," said Brad, "to get more respect from people." That was Brad's main concern: that people on the trading floor, even at RBC, would take one look at Ronan and see a guy in a yellow jumpsuit who'd just emerged from some manhole. Ronan didn't even pretend to know what happened on a trading floor. "He had questions that were unbelievably rudimentary but that were necessary," said Brad. "He didn't know what 'bid' and 'offer' was. He didn't know what it meant to 'cross the spread.'"

On the side, without making a big deal of it, Brad started to teach Ronan the language of trading. A "bid" was an attempt to buy stock, an "offer" an attempt to sell it. To cross the spread, if you were selling, meant to accept the bidder's price, or, if you were buying, the offering price. "This fucking guy didn't laugh at me," said Ronan. "He sat down and explained it." That was their private deal: Brad would teach Ronan about trading, and Ronan would teach Brad about technology.

Right away there was something to teach. Brad and his team were having trouble turning Thor into a product they could sell to investors. The investors they'd told about their discovery were clearly eager to buy Thor and use it for themselves— T. Rowe Price's Gitlin had more or less tried to buy it on the spot—but Thor now had its problems. The experiment of arriving at the exchanges at the same time had worked perfectly—the first time. It proved hard to repeat, because it was difficult to coax thirteen light signals to arrive in thirteen different stock exchanges spread across northern New Jersey within 350 microseconds of each other—or roughly 100 microseconds less than the time they had calculated it would take some high-speed trader to front-run their order. They'd succeeded the first time by estimating the differences in travel time it took to send the messages to the various exchanges, and by building the equivalent delays into their software. But the travel times were never the same. They had no control over the path the signals took to get to the exchanges, or how much traffic was on the network. Sometimes it took 4 milliseconds for their stock market orders to arrive at the New York Stock Exchange; other times, it took 7 milliseconds. When the travel time differed from their guesses of what it would be, the market, once again, vanished.

In short, Thor was inconsistent; and it was inconsistent, Ronan explained, because the paths the electronic signals took from Brad's desk to the various exchanges were inconsistent. Ronan could see that these traders hadn't thought much about the physical process by which their signals traveled to the New Jersey stock exchanges. "I realized very quickly," he said, "and they'll admit this, so I mean no disrespect, that they had no fucking clue what they were doing." The signal sent from Brad's desk arrived at the New Jersey exchanges at different times because some exchanges were farther from Brad's desk than others. The fastest any high-speed trader's signal could travel from the first exchange it reached to the next one was 465 microseconds, or one two-hundredths of the time it takes to blink your eye, if you have a talent for it. That is, for Brad's trading orders to interact with the market as displayed on his trading screens, they needed to arrive at all the exchanges within a 465-microsecond window. The only way to do that, Ronan told his new colleagues at RBC, was to build and control your own fiber network.

To make his point, Ronan brought in oversized maps of New Jersey showing the fiber-optic networks built by telecom companies. On the maps you could see just how a signal traveled from Brad's trading station at One Liberty Plaza to the exchanges. When he unrolled his first map, a guy who worked in RBC's network support team burst out, "How the fuck did

you get those? They're telecom property! They're proprietary!"
Ronan explained, "When they said they wouldn't give them to
me because they were proprietary, I said, 'Well, then, propri-
etarily fuck off.'" The high-frequency traders were paying the
telecom carriers too much to be denied whatever they wanted,
and Ronan had been the agent of their desires. "These maps are
like fucking gold," he said. "But I had brought them so much
business that they would let me see inside their freaking wife's
underwear drawer if I asked them to."

The maps told a story: Any trading signal that originated in
lower Manhattan traveled up the West Side Highway and out
the Lincoln Tunnel. Perched immediately outside the tunnel, in
Weehawken, New Jersey, was the BATS exchange. From BATS
the routes became more complicated, as they had to find their
way through the clutter of the Jersey suburbs. "New Jersey is
now carved up like a Thanksgiving turkey," said Ronan. One
way or another, they traveled east to Secaucus, the location of
the Direct Edge family of exchanges founded by Goldman Sachs
and Citadel, and south to the Nasdaq family of exchanges in
Carteret. The New York Stock Exchange further complicated
the story. In early 2010, NYSE still had its computer servers in
lower Manhattan, at 55 Water Street. (They moved them to
distant Mahwah, New Jersey, that August.) As it was less than a
mile from Brad's desk, NYSE appeared to be the stock market
closest to him; but Ronan's maps showed the incredible indirec-
tion of optic fiber in Manhattan. "To get from Liberty Plaza
to Fifty-five Water Street, you might go through Brooklyn,"
he explained. "You can go fifty miles to get from Midtown to
downtown. To get from a building to a building across the street
you could travel fifteen miles." It was a ten-minute walk from
RBC's office at Liberty Plaza to the New York Stock Exchange.

But from a computer's point of view, the New York Stock Exchange was further from RBC's offices than Carteret.

To Brad the maps explained, among other things, why the market on BATS had proved so accurate. The reason they were always able to buy or sell 100 percent of the shares listed on BATS was that BATS was always the first stock market to receive their orders. News of their buying and selling hadn't had time to spread throughout the marketplace. "I was like, 'Holy shit, BATS is just closest to us.' It's right outside the freaking tunnel." Inside BATS, high-frequency trading firms were waiting for news that they could use to trade on the other exchanges. They obtained that news by placing very small bids and offers, typically for 100 shares, for every listed stock. Having gleaned that there was a buyer or seller of Company X's shares, they would race ahead to the other exchanges and buy or sell accordingly. (The race they needed to win was not a race against the ordinary investor, who had no clue what was happening to him, but against other high-speed traders.) The orders resting on BATS were typically just the 100-share minimum required for an order to be at the front of any price queue, as their only purpose was to tease information out of investors. The HFT firms posted these tiny orders on BATS—orders to buy or sell 100 shares of basically every stock traded in the U.S. market—not because they actually wanted to buy and sell the stocks but because they wanted to find out what investors wanted to buy and sell before they did it. BATS, unsurprisingly, had been created by high-frequency traders.

The funny thing was that a lot of what Ronan had seen and heard didn't make sense to him: He didn't know what he knew. Brad now helped him to understand. For instance, Ronan had noticed the HFT guys creating elaborate tables of the time, measured in microseconds, it took for a stock market order to travel from any given brokerage house to each of the exchanges. "Latency tables," these were called. The times were subtly different for every brokerage house—they depended upon where the brokerage house physically was located and which fiber networks it leased in New Jersey. These tables took trouble to create and were of obvious value to high-frequency traders, but Ronan had no idea why. This was the first Brad had heard of latency tables, but he knew exactly why they had been created: They enabled high-frequency traders to identify brokers by the time their orders took to travel from one exchange to the other. Once you had figured out which broker was behind any given stock market order, you could discern patterns in each broker's behavior. If you knew which broker had just come into the market with an order to buy 1,000 shares of IBM, you might further guess whether those 1,000 shares were the entire order or a part of a much larger order. You might also guess how the broker might distribute the order among the various exchanges and how much above the current market price for IBM shares the broker might be willing to pay. The HFT guys didn't need perfect information to make riskless profits; they only needed to skew the odds systematically in their favor. But, as Brad put it, "What you're looking for ultimately is large brokers who are behaving idiotically with their customers' orders. That's the real gold mine."

He also knew that Wall Street brokers had a new incentive to behave idiotically, because he had himself succumbed to the temptation. When Wall Street decided where to route their clients' stock market orders, they were now greatly influenced by the new system of kickbacks paid and fees charged to them by the exchanges: If a big Wall Street broker stood to be paid to send an order to buy 10,000 shares of IBM to BATS but was charged to send the same order to the New York Stock Exchange, it would program its routers to send the customer's order to BATS. The router, designed by human beings, took on a life of its own.

Along with the trading algorithms, the routers were a critical piece of technology in the automated stock markets. Both are designed and built by people who work for the Wall Street broker. Both do the thinking that people used to do, but the intellectual tasks they perform are different. The algorithm does its thinking first: It decides how to slice up any given order. Say you want to buy 100,000 shares of XYZ Company at no more than $25 a share, when the market shows a total of 2,000 shares offered at $25. To simply attempt to buy 100,000 shares all at once would create havoc in the market and drive the price higher. The algorithm decides how many shares you buy, when to buy them, and the price to pay. For example, it may instruct the router to carve the 100,000-share order into twenty pieces, and to buy 5,000 shares every five minutes, so long as the price is no higher than $25.

The router determines *where* the order is sent. For instance, a router might instruct the order to go first to a Wall Street firm's dark pool before going to the exchanges. Or it might instruct the order to go first to any exchange that will pay the broker to trade, and only then to exchanges on which the broker will be compelled to pay to trade. (This is a so-called sequential cost-effective router.) To illustrate how stupid routing can be, say you have told your Wall Street broker—to whom you are paying a commission—that you wish to buy 100,000 shares of Company XYZ at $25 and now, conveniently, there are 100,000 shares for sale at $25, 10,000 on each of ten different exchanges, all of which will charge the broker to trade on your behalf (though far less than the commission you have paid to him). There are, however, another 100 shares for sale, also at $25, on the BATS exchange—which will pay the broker for the trade. The sequential cost-effective router will go first to BATS and buy the 100 shares—and cause the other 100,000 shares to vanish into the paws of high-frequency traders (in the bargain relieving the broker of the obligation to pay to trade). The high-frequency traders can then turn around and sell the shares of Company XYZ at a higher price, or hold onto the shares for a few seconds more, while you, the investor, chase Company XYZ's shares even higher. In either case, the result is unappealing to the original buyer of Company XYZ's shares.

That is but the most obvious of many examples of routing stupidity. The customer (you, or someone investing on your behalf) is typically entirely oblivious to the inner workings of both algorithms and routers: Even if he demanded to know how his order was routed, and his broker told him, he would never be sure what was said was true, as he has no sufficiently detailed record of what shares traded and when they traded.

The brokers' routers, like bad poker players, all had a conspicuous tell. The tell might be a glitch in their machines rather than a twitch of their facial muscles, but it was just as valuable to the HFT guys on the other side of the table.

Once Brad had explained all of this to Ronan, he didn't need to explain it again. "It was, 'Oh shit, some of the things I overheard now make more sense,'" said Ronan.

With Ronan's help, the RBC team designed their own fiber network and turned Thor into a product that could be sold to investors. The sales pitch was absurdly simple: *There is a new predator in the financial markets. Here is how he operates, and we have a weapon you can use to defend yourself against him.* The argument about whether RBC should leap into bed with high-frequency traders ended. Brad's new problem was spreading the word of what he now knew to the U.S. investing public. Seeing how shocked people were by what Ronan had to say, and how interested they were in it, and no longer needing Ronan to persuade his bosses that something strange and new was afoot, Brad decided to set Ronan loose on Wall Street's biggest customers. "Brad calls me in and says, 'What if we stop calling you Head of High-Frequency Trading Strategy and make you Head of Electronic Trading Strategy?,'" said Ronan, who had no idea what either title actually meant. "I called my wife and said, 'I think they just promoted me.'"

A few days later, Ronan went with Brad to his first Wall Street meeting. "Right before the meeting, Brad says, 'What are you going to say? What have you prepared?' I hadn't prepared anything, so I said, 'I'll just wing it.'" He now had a pretty good idea why Brad had given him a new job title. "My role was to walk around and say to clients, 'Don't you understand you're being fucked?'" The man on the other end of this first extemporaneous presentation—the president of a $9 billion hedge fund—recalls the encounter this way: "I know I have a three-hundred-million-dollar problem on a nine-billion-dollar hedge fund." (That is, he knows that the cost of not being able to trade at the stated market prices is costing him $300 million a year.) "But I don't know exactly what the problem is. As he's talking, I'm saying to myself, RBC doesn't even know what they are doing. And who are these guys? They aren't traders. They're not salesguys. And they're not quants. So what are they? And then they say they have a solution to the world's problems. And you're like: 'What? How on earth can I even trust you?' And then they totally explain my problem." Between them, Brad and Ronan told this hedge fund manager all they had learned. They explained, in short, how the informational value of everything this man did with money was being auctioned by brokers and exchanges to high-frequency trading firms so that they might exploit him. That was why he had a $300 million problem on a $9 billion fund.

After Brad and Ronan had left his office, the president of this big hedge fund, who had never before thought of himself as prey, reconsidered the financial markets. He sat at his desk watching both his personal online brokerage account and his $1,800-a-month Bloomberg terminal. In his private brokerage account he set out to buy an exchange-traded fund (ETF) comprised of Chinese construction companies. Over several hours he watched the price of the fund on his Bloomberg terminal. It was midnight in China, nothing was happening, and the ETF's price didn't budge. He then clicked the Buy button on his online brokerage account screen, and the price on the Bloomberg screen jumped. Most people who used online brokerage accounts didn't have Bloomberg terminals that enabled them to monitor the market in something close to real time. Most investors never would know what happened in the market after they pressed the Buy button. "I hadn't even hit Execute," says the hedge fund president. "I hadn't done anything but put in a ticker symbol and a quantity to buy. And the market popped." Then, after he had bought his ETF at a higher price than originally listed, the hedge fund president received a confirmation saying that the trade had been executed by Citadel Derivatives. Citadel was one of the biggest high-frequency trading firms. "And I wondered, Why is my online broker sending my trades to Citadel?"

Brad had observed and encouraged a lot of Wall Street careers, but, as he said, "I'd never seen anyone's star rise as quickly as Ronan's did. He just took off." Ronan, for his part, couldn't quite believe how ordinary the people on Wall Street were. "It's a whole industry of bullshit," he said. The first thing that struck Ronan about a lot of the big investors he met was their insecurity. "People in this industry don't want to admit they don't know something," he said. "Almost never do they say, 'No, I don't know. Tell me.' I'd say, 'Do you know what co-location is?' And they'd say, 'Oh yeah, I know about co-location.' Then I'd say, 'You know, HFT now puts their servers in the same building with the exchange, as close as possible to the exchange's matching engine, so they get market data before everyone else.' And people are like, 'What the fuck??!! That's got to be illegal!' We met with hundreds of people. And no one knew about it." He was also surprised to find how wedded they were to the big Wall Street banks, even when those banks failed them. "In HFT there was no loyalty whatsoever," he said. Over and over again, investors would tell Ronan and Brad how outraged they were that the big Wall Street firms that handled their stock market orders had failed to protect them from this new predator. Yet they were willing to give RBC only a small percentage of their trades to execute. "This was the biggest confusion to me about Wall Street," said Ronan. " 'Wait, you're telling me you can't pay us because you need to pay all these other people who are trying to screw you?' "

Maybe because Ronan was so unlike a Wall Street person, he was granted special access and was able to get inside the heads of the Wall Street people to whom he spoke. "After that first meeting, I told him there was no point in us even being in the same meeting," said Brad. "We needed to divide and conquer."

By the end of 2010, Brad and Ronan between them met with roughly five hundred professional stock market investors who controlled, among them, many trillions of dollars in assets. They

never created a PowerPoint; they never did anything more for-
mal than sit down and tell people everything they knew in plain
English. Brad soon realized that the most sophisticated investors
didn't know what was going on in their own market. Not the
big mutual funds, Fidelity and Vanguard. Not the big money
management firms like T. Rowe Price and Janus Capital. Not
even the most sophisticated hedge funds. The legendary investor David Einhorn, for instance, was shocked; so was Dan Loeb,
another prominent hedge fund manager. Bill Ackman ran a
famous hedge fund, Pershing Square, that often made bids for
large chunks of companies. In the two years before Brad turned
up in his office to explain what was happening, Ackman had
started to suspect that people might be using the information
about his trades to trade ahead of him. "I felt that there was a
leak every time," says Ackman. "I thought maybe it was the
prime broker. It wasn't the kind of leak that I thought." A salesman Brad hired at RBC from Merrill Lynch to help him market Thor recalls one big investor calling to say, "You know,
I thought I knew what I did for a living but apparently not,
because I had no idea this was going on."

Then came the so-called flash crash. At 2:45 on May 6, 2010,
for no obvious reason, the market fell six hundred points in a
few minutes. A few minutes later, like a drunk trying to pretend he hadn't just knocked over the fishbowl and killed the
pet goldfish, it bounced right back up to where it was before. If
you weren't watching closely you could have missed the entire
event—unless, of course, you had placed orders in the market to buy or sell certain stocks. Shares of Procter & Gamble,
for instance, traded as low as a penny and as high as $100,000.
Twenty thousand different trades happened at stock prices more
than 60 percent removed from the prices of those stocks just

moments before. Five months later, the SEC published a report blaming the entire fiasco on a single large sell order, of stock market futures contracts, mistakenly placed on an exchange in Chicago by an obscure Kansas City mutual fund.

That explanation could only be true by accident, because the stock market regulators did not possess the information they needed to understand the stock markets. The unit of trading was now the microsecond, but the records kept by the exchanges were by the second. There were one million microseconds in a second. It was as if, back in the 1920s, the only stock market data available was a crude aggregation of all trades made during the decade. You could see that at some point in that era there had been a stock market crash. You could see nothing about the events on and around October 29, 1929. The first thing Brad noticed as he read the SEC report on the flash crash was its old-fashioned sense of time. "I did a search of the report for the word 'minute,'" said Brad. "I got eighty-seven hits. I then searched for 'second' and got sixty-three hits. I then searched for 'millisecond' and got four hits—none of them actually relevant. Finally, I searched for 'microsecond' and got zero hits." He read the report once and then never looked at it again. "Once you get a sense of the speed with which things are happening, you realize that explanations like this—someone hitting a button—are not right," he said. "You want to see a single time-stamped sheet of every trade. To see what followed from what. Not only does it not exist, it *can't* exist, as currently configured."

No one could say for sure what caused the flash crash—for the same reason no one could prove that high-frequency traders were front-running the orders of ordinary investors. The data didn't exist. But Brad sensed that the investment community was not persuaded by the SEC's explanation and by the assur-

ances of the stock exchanges that all was well inside them. A
lot of them asked the same question he was asking himself: Isn't
there a much deeper question of how this one snowball caused
a deadly avalanche? He watched the most sophisticated investors respond after Duncan Niederauer, the CEO of the New
York Stock Exchange, embarked on a goodwill tour, the purpose of which seemed to be to explain why the New York Stock
Exchange had nothing to do with the flash crash. "That's when
a light went off," said Danny Moses, of Seawolf Capital, a hedge
fund that specialized in stock market investments. He had heard
Brad and Ronan's pitch. "Niederauer was saying, 'Hey, have
confidence in us. It wasn't us.' Wait a minute: I never thought it
was you. Why should I be concerned that it was you? It was like
your kid walks into your house and says to you, 'Dad, I didn't
dent your car.' Wait, there's a dent in my car?"

After the flash crash, Brad no longer bothered to call investors
to set up meetings. His phone rang off the hook. "What the flash
crash did," said Brad, "was it opened the buy side's willingness
to understand what was going on. Because their bosses started
asking questions. Which meant that our telling the truth, and
explaining it to them, fit perfectly."

A few months later, in September 2010, another strange,
albeit more obscure, market event occurred, this time in the
Chicago suburbs. A sleepy stock exchange called the CBSX,
which traded just a tiny fraction of total stock market volume,
announced that it was going to invert the usual system of fees
and kickbacks. It was now going to pay people to "take" liquidity and charge people to "make" it. Once again, this struck Brad
as bizarre: Who would make markets on exchanges if they had
to pay to do it? But then the CBSX exploded with activity.
Over the next several weeks, for example, it handled a third of

the total volume of the shares traded in Sirius, the satellite radio company. Brad knew that Sirius was a favorite stock of HFT firms—but he couldn't understand why it was suddenly trading in huge volume in Chicago. Obviously, when they saw they could be paid to "take" on the CBSX, the big Wall Street brokers all responded by reprogramming their routers so that their customers' orders were sent to the CBSX. But who was on the other side of their trades, paying more than ever had been paid for the privilege?

That's when Ronan told Brad about a new company called Spread Networks. Spread Networks, as it turned out, had tried to hire Ronan to sell its precious line to high-frequency traders. They'd walked Ronan through their astonishing tunneling project and their business plans. "I told them they were fucking bananas," said Ronan. "They said they were going to sell two hundred of these things. I came up with a list of twenty-eight firms who would potentially buy the line. Plus they were charging ten point six million dollars up front for five years' worth of service, and they wanted to pay me twelve grand for each one I sold. Which is just an insult. You might as well ask me to blow you while I'm doing it."

Ronan mentioned this unpleasant experience to Brad, who naturally said, "You're telling me this *now*?" Ronan explained that he hadn't been able to mention Spread before because he had signed a non-disclosure agreement with the company. The agreement had expired that day, and so now he was free to disclose not only what Spread had done but for whom they had done it: not just HFT firms like Knight and Citadel but also the big Wall Street banks—Morgan Stanley, Goldman Sachs, and others. "You couldn't prove what these guys were doing was a big deal, because they were so guarded about how much money they were making," said Brad. "But you could see how big a deal it was by how much they spent. And now the banks were involved. I thought, Oh shit, this isn't just HFT shops. This is industry-wide. It's systemic."

Ronan offered an explanation for what had just happened on the CBSX: Spread Networks had flipped its switch and turned itself on just two weeks earlier. CBSX then inverted its pricing. By inverting its pricing—by paying brokers to execute customers' trades for which they would normally be charged a fee—the exchange enticed the brokers to send their customers' orders to the CBSX so that they might be front-run back to New Jersey by high-frequency traders using Spread Networks. The information that high-frequency traders gleaned from trading with investors in Chicago they could use back in the markets in New Jersey. It was now very much worth it to them to pay the CBSX to "make" liquidity. It was exactly the game they had played on BATS, of enticing brokers to reveal their customers' intentions so that they might exploit them elsewhere. But racing a customer order from Weehawken to other points in New Jersey was hard compared to racing it from Chicago on Spread's new line.

Spread was another piece of what was becoming a fantastically elaborate puzzle. The team Brad was assembling at RBC didn't have all the pieces to the puzzle—not yet—but they had more of them than anyone else willing to talk openly on the subject. The reactions of investors to what they already knew they considered as simply more pieces of the puzzle. Every now and then—perhaps 5 percent of the time—Brad or Ronan met some investor who didn't care to know about the puzzle, someone who didn't want to hear their story. Whenever Brad returned from one of these meetings, he'd discover that the person to whom he had just spoken depended, one way or another, on the revenues flowing to high-frequency traders. Every now and again—maybe another 5 percent of the time—they met with an investor who was completely terrified. "They knew so little, and they'd be so scared inside their own firms that they'd rather the meeting never happened," said Brad. But most of the hundreds of big-time investors with whom Brad and Ronan spoke had the same reaction as T. Rowe Price's Mike Gitlin: They knew something was very wrong, but they didn't know what, and now that they knew they were outraged. "Brad was the honest broker," said Gitlin. "I don't know how many knew it, but he was the only guy who would say it. He was saying, 'I'm here and I'm watching it and we're a party to it and the whole thing is rigged.' He exposed people who were bad actors, and a lot of people in this industry are afraid to do that. He was saying, 'This is just offensive.'" Vincent Daniel, the head strategist at Seawolf, put it another way. He took a long look at this unlikely pair—a Canadian Asian guy from this bank no one cared about, and this Irish guy who was doing a fair impression of a Dublin handyman—who had just told him the most incredible true story he had ever heard, and said, "Your biggest competitive advantage is that you don't want to fuck me."

Trust on Wall Street was still—just—possible. The big investors who trusted Brad began to share whatever information they could get their hands on from their other brokers—information Brad was never meant to see. For instance, several demanded to know from their other Wall Street brokers what percentage of the trades executed on their behalf were executed inside the brokers' dark pools. These dark pools contained the murkiest financial incentives in the new stock market. Goldman Sachs and Credit Suisse ran the most prominent dark pools. But every brokerage firm strongly encouraged investors who wanted to buy or sell big chunks of stock to do so in that firm's dark pool. In theory, the brokers were meant to find the best price for their customers. If the customer wanted to buy shares in Chevron, and the best price happened to be on the New York Stock Exchange, the broker was not supposed to stick the customer with a worse price inside their dark pool. But the dark pools were opaque. Their rules were not published. No outsider could see what went on inside them. It was entirely possible that a broker's own traders were trading against the customers in the dark pool: There were no rules against it. And while the brokers often protested that there were no conflicts of interest inside their dark pools, all the dark pools exhibited the same strange property: A huge percentage of the customer orders sent into a dark pool were executed inside the pool. Brad knew this because a handful of the world's biggest stock market investors had shared their information with him—so that he might help them figure out what was going on.

It was hard to explain. A broker was expected to find the best possible price in the market for his customer. The Goldman Sachs dark pool—to take one example—was less than 2 percent of the entire stock market. So why did nearly 50 percent of the customer orders routed into Goldman's dark pool end up being executed inside that pool—rather than out in the wider market? Most of the brokers' dark pools constituted less than 1 percent of the entire market, and yet somehow those brokers found the best price for their customers between 15 and 60 percent of the time. (So-called rates of internalization varied from broker to broker.) And because the dark pool was not required to say exactly when it had executed a trade, and the broker did not typically tell his investors where it had executed a trade, much less the market conditions at the moment of execution, the customer lived in darkness. Even a giant investor like T. Rowe Price simply had to take it on faith that Goldman Sachs or Merrill Lynch had acted in its interest, despite the obvious financial incentives *not* to do so. As Mike Gitlin said, "It's just very hard to prove that any broker-dealer is routing the trades to someplace other than the place that is best for you. You couldn't SEE what any given broker was doing." If an investor as large as T. Rowe Price, which acted on behalf of millions of small investors, was unable to obtain from its stockbrokers the information it needed to determine if the brokers had acted in their interest, what chance did the little guy have?

In this environment, the effect of trying to help investors see what was happening to their money was revolutionary. The Royal Bank of Canada had never been anything more than the most trivial player in the U.S. stock market. At the end of 2010, Brad saw a report from Greenwich Associates, the firm used by Wall Street banks to evaluate their standing in relation to their peers. Greenwich Associates interviews the investors who use Wall Street's services and privately reports their findings to the Wall Street firms. In 2009, RBC had—at number 19—been far down Greenwich Associates' stock market rankings. At the end of 2010, after only six months of Thor, RBC was ranked number 1. Greenwich Associates called RBC to ask what on earth was going on within the bank. In the history of their rankings, they said, they had never seen a firm jump more than three spots.

At the same time, this movement spawned by Brad Katsuyama's unhappiness with Wall Street was starting to feel less like a business than a cause. Brad was no radical. As he put it, "There's a difference between choosing a crusade and having it thrust on you." He'd never really thought all that much about how he fit into the bigger picture, and certainly never considered himself a character upon a stage. He'd never run for student council. He'd never had anything to do with politics. "It's always seemed to me that the things you need to do to influence change had to do with glad-handing," he said. "It just felt so phony." This didn't feel phony. This felt like a situation in which a person, through his immediate actions, might change the world. After all, he was now educating the world's biggest money managers about the inner workings of the stock market, which strongly suggested to him that no one else on Wall Street was willing to teach them how their investment dollars were being abused. The more he understood the inner workings of the financial system, the better he might inform the investors, big and small, who were being abused by that system. And the more pressure they might bring to bear on the system to change.

The deep problem with the system was a kind of moral inertia. So long as it served the narrow self-interests of everyone inside it, no one on the inside would ever seek to change it, no matter how corrupt or sinister it became—though even to use words like "corrupt" and "sinister" made serious people uncomfortable, and so Brad avoided them. Maybe his biggest concern, when he spoke to investors, was that he'd be seen as just another nut with a conspiracy theory. One of the compliments that made him happiest was when a big investor said, "Thank God, finally there's someone who knows something about high-frequency trading who isn't an Area 51 guy." Because he wasn't a radical, it took him a while to figure out that fate and circumstance had created for him a dramatic role, which he was obliged to play. One night he actually turned to Ashley, now his wife, and said, "It feels like I'm an expert in something that badly needs to be changed. I think there's only a few people in the world who can do anything about this. If I don't do something right now—me, Brad Katsuyama—there's no one to call."

CHAPTER FOUR

TRACKING THE PREDATOR

B y the end of 2010 they'd built a marketable weapon. The weapon promised to defend investors in the U.S. stock market from what appeared to be a new kind of market predator. About that predator they knew surprisingly little. Apart from Ronan, Brad knew no one from inside the world of high-frequency trading. He had only a vague idea of that world's reach, or its political influence. From Ronan he knew that the HFT firms enjoyed special relationships with the public stock exchanges, but he knew nothing about their dealings with the big Wall Street banks tasked with guarding the interests of investors. Then again, many of the people who worked inside the Wall Street banks seemed to have only the faintest idea of what those banks were up to. If you worked for a big Wall Street bank, the easiest way to find out what other banks were up to was to seek out their employees who were looking for new jobs and interview them. In the wake of the financial crisis, the too-big-to-fail end of Wall Street was in turmoil, and Brad was able to talk to people who, just a few years before, would never have considered working for the Royal Bank of Canada. By the time he was finished picking their collective brains, he had spoken to more than a hundred employees at too-big-to-fail banks but hired only about thirty-five of them. "They all wanted jobs," he said. "It's not that they wouldn't tell me. It's that they didn't know how their own electronic systems worked."

The thread running through all these people, even the ones he didn't hire, was their fear and distrust of the system. John Schwall was a curious case in point. Schwall's father had been a firefighter on Staten Island, like his father before him. "Every male on my father's side is a fireman," Schwall said. "I wanted to do something more." More meant getting a master's in engineering from the Stevens Institute of Technology, in Hoboken, New Jersey. In the late 1990s he took a job at Banc of America Securities,* where he rose to a position with an important-sounding title: Head of New Products. His job description was more glamorous than his job. John Schwall was the guy behind the scenes who handled the boring details, like managing relations between the traders on the floor and the tech geeks who built stuff for them, or ensuring that the bank complied with new stock market regulations. He routinely ranked in the top 1 percent of all employees in Banc of America's reviews of its personnel, but his status in a Wall Street bank was akin to head butler to a British upper-class family. To the grunts in the back office he might have seemed like a big shot, but to the traders who made the money he did not.

---

* It is irritating to read about an American bank that insists on calling itself a banc. The banc in this case was pushed to do so, as the securities divisions within American banks (here, Bank of America) are prohibited by regulators from referring to themselves as banks.

Whatever frustration this caused him he buried. Given an excuse to feel loyalty for his company, he seized it. September 11, 2001, for instance. Schwall's desk was in the North Tower of the World Trade Center, on the eighty-first floor. By sheer fluke he had been late to work that morning—the only day in 2001 he would report late to work—and he'd watched the first plane hit, thirteen floors above his desk, from the window of a distant bus. Several of his colleagues died that day, and so had some Staten Island firemen he'd known. Schwall seldom spoke of the event, but privately he believed that, had he been at his desk when the plane hit, his instinct would have been to go up the stairs rather than down them. The guilt he felt for not having been on hand to help somehow became, in his mind, a debt he owed to his colleagues and to his employer. Which is to say that Schwall wanted to feel toward a Wall Street bank what a fireman is meant to feel toward his company. "I thought I'd be at Banc of America forever," he said.

Then came the financial crisis, and, in 2008, the acquisition, by Bank of America, of a collapsing Merrill Lynch. What happened next upended Schwall's worldview. Merrill Lynch had been among the most prolific creators of the very worst subprime mortgage bonds. Had they been left to the mercy of the market—had Bank of America not saved them—the Merrill Lynch people would have been tossed out on the street. Instead, right before their acquisition, they awarded themselves massive bonuses that Bank of America wound up having to pay. "It was incredibly unfair," said Schwall. "It was incredibly unjust. My stock in this company I helped to build for nine years goes into the shitter, and these assholes pay themselves record bonuses. It was a fucking crime." Even more incredibly, the Merrill Lynch people ended up in charge of Bank of America's equity division and set about firing most of the people in it. A lot of those people had been good, loyal employees of the bank. "Wall Street is corrupt, I decided," said Schwall afterwards. "There is no corporate loyalty to employees."

Schwall was one of the few Banc of America people who kept his job: Merrill Lynch had no one to replace him. He hid his true feelings, but he no longer trusted his employer. And he sensed, for the first time in his career, that his employer did not trust him. One day he sent himself an email from his personal account to his work account—he was helping out some friends who had been fired by the bank and who wanted to start a small brokerage firm. His boss called him to ask him about it. *What the hell are they doing monitoring my incoming emails?* Schwall wondered.

His ability to monitor his superiors exceeded their ability to monitor him, and he began to do it. "There was a lot of unspoken animosity," he said. He noticed the explosion of trading activity inside of Merrill Lynch's dark pool fueled by high-frequency traders. He saw that Merrill Lynch created a new revenue line, to account for the money paid to them by high-frequency trading firms for access to the Merrill Lynch dark pool. He noticed that the guy who had built the Merrill Lynch electronic trading platform was one of the highest-paid people in all of Merrill Lynch—and he'd nevertheless quit to create a company that would cater to HFT firms. He noticed letters sent on bank letterhead to the Securities and Exchange Commission arguing against further stock market regulation. He saved one in which the bank's lawyers wrote that "despite numerous changes in recent years in both market structure and participant behavior, the equity market is functioning well today." One day he heard a rumor that the Merrill people had assigned an analyst to produce a report to prove that Merrill's stock market customers were better off because of whatever happened inside Merrill's dark pool. There was apparently some controversy around this report. Schwall filed that rumor away for later use.

Schwall wanted to think of himself as a guy who lived by a few simple principles, a good soldier. After the financial crisis he was more like the Resentful Butler. He had a taste for asking complicated questions, and for tracking the answers into whatever rabbit hole they might lead him. He had, in short, an obsessive streak.

It wasn't until after he'd hired Schwall away from Bank of America to work for RBC that Brad noticed this side of Schwall. He should have seen it before, simply from Schwall's chosen role on Wall Street: product manager. A product manager, to be any good, had to be obsessive. The role had been spawned by the widespread belief that traders didn't know how to talk to computer geeks and that computer geeks did not respond rationally to big, hairy traders hollering at them. A product manager stood between the two groups, to sort out which of the things the traders wanted that were the most important and how best to build them. For instance, an RBC stock market trader might demand a button on his screen that said "Thor," which he could hit when he wanted Thor to execute his order to buy stock. To design that button might require twenty pages of mind-numbingly detailed specifications. That's where Schwall came in. "He goes into details that no one else will go into, because for some reason that's what he likes to do," said Brad.

The first hint that Schwall's obsession with detail might take a sharp turn into some private cul-de-sac came in company meetings. "He'd go off on complete tangents," said Brad. "Semi-related but outer space–type stuff." Another way Brad saw how

Schwall's mind worked was in a fight that Schwall picked not long after he started working at RBC. The bank had declined an offer to serve as a lead sponsor for a charity called Wings Over Wall Street. Wings Over Wall Street raised money to combat amyotrophic lateral sclerosis (ALS)—Lou Gehrig's disease. In response, and without explaining why, Schwall blasted a system-wide email explaining the importance of ALS research and encouraging all RBC employees to get behind Wings Over Wall Street. The RBC executives who had made the original decision understandably saw this rogue email as a political act intended to undermine their authority. For no apparent reason, Schwall had alienated a bunch of important people who had the power to fire him.

Brad now found himself between his new, extremely valuable employee and a top RBC executive who wanted his scalp. When pressed, Schwall finally explained to Brad that his mother had just died of ALS. "And he hadn't thought to mention it," said Brad. "He'd spent years trying to figure out how to help his mother. The fact his mother died of the disease would have won the argument, and he never mentions it. He said it would have been underhanded and unprincipled." Schwall's problem wasn't an uncharming taste for corporate politics but a charming ineptitude at playing them, Brad decided. ("Anyone who was politically astute never would have done this.") He nevertheless stumbled into politics often enough and played them badly enough that Brad finally came up with a name for the resulting mess: a Schwalling. "A Schwalling is when he does something unintentionally idiotic that makes him look stupid," said Brad.

All Schwall would say is, "I just sort of get crazy from time to time." He'd become obsessed with something, and his obsessions sent him on a trip to a place from which the journey's origin could no longer be glimpsed. The result was a lot of activity without an obvious motive.

Thor had triggered Schwall's private process. Thor, and what it implied about the U.S. financial system, became Schwall's greatest obsession. Before Brad explained to him how Thor worked and why, Schwall hadn't thought twice about the U.S. stock markets. After he met Brad, he was certain that the market at the heart of capitalism was rigged. "As soon as you realize this," he said, "as soon as you realize that you are not able to execute your orders because someone else is able to identify what you are trying to do and race ahead of you to the other exchanges, it's over," he said. "It changes your mind." He stewed on the situation; the longer he stewed, the angrier he became. "It really just pissed me off," he said. "That people set out this way to make money from everyone else's retirement account. I knew who was being screwed, people like my mom and pop, and I became hell-bent on figuring out who was doing the screwing." He reconsidered what he'd seen at Merrill Lynch after they had taken over Bank of America's stock trading department. He hunted down the analyst who had done the controversial analysis of Merrill's dark pool, for instance. The analyst told him that he had found that the dark pool was actually costing the customers (while profiting Merrill Lynch), but that management did not want to hear it. "They kept on telling him to change his report," said Schwall. "He was basically told that he had to find a different way to do it to get the answer they needed."

Early one Monday morning, in the summer of 2011, Brad had a call from Schwall. "He said, 'Hey, I'm not coming in today,'" recalls Brad. "And I said, 'What's going on?' He just said, 'Trust me.' Then he disappeared."

The previous night Schwall had gone out into his backyard,

with nothing but a cigar, a chair, and his iPad. "I had the belief that some people were perpetuating a fraud. When you think HFT, what do you think? You think nothing. You don't have a person. You don't have a face. You think a *computer*. But there are specific people behind this." He'd started by Googling "front-running" and "Wall Street" and "scandal." What he was looking for, at first, was the cause of the problem Thor had solved: How was it legal for a handful of insiders to operate at faster speeds than the rest of the market and, in effect, steal from investors? He soon had his answer: Regulation National Market System. Passed by the SEC in 2005 but not implemented until 2007, Reg NMS, as it became known, required brokers to find the best market prices for the investors they represented. The regulation had been inspired by charges of front-running made in 2004 against two dozen specialists on the floor of the old New York Stock Exchange—a charge the specialists settled by paying a $241 million fine.

Up till then the various brokers who handled investors' stock market orders had been held to the loose standard of "best execution." What that meant in practice was subject to interpretation. If you wanted to buy 10,000 shares of Microsoft at $30 a share, and the broker went into the market and saw that there were only 100 shares offered at $30, he might choose not to buy those hundred shares and wait until more sellers turned up. He had the discretion not to spook the market, and to play your hand on your behalf as smartly as he could. After the brokers abused the trust implicit in that discretion once too often, the government took the discretion away. Reg NMS replaced the loose notion of best execution with the tight legal one of "best price." To define best price, Reg NMS relied on the concept of the National Best Bid and Offer, known as the NBBO. If an investor wished to buy 10,000 shares of Microsoft, and 100 shares were offered on the BATS exchange at $30 a share, while the full 10,000 listed on the other twelve exchanges were offered at $30.01, his broker was required to purchase the 100 shares on Bats at $30 before moving on to the other exchanges. "It mandated routing to more exchanges than you might otherwise have to go to," said Schwall. "And so it created more opportunities for people to front-run you." The regulation also made it far easier for high-frequency traders to predict where brokers would send their customers' orders, as they must send them first to the exchange that offered the best market price.

That would have been fine but for the manner in which the best market price was calculated. The new law required a mechanism for taking the measure of the entire market—for creating the National Best Bid and Offer—by compiling all the bids and offers for all U.S. stocks in one place. That place, inside some computer, was called the Securities Information Processor, which, because there is no such thing on Wall Street as too many acronyms, became known as the SIP. The thirteen stock markets piped their prices into the SIP, and the SIP calculated the NBBO. The SIP was the picture of the U.S. stock market most investors saw.

Like a lot of regulations, Reg NMS was well-meaning and sensible. If everyone on Wall Street abided by the rule's spirit, the rule would have established a new fairness in the U.S. stock market. The rule, however, contained a loophole: *It failed to specify the speed of the SIP.* To gather and organize the stock prices from all the exchanges took milliseconds. It took milliseconds more to disseminate those calculations. The technology used to perform these calculations was old and slow, and the exchanges apparently had little interest in improving it. There was no rule against high-frequency traders setting up computers inside the exchanges and building their own, much faster, better cared for version of the SIP. That's exactly what they'd done, so well that there were times when the gap between the high-frequency traders' view of the market and that of ordinary investors could be twenty-five milliseconds, or twice the time it now took to travel from New York to Chicago and back again.

Reg NMS was intended to create equality of opportunity in the U.S. stock market. Instead it institutionalized a more pernicious inequality. A small class of insiders with the resources to create speed were now allowed to preview the market and trade on what they had seen.

Thus—for example—the SIP might suggest to the ordinary investor in Apple Inc. that the stock was trading at 400–400.01. The investor would then give his broker his order to buy 1,000 shares at the market price, or $400.01. The infinitesimal period of time between the moment the order was submitted and the moment it was executed was gold to the traders with faster connections. How much gold depended on two variables: a) the gap in time between the public SIP and the private ones and b) how much Apple's stock price bounced around. The bigger the gap in time, the greater the chance that Apple's stock price would have moved; and the more likely that a fast trader could stick an investor with an old price. That's why volatility was so valuable to high-frequency traders: It created new prices for fast traders to see first and to exploit. It wouldn't matter if some people in the market had an early glimpse of Apple's price if the price of Apple's shares never moved.

Apple's stock moved a lot, of course. In a paper published in February 2013, a team of researchers at the University of California, Berkeley, showed that the SIP price of Apple stock and the price seen by traders with faster channels of market information differed 55,000 times in a single day. That meant that there were 55,000 times a day a high-frequency trader could exploit the SIP-generated ignorance of the wider market. Fifty-five thousand times a day, he might buy Apple shares at an outdated price, then turn around and sell them at the new, higher price, exploiting the ignorance of the slower-footed investor on either end of his trades. And that was only the most obvious way a high-frequency trader might use his advance view of the market to make money.

Schwall already knew a lot about the boring nitty-gritty details of Reg NMS, as he had been in charge of implementing the new rule for the whole of Bank of America. He'd seen to the bank's need to build so-called smart order routers that could figure out which exchange had the official best price of any given stock (the NBBO) and send the customers' orders to that exchange. By complying with Reg NMS, he now understood, the smart order routers simply marched investors into various traps laid for them by high-frequency traders. "At that point I just got very, very pissed off," he said. "That they are ripping off the retirement savings of the entire country through systematic fraud and people don't even realize it. That just drives me up the fucking wall."

His anger expressed itself in a search for greater detail. When he saw that Reg NMS had been created to correct for the market manipulations of the old NYSE specialists, he wanted to know: How had *that* corruption come about? He began another search. He discovered that the New York Stock Exchange specialists had been exploiting a loophole in some earlier regulation— which of course just led Schwall to ask: What event had led the SEC to create *that* regulation? Many hours later he'd clawed his way back to the 1987 stock market crash, which, as it turned out, gave rise to the first, albeit crude, form of high-frequency trading. During the 1987 crash, Wall Street brokers, to avoid having to buy stock, had stopped answering their phones, and small investors were unable to enter their orders into the market. In response, the government regulators had mandated the creation of an electronic Small Order Execution System so that the little guy's order could be sent into the market with the press of a key on a computer keyboard, without a stockbroker first taking it from him on the phone. Because a computer was able to transmit trades must faster than humans, the system was soon gamed by smart traders, for purposes having nothing to do with the little guy.* At which point Schwall naturally asked: From whence came the regulation that had made brokers feel comfortable not answering their phones in the midst of the 1987 stock market crash?

As it turns out, when you Google "front-running" and "Wall Street" and "scandal," and you are hell-bent on following the search to its conclusion, the journey cannot be finished in an evening. At five o'clock Monday morning Schwall finally went back inside his house. He slept for two hours, then rose and called Brad to tell him he wasn't coming to work. Then he set off for a Staten Island branch of the New York Public Library. "There was quite a bit of vengeance on my mind," he said. As a high school junior Schwall had been New York City's wrestling champion in the 119-pound division. "He's the nicest guy in the world most of the time," said Brad. "But then sometimes he's not." A streak of anger ran through him, and exactly where

---

* A year later, in 2012, *Wall Street Journal* reporter Scott Patterson would write an excellent history of the early electronic traders called *Dark Pools*.

it came from Schwall could not say, but he knew perfectly well what triggered it: injustice. "If I can fix something and fuck these people who are fucking the rest of this country, I'm going to do it," he said. The trigger for his most recent burst of feeling was Thor, but if you had asked him on Wednesday morning why he was still digging around the Staten Island library instead of going to work, Schwall wouldn't have thought to mention Thor. Instead he would have said, "I am trying to understand the origins of every form of front-running in the history of the United States."

Several days later he'd worked his way back to the late 1800s. The entire history of Wall Street was the story of scandals, it now seemed to him, linked together tail to trunk like circus elephants. Every systemic market injustice arose from some loophole in a regulation created to correct some prior injustice. "No matter what the regulators did, some other intermediary found a way to react, so there would be another form of front-running," he said. When he was done in the Staten Island library he returned to work, as if there was nothing unusual at all about the product manager having turned himself into a private eye. He'd learned several important things, he told his colleagues. First, there was nothing new about the behavior they were at war with: The U.S. financial markets had always been either corrupt or about to be corrupted. Second, there was zero chance that the problem would be solved by financial regulators; or, rather, the regulators might solve the narrow problem of front-running in the stock market by high-frequency traders, but whatever they did to solve the problem would create yet another opportunity for financial intermediaries to make money at the expense of investors.

Schwall's final point was more aspiration than insight. For

the first time in Wall Street history, the technology existed that eliminated entirely the need for financial intermediaries. Buyers and sellers in the U.S. stock market were now able to connect with each other without any need of a third party. "The way that the technology had evolved gave me the conviction that we had a unique opportunity to solve the problem," he said. "There was no longer any need for any human intervention." If they were going to somehow eliminate the Wall Street middlemen who had flourished for centuries, they needed to enlarge the frame of the picture they were creating. "I was so concerned that we were talking about what we were doing as a solution to high-frequency trading," he said. "It was bigger than that. The goal had to be to eliminate *any* unnecessary intermediation."

BRAD FOUND IT odd that his product manager had set off to investigate the history of Wall Street scandal—it was a bit like an offensive lineman choosing to skip practice to infiltrate the opposing team's locker room. But Schwall's side career as a private eye, at least at first, struck him as a harmless digression, of a piece with Schwall's tendency in meetings to go off on tangents. "Once he gets on one of these bents it's better just to let him go," said Brad. "That's just him working eighteen-hour days instead of fourteen-hour days."

Besides, they now had far bigger problems. By the middle of 2011, Thor's limitations were visible. "We had this meteoric rise in our business the first year and then it flatlines," said Brad. In an open market, when customers were offered a new and better product, they ditched their old product for it. Wall Street banks weren't subject to the usual open market forces. Investors paid Wall Street banks for all sorts of reasons: for research, to keep them sweet, to get private access to corporate executives, or simply because they had always done so. The way that they paid them was to give them their trades to execute—that is, they believed they needed to allocate some very large percentage of their trades to the big Wall Street banks simply to maintain existing relations with them. RBC's clients were now routinely calling to say, "Hey, we love using Thor, but there is only so much business we can do with you because we have to pay Goldman Sachs and Morgan Stanley."

The Royal Bank of Canada was running away with the title of Wall Street's most popular broker by peddling a tool whose only purpose was to protect investors from the rest of Wall Street. The investors refused to draw the obvious conclusion that they should have a lot less to do with the rest of Wall Street. RBC had become the number-one-rated stockbroker in America and yet was still only the ninth best paid: They would never attract more than a tiny fraction of America's stock market trades, and that fraction would never be enough to change the system. A guy Ronan knew at the big high-frequency trading shop Citadel called him one day and put the matter in a nutshell: *I know what you're doing. It's genius. And there's nothing we can do about it. But you are only two percent of the market.*

On top of that, the big Wall Street banks, seeing RBC's success, were seeking to undermine it or at least to pretend to replicate it. "The tech people at other firms are calling me and saying, 'I want to do Thor. How does Thor work?'" recalled Allen Zhang. The business people at the banks were now calling Ronan and Rob and offering them multiples of what they earned at RBC to leave. The whole of Wall Street had been in something like a two-year hiring freeze, and yet these big banks were suggesting to Ronan—who had spent the past fifteen years unable to get his foot in the door of any bank—that they'd pay him as much as $1.5 million to join them. Headhunters called Brad and told him that, if he was willing to leave RBC for a competitor, the opening bid was $3 million a year, guaranteed. Just to keep his team in place, Brad arranged for RBC to create a pool of money and set it aside: If the guys hung around for three years, they would be handed the money and would wind up being paid something closer to their market value. RBC agreed to do it, probably because Brad did not ask for a piece of the action himself and continued to work for far less than he could have made elsewhere.

The bank's marketing department proposed to Brad, as a way to get some media attention for Thor, that he apply for a *Wall Street Journal* Technology Innovation Award. Brad had never heard of the *Wall Street Journal*'s Technology Innovation Awards, but he thought that he might use the *Wall Street Journal* to tell the world just how corrupt the U.S. stock market had become. His bosses at RBC, when they got wind of his plans, wanted him to attend a lot of meetings—to discuss what he might say to the *Wall Street Journal*. They worried about their relationships with other Wall Street banks and with the public exchanges. "They didn't want to ruffle anyone's feathers," says Brad. "There was not a lot I couldn't say in a small closed forum, but they didn't want me saying it openly." He soon realized that, while RBC would allow him to apply for awards, it would not let him describe publicly what Thor had inadvertently exposed: the manner in which HFT firms front-ran ordinary investors; the conflict of interest that brokers had when they were being paid by the exchanges to route orders; the conflict of interest the exchanges had when they were being paid a billion dollars a year by HFT firms for faster access to market data; the implications of an exchange paying brokers to "take" liquidity; that Wall Street had found a way to bill investors without showing them the bill. "I had about eight things I wanted to say to the *Journal*," said Brad. "By the time I got through all these meetings, there was nothing to say. I was only allowed to say one of them—that we had found a way to route orders so they arrived at the exchanges simultaneously."

That was the problem with being RBC nice: It rendered you incapable of going to war with nasty. Before Brad said anything at all to the *Wall Street Journal*, RBC's upper management felt they needed to inform the U.S. regulators of what little he planned to say. They asked Brad to prepare a report on Thor for the SEC and then flew themselves down from Canada to join him in a big meeting with the SEC's Division of Trading and Markets staff. "It was more about not wanting them to be embarrassed about not knowing about Thor than it was us thinking they were going to do something about it," Brad said. He had no idea what a meeting at the SEC was supposed to be like and prepared as if he were testifying before Congress. As he read straight from the document he had written, the people around the table listened, stoned-faced. "I was scared shitless," he said. When he was finished, an SEC staffer said, *What you are doing is not fair to high-frequency traders. You're not letting them get out of the way.*

Excuse me? said Brad.

The SEC staffer argued that it was unfair that high-frequency traders couldn't post phony bids and offers on the exchanges to extract information from actual investors without running the risk of having to stand by them. It was unfair that Thor forced them to honor the markets they claimed to be making. Brad just looked at the guy: He was a young Indian quant.

Then a second staffer, a much older guy, raised his hand and said, *If they don't want to be on the offer they shouldn't be there at all.*

A lively argument ensued, with the younger SEC staffers taking the side of high-frequency trading and the older half taking Brad's point. "There was no clear consensus," said Brad. "But it gave me a sense that they weren't going to be doing anything anytime soon."* After the meeting, RBC conducted a study, never released publicly, in which they found that more than two hundred SEC staffers since 2007 had left their government jobs to work for high-frequency trading firms or the firms that lobbied Washington on their behalf. Some of these people had played central roles in deciding how, or even whether, to regulate high-frequency trading. For instance, in June 2010, the associate director of the SEC's Division of Trading and Markets, Elizabeth King, had quit the SEC to work for Getco. The SEC, like the public stock exchanges, had a kind of equity stake in the future revenues of high-frequency traders.

The argument in favor of high-frequency traders had beaten the argument against them to the U.S. regulators. It ran as follows: Natural investors in stocks, the people who supply capital to companies, can't find each other. The buyers and sellers of any given stock don't show up in the market at the same time, so they needed an intermediary to bridge the gap, to buy from the seller and to sell to the buyer. The fully computerized market moved too fast for a human to intercede in it, and so the high-frequency traders had stepped in to do the job. Their

---

* "There's a culture in the SEC of not getting into a dialogue with any individual who comes in," says a staffer who listened to Brad Katsuyama's presentation. "They don't want to give any one person an unfair peek at the way the SEC thinks. But it's a very defensive culture. And there were people in the room who had written some of the rules he was implicitly criticizing."

importance could be inferred from their activity: In 2005 a quarter of all trades in the public stock markets were made by HFT firms; by 2008 that number had risen to 65 percent. Their new market dominance—so the argument went—was a sign of progress, not just necessary but good for investors. Back when human beings sat in the middle of the stock market, the spreads between the bids and the offers of any given stock were a sixteenth of a percentage point. Now that computers did the job, the spread, at least in the more actively traded stocks, was typically a penny, or one-hundredth of 1 percent. That, said the supporters of high-frequency trading, was evidence that more HFT meant more liquidity.

The arguments against the high-frequency traders hadn't spread nearly so quickly—at any rate, Brad didn't hear them from the SEC. A distinction cried out to be made, between "trading activity" and "liquidity." A new trader could leap into a market and trade frantically inside it without adding anything of value to it. Imagine, for instance, that someone passed a rule, in the U.S. stock market as it is currently configured, that *required* every stock market trade to be front-run by a firm called Scalpers Inc. Under this rule, each time you went to buy 1,000 shares of Microsoft, Scalpers Inc. would be informed, whereupon it would set off to buy 1,000 shares of Microsoft offered in the market and, without taking the risk of owning the stock for even an instant, sell it to you at a higher price. Scalpers Inc. is prohibited from taking the slightest market risk; when it buys, it has the seller firmly in hand; when it sells, it has the buyer in hand; and at the end of every trading day, it will have no position at all in the stock market. Scalpers Inc. trades for the sole purpose of interfering with trading that would have happened without it. In buying from every seller and selling to every buyer, it winds up: a) doubling the trades in the marketplace and b) being exactly 50 percent of that booming volume. It adds nothing to the market but at the same time might be mistaken for the central player in that market.

This state of affairs, as it happens, resembles the United States stock market after the passage of Reg NMS. From 2006 to 2008, high-frequency traders' share of total U.S. stock market trading doubled, from 26 percent to 52 percent—and it has never fallen below 50 percent since then. The total number of trades made in the stock market also spiked dramatically, from roughly 10 million per day in 2006 to just over 20 million per day in 2009.

"Liquidity" was one of those words Wall Street people threw around when they wanted the conversation to end, and for brains to go dead, and for all questioning to cease. A lot of people used it as a synonym for "activity" or "volume of trading," but it obviously needed to mean more than that, as activity could be manufactured in a market simply by adding more front-runners to it. To get at a useful understanding of liquidity and the likely effects of high-frequency trading on it, one might better begin by studying the effect on investors' willingness to trade once they sense that they are being front-run by this new front-running entity. Brad himself had felt the effect: When the market as displayed on his screens became illusory, he became less willing to take risk in that market—to provide liquidity. He could only assume that every other risk-taking intermediary— every other useful market participant—must have felt exactly the same way.

The argument for HFT was that it provided liquidity, but what did this mean? "HFT firms go home flat every night," said Brad. "They don't take positions. They are bridging an amount of time between buyers and sellers that's so small that no one even knows it exists." After the market was computerized and decimalized, in 2000, spreads in the market had narrowed—that much was true. Part of that narrowing would have happened anyway, with the automation of the stock market, which made it easier to trade stocks priced in decimals rather than in fractions. Part of that narrowing was an illusion: What appeared to be the spread was not actually the spread. The minute you went to buy or sell at the stated market price, the price moved. What Scalpers Inc. did was to hide an entirely new sort of activity behind the mask of an old mental model—in which the guy who "makes markets" is necessarily taking market risk and providing "liquidity." But Scalpers Inc. took no market risk.*

In spirit Scalpers Inc. was less a market enabler than a weird sort of market burden. Financial intermediation is a tax on capital; it's the toll paid by both the people who have it and the people who put it to productive use. Reduce the tax and the rest of the economy benefits. Technology should have led to a reduction in this tax; the ability of investors to find each other without the help of some human broker might have eliminated the tax altogether. Instead this new beast rose up in the middle of the market and the tax increased—by billions of dollars. Or had it? To measure the cost to the economy of Scalpers Inc., you needed to know how much money it made. That was not possible. The new intermediaries were too good at keeping their

---

* In early 2013, one of the largest high-frequency traders, Virtu Financial, publicly boasted that in five and a half years of trading it had experienced just one day when it hadn't made money, and that the loss was caused by "human error." In 2008, Dave Cummings, the CEO of a high-frequency trading firm called Tradebot, told university students that his firm had gone four years without a single day of trading losses. This sort of performance is possible only if you have a huge informational advantage.

profits secret.* Secrecy might have been the signature trait of the
entities who now sat at the middle of the stock market: You had
to guess what they were making from what they spent to make
it. Investors who eyeballed the situation did not find reason for
hope. "There used to be this guy called Vinny who worked on
the floor of the stock exchange," said one big investor who had
observed the market for a long time. "After the markets closed
Vinny would get into his Cadillac and drive out to his big house
in Long Island. Now there is the guy called Vladimir who gets
into his jet and flies to his estate in Aspen for the weekend. I
used to worry a little about Vinny. Now I worry a lot about
Vladimir."

Apart from taking some large sum of money out of the market,
and without taking risk or adding anything of use to that market, Scalpers Inc. had other, less intended consequences. Scalpers
Inc. inserted itself into the middle of the stock market not just as
an unnecessary middleman but as a middleman with incentives
to introduce dysfunction into the stock market. Scalpers Inc.
was incentivized, for instance, to make the market as volatile
as possible. The value of its ability to buy Microsoft from you
at $30 a share and to hold the shares for a few microseconds—
knowing that, even if the Microsoft share price began to fall, it
could turn around and sell the shares at $30.01—was determined
by how likely it was that Microsoft's share price, in those magi-
cal microseconds, would rise in price. The more volatile Microsoft's share price, the higher Microsoft's stock price might move

---

* A former employee of Citadel who also once had top secret security clearance at the
Pentagon says, "To get into the Pentagon and into my area, it took two badge swipes.
One to get into the building and one to get into my area. Guess how many badge swipes
it took me to get to my seat at Citadel? Five."

during those microseconds, and the more Scalpers Inc. would be able to scalp. One might argue that intermediaries have always profited from market volatility, but that is not really true. The old specialists on the New York Stock exchange, for instance, because they were somewhat obliged to buy in a falling market and to sell in a rising one, often found that their worst days were the most volatile days. They thrived in times of relative stability.

Another incentive of Scalpers Inc. is to fragment the marketplace: The more sites at which the same stocks changed hands, the more opportunities to front-run investors from one site to another. The bosses at Scalpers Inc. would thus encourage new exchanges to open, and would also encourage them to place themselves at some distance from each other. Scalpers Inc. also had a very clear desire to maximize the difference between the speed of their private view of the market and the view afforded the wider public market. The more time that Scalpers Inc. could sit with some investor's stock market order, the greater the chance that the price might move in the interim. Thus an earnest employee of Scalpers Inc. would look for ways either to slow down the public's information or to speed up his own.

The final new incentive introduced by Scalpers Inc. was perhaps the most bizarre. The easiest way for Scalpers Inc. to extract the information it needed to front-run other investors was to trade with them. At times it was possible to extract the necessary information without having to commit to a trade. That's what the "flash order" scandal had been about: high-frequency traders being allowed by the exchanges to see other people's orders before anyone else, without any obligation to trade against them. But for the most part, if you wanted to find out what some big investor was about to do, you needed to do a little bit of it with him. For instance, to find out that, say, T. Rowe Price wanted to buy 5 million shares of Google Inc., you needed to sell some Google to T. Rowe Price. That initial market contact between any investor and Scalpers Inc. was like the bait in a trap—a loss leader. For Scalpers Inc., the goal was to spend as little as possible to acquire the necessary information—to make those initial trades, the bait, as small as possible.

To an astonishing degree, since the implementation of Reg NMS, the U.S. financial markets had evolved to serve the narrow interests of Scalpers Inc. Since the mid-2000s, the average trade size in the U.S. stock market had plummeted, the markets had fragmented, and the gap in time between the public view of the markets and the view of high-frequency traders had widened. The rise of high-frequency trading had been accompanied also by a rise in stock market volatility—over and above the turmoil caused by the 2008 financial crisis. The price volatility within each trading day in the U.S. stock market between 2010 and 2013 was nearly 40 percent higher than the volatility between 2004 and 2006, for instance. There were days in 2011 in which volatility was higher than in the most volatile days of the dot-com bubble.

The financial crisis brought with it a great deal of stock market volatility; perhaps people just assumed that there was supposed to be an unusual amount of drama in the stock market evermore. But then the financial crisis abated and the drama remained. There was no good explanation for this, but Brad now had a glimmer of one. It had to do with the way a front-runner operates. A front-runner sells you a hundred shares of some stock to discover that you are a buyer and then turns around and buys everything else in sight, causing the stock to pop higher (or the opposite, if you happen to be a seller). The Royal Bank of Canada had tested the effects on stock market volatility of using

Thor, which stymied front-runners, rather than the standard order routers used by Wall Street, which did not. The sequential cost-effective router responded to the kickbacks and fees of the various exchanges and went to those exchanges first that paid them the most to do so. The spray router—which, as its name suggests, just sprayed the market and took whatever stock was available, or tried to—did not make any effort to compel a stock market order to arrive at the different exchanges simultaneously. Every router, when it bought stock, tended to drive the price of that stock a bit higher. But when the stock had settled—say, ten seconds later—it settled differently with each router. The sequential cost-effective router caused the share price to remain higher than the spray router did, and the spray router caused it to move higher than Thor did. "I have no scientific evidence," said Brad. "This is purely a theory. But with Thor the HFT firms are trying to cover their losses. *I'm short when I don't want to be, so I need to buy to cover, quickly.*" The other two routers enabled HFT to front-run, so they wound up being long the stock. "[With] the other two, HFT is in a position to trade around a winning position," said Brad, "and they can do whatever they can do to force the stock even higher." (Or lower, if the investor who triggered the activity is a seller.) They had, in those privileged microseconds, the reckless abandon of gamblers playing with house money.

The new choppiness in the public U.S. stock markets was spreading to other financial markets, as they, too, embraced high-frequency traders. It was what investors most noticed: They were less and less able to buy and sell big chunks of stock in a gulp. Their frustration with the public stock exchanges had led the big Wall Street banks to create private exchanges: dark pools. By the middle of 2011, roughly 30 percent of all stock market trades occurred off the public exchanges, most of them in dark pools. The appeal of these dark pools—said the Wall Street banks—was that investors could expose their big stock market orders without fear that those orders would be exploited.

WHAT BOTHERED RICH Gates, at least at first, was the tone of the pitch he was hearing from the big Wall Street banks. All through 2008 and 2009 they would come to his office and tell him why he needed their algorithms to defend himself in the stock market. *This algo is like a tiger that lurks in the woods and waits for the prey and then jumps on it.* Or: *This algo is like an anaconda in a tree.* The algos had names like Ambush and Nighthawk and Raider and Dark Attack and Sumo. Citi had one called Dagger, Deutsche Bank had Slicer, and Credit Suisse had one named Guerrilla, which came, in the bank's flip-chart presentation, with a menacing drawing of Che Guevara wearing a beret and scowling. What the hell was that about? Their very names made Rich Gates wary; he also didn't like how loudly the brokers selling them told him they'd come to protect him. Protect him from what? Why did he need protection? From whom did he need to be protected? "I'm immediately skeptical of people saying they are looking out for my interests," Gates said. "Especially on Wall Street."

Gates ran a mutual fund, TFS Capital, that he had created in 1997 with friends from the University of Virginia. He liked to think of himself as a hick, but in truth he was a keenly analytical math geek in the perfectly pleasant Philadelphia suburb of West Chester. He managed nearly $2 billion belonging to 35,000 small investors but still positioned himself, even in his own mind, as an industry outsider. He believed that mutual funds were less often exercises in smart money management than in creepy marketing, and that many of the people who ran mutual funds should be doing something else with their lives. Back in 2007, to make this point, he dug out of a stack of league tables America's worst-performing mutual fund: the Phoenix Market Neutral Fund. Over the prior decade, Gates's firm had earned its investors returns of 10 percent per year. Over that same period, the Phoenix Market Neutral Fund had *lost* .09 percent a year for its investors—the investors would have been better off hopping over the fence of the president of the Phoenix Market Neutral Fund's home and burying the money in his backyard. Gates wrote a letter to the Phoenix president saying, in effect, *You are so obviously inept at managing money that you could do your investors a favor by turning over all of your assets to me and letting me run them for you.* The president failed to reply.

The machismo of Wall Street's algorithms, combined with what struck Gates as a lot of nonsensical talk about the need for trading speed, stirred his naturally suspicious mind. "I just noticed a lot of bullshit," he said. He and his colleagues devised a test to see if there was anything in this new stock market to fear. The test, specifically, would show him if, when he entered an order into one of Wall Street's dark pools, he wound up getting ripped off by some unseen predator. He started by identifying stocks that didn't trade very often. Chipotle Mexican Grill, for instance. He sent in an order to a single Wall Street dark pool to buy that stock at the "mid-market" price. Say, for example, that the shares of Chipotle Mexican Grill were trading at 100–100.10. Gates would submit his bid to buy a thousand shares of Chipotle at $100.05. There it would normally just sit until some other investor came along and lowered his price from $100.10 to $100.05. Gates didn't wait for that to happen. Instead, a few seconds later, he sent a second order to one of the public exchanges, to *sell* Chipotle at $100.01.

What should have happened next was that his order in the dark pool should have been filled at $100.01, the official new best price in the market. He should have been able to buy from himself the shares he was selling at $100.01. But that's not what happened. Instead, before he could blink his eye, he had made two trades. He had bought Chipotle from someone inside the Wall Street dark pool at $100.05 and sold it to someone else on the public exchange for $100.01. He'd lost 4 cents by, in effect, trading with himself. Only he hadn't traded with himself; some third party had obviously used the sell order he had sent to the public exchange to exploit the buy order he had sent to the dark pool.

Gates and his colleagues wound up making hundreds of such tests, with their own money, in several Wall Street dark pools. In the first half of 2010 there was only one Wall Street firm in whose dark pool the test came back positive: Goldman Sachs. In the Goldman dark pool, Sigma X, he got ripped off a bit more than half the time he ran the test. As Gates traded in lightly traded stocks, and high-frequency trading firms were overwhelmingly interested in heavily traded ones, these tests would have been vastly more likely to generate false negatives than false positives. Still, he was a bit surprised that Goldman, and only Goldman, seemed to be running a pool that allowed someone else to front-run his orders to the public stock exchanges. He called his broker at Goldman. "He said it wasn't fair," said Gates, "because it wasn't just them. He said, 'It's happening all over. It's not just us.'"

Gates was dutifully shocked. "When I first saw the results of these tests, I thought: This obviously is not right. As far as he could tell, no one seemed much to care that 35,000 small investors could be so exposed to predation inside Wall Street's most prominent bank. "I'm amazed that people don't ask the questions," he said. "That they don't dig deeper. If some schmuck in West Chester, PA, can figure it out, I've got to believe other people did, too." Outraged, Gates called a reporter he knew at the *Wall Street Journal*. The reporter came to see Gates's tests and seemed interested, but two months later there was still no piece in the *Journal*—and Gates sensed that there might never be. (Among other things, the reporter was uncomfortable mentioning Goldman Sachs by name.) At which point Gates noticed that the Dodd-Frank Wall Street Reform and Customer Protection Act, soon to be passed, contained a whistle-blower provision. "I'm like, 'Holy crap, I'm trying to out this anyway. If I can get paid, too—great.'"

The people who worked in the SEC's Division of Trading and Markets were actually great—nothing like what the public imagined. They were smart and asked good questions and even spotted small mistakes in Gates's presentation, which he appreciated—though, as with Brad Katsuyama, they gave him no idea how they might respond to the information he'd given them. They wondered, shrewdly, exactly who was ripping off investors in Goldman's dark pool. "They wanted to know if Goldman Sachs's prop group was on the other side of the trade," said Gates. He had no answer for that. "They don't tell you who took the other side of the trade," he said. All he knew was that he'd been ripped off, in exactly the way you might expect to be ripped off, when you can't see the market trading in real time and others can.

And that, at least for a few months, was that. "After I blew the whistle, I laid low," Gates said. "I just wanted to focus on our business. I don't get off throwing bombs." Then came the flash

crash, and the *Wall Street Journal*'s interest was rekindled. The
paper published a piece on Rich Gates's tests—without mentioning Goldman Sachs by name. "I think it's going to set the
world on fire," said Gates. "It didn't do anything. There are fifteen comments at the bottom of the piece on the Web, and all of
them are Russian mail order brides." But the piece led a person
close to both the BATS exchange and Credit Suisse to get in
touch with Gates with a suggestion: Run your tests again, specifically on the BATS exchange and the Credit Suisse dark pool
called Crossfinder. Just to see. Toward the end of 2010, Gates ran
another round of tests.

Sure enough, he was able to get himself ripped off, in exactly
the same way he had been ripped off in the Goldman Sachs
dark pool—on the BATS exchange, and inside the Credit Suisse
dark pool, and in some other places, too. At Goldman Sachs,
however, the tests were now negative. "When we did it the
first time," he said, "it worked at Goldman but nowhere else.
When we did it six months later it didn't work at Goldman, but
it worked everywhere else."

IN MAY 2011, the small team Brad had created—Schwall, Ronan,
Rob Park, a couple of others—sat around a table in Brad's office,
surrounded by the applications of past winners of the *Wall Street
Journal*'s Technology Innovation Awards. As it turned out,
RBC's marketing department had informed them of the awards
the day before submissions were due—so they were scrambling
to figure out in which of several categories they belonged, and
how to make Thor sound life-changing. "There were papers
everywhere," said Rob. "No one sounded like us. There were
people who had, like, cured cancer." "It was stupid," said Brad,

"there wasn't even a category to put us into. I think we ended up applying under *Other*."

With the purposelessness of the exercise hanging in the air, Rob said, "I just had a sick idea." Rob's idea was to license the technology to one of the exchanges. (Schwall had patented Thor for RBC.) The line between Wall Street brokers and exchanges had blurred. The big Wall Street banks now ran their own private exchanges. The stock exchanges, for their part, were making a bid to become brokers. The bigger ones now offered a service that enabled brokers to simply hand them their stock market orders, which they would then route. To their own exchange, of course, but also to others. The service was used mainly by small regional brokerage firms that didn't have their own routers, but this brokerage-like service opened up, at least in Rob's mind, a new possibility. If just one of the exchanges was handed the tool for protecting investors from market predators, the small brokers from around the country might flock to it, and it might become the mother of all exchanges.

"Screw that," said Brad. "Let's just create our own stock exchange."

"We just sat there for a while," said Rob. "Kind of staring at each other. *Create your own stock exchange.* What does that even mean?"

A few weeks later Brad flew to Canada and sold his bosses on the idea of an RBC-led stock exchange. Then, in the fall of 2011, he canvassed a handful of the world's biggest money managers (Janus Capital, T. Rowe Price, BlackRock, Wellington, Southeastern Asset Management) and some of its most influential hedge fund managers (David Einhorn, Bill Ackman, Daniel Loeb). They all had the same reaction. They loved the idea of a stock exchange that protected investors from Wall Street's pred-

ators. They also thought that a new stock exchange, to be cred-
ibly independent of Wall Street, could not be created by a Wall
Street bank. Not even a bank as nice as RBC. If Brad wanted to
create the mother of all stock exchanges, he would need to quit
his job and do it on his own.

The challenges were obvious. He'd need to find money. He'd
need to persuade a lot of highly paid people to quit their Wall
Street jobs to work for tiny fractions of their current salaries—
and possibly even supply the capital to pay themselves to work.
"I was asking: Can I get the people I need? How long can we
survive without getting paid? Will our significant others let us
do this?" He also needed to find out if the nine big Wall Street
banks that controlled nearly 70 percent of all stock market orders*
would be willing to send those orders to a truly safe exchange.
It would be far more difficult to start an exchange premised on
fairness if the banks that controlled the vast majority of the customers' orders were committed to unfairness.

For a surprisingly long time, Brad had reserved final judgment about the biggest Wall Street banks. "I held out a degree
of hope that the people at [each] bank who handled the clients'
orders were removed from the prop group," he said. His hope
sprang mainly from his own experience: At RBC, where he
handled the clients' orders, he barely knew the prop traders and
had no idea what they were doing. There was a reason for this:
RBC had not created a dark pool, because Brad had killed the
idea. Still, he knew that each of the big Wall Street banks had its
own internal politics, and that there were people in each of them

---

* Those nine banks, in order of their (fairly evenly distributed) 2011 market share, from
highest to lowest: Credit Suisse, Morgan Stanley, Bank of America, Merrill Lynch,
Goldman Sachs, J.P. Morgan, Barclays, UBS, Citi, Deutsche Bank.

who wanted to act in the long-term interests of their firms and do the right thing by their customers. His hope was that some of these people, in some of these places, had power.

John Schwall's private investigations put an end to that hope. By the fall of 2011 Schwall had become something like a connoisseur of the uses of LinkedIn to find stuff out about people in and around high-frequency trading. He'd put a face on high-frequency trading, or rather two faces. "I began to anticipate that certain people were in on the game," said Schwall. "I'd connect to them so that I could see their network. There were maybe twenty-five guys I called kingpins—the people who actually knew what was going on." At the very top of the food chain were a lot of white guys in their forties whose careers could be traced back, one way or another, to the early electronic stock exchanges born of the regulations passed after the crash of 1987—Wall Street guys who might have some technical background but whose identity was more trader than programming geek.

The new players in the financial markets, the kingpins of the future who had the capacity to reshape those markets, were a different breed: the Chinese guy who had spent the previous ten years in American universities; the French particle physicist from FERMAT lab; the Russian aerospace engineer; the Indian PhD in electrical engineering. "There were just *thousands* of these people," said Schwall. "Basically all of them with advanced degrees. I remember thinking to myself how unfortunate it was that so many engineers were joining these firms to exploit investors rather than solving public problems." These highly trained scientists and technicians tended to be pulled onto Wall Street by the big banks and then, after they'd learned the ropes, to move on to smaller high-frequency trading shops. They behaved more like free agents than employees of a big corporation. In their LinkedIn profiles, for instance, they revealed all sorts of information that their employers almost certainly would not want revealed. Here Schwall stumbled upon the predator's weakness: The employees of the big Wall Street banks felt no more loyalty toward the banks than the banks felt toward them.

The employees of Credit Suisse offered the clearest example. Credit Suisse's dark pool, Crossfinder, vied with Goldman Sachs's Sigma X to be Wall Street's biggest private stock exchange. Credit Suisse's biggest selling point to investors was that it put their interests first and protected them from whatever it was that high-frequency traders were doing. Back in October 2009, the head of Advanced Execution Services (AES) at Credit Suisse, Dan Mathisson, had testified before a U.S. Senate Banking, Housing, and Urban Affairs Committee at a hearing on dark pools. "The argument that dark pools are somehow part of the high-frequency trading debate simply does not make sense," he'd said. "High-frequency traders make their money by digesting publicly available information faster than others; dark pools hide order information from everyone."

That, Schwall thought, because Brad had explained it all to him, was simply wrong. It was true that when, say, a pension fund gave a Wall Street bank an order to buy 100,000 shares of Microsoft, and the Wall Street bank routed the order to the dark pool, the wider world was not informed. But that was just the beginning of the story. The pension fund did not know the rules of the dark pool, and could not see how the buy order was handled inside of it. The pension fund would not be able to say, for example, whether the Wall Street bank allowed its own proprietary traders to know of the big buy order, or if those traders had used their (faster than the dark pool) market connections to front-run the order on the public exchanges. Even if the Wall Street bank resisted the temptation to trade for itself against its own customers, there was virtually no chance they resisted the temptation to sell access to the dark pool to high-frequency traders. The Wall Street banks did not disclose which high-speed trading firms had paid them for special access to their dark pools, or how much they had paid, but selling that access was standard practice.

Raising, again, the obvious question: *Why would anyone pay for access to the customers' orders inside a Wall Street bank's dark pool?* The straight answer was that a customer's stock market order, inside a dark pool, was fat and juicy prey. The order was typically large, and its movements were especially predictable: Each Wall Street bank had its own detectable pattern for handling orders. The order was also slow, because of the time it was forced to spend inside the dark pool before accessing the wider market. As Brad had put it, "You could front-run an order in a dark pool on a bicycle." The pension fund trying to buy 100,000 shares of Microsoft could, of course, specify that the Wall Street bank not take its orders to the public exchanges at all but simply rest it, hidden, inside the dark pool. But an order hidden inside a dark pool wasn't very well hidden. Any decent high-frequency trader who had paid for a special connection to the pool would ping the pool with tiny buy and sell orders in every listed stock, searching for activity. Once they'd discovered the buyer of Microsoft, they'd simply wait for the moment when Microsoft ticked lower on the public exchanges and sell it to the pension fund in the dark pool at the stale, higher "best" price (as Rich Gates's tests had demonstrated). It was riskless, larcenous, and legal—made so by Reg NMS. The way Brad had described it, it was as if only one gambler were permitted to know the scores of last week's NFL games, with no one else aware of his knowledge. He places bets in the casino on every game and waits for other gamblers to take the other side of those bets. There's no guarantee that anyone will do so; but if they do, he's certain to win.

In his investigation of the people who managed Credit Suisse's dark pool, one of the first things Schwall noticed was the guy in charge of electronic trading: Josh Stampfli, who had joined Credit Suisse after seven years spent working for Bernie Madoff. (Madoff had pioneered the idea of paying brokers for the right to execute the brokers' customers' orders, which should have told people something but apparently did not.) This, of course, only heightened Schwall's suspicions, and sent him digging around in old articles in trade journals about Credit Suisse's dark pool.* There he found references and allusions that made sense only if Credit Suisse had planned, right from the start, to be deeply involved with high-frequency trading firms. For instance, in April 2008 a guy named Dmitri Galinov, a director and the head of liquidity strategy at Credit Suisse, had told the *Securities Technology Monitor* that many of Credit Suisse's "clients" had placed computer servers in Weehawken, New Jersey, to be closer to Credit Suisse's dark pool. The only people who put servers next to dark pools in Weehawken were Ronan's old clients—the high-frequency trading firms. No stock market investor went to such lengths to shave microseconds off trading time.

"Client," to Credit Suisse, appeared to Schwall to be a category that included "high-frequency trading firms." Schwall's suspicion that Credit Suisse wanted to service HFT while not seeming to do so grew after he read an interview Dan Mathisson gave to the *New York Times* in November 2009.

---

* Stampfli has not been charged with any wrongdoing.

Q: Who are your clients at CrossFinder [*sic*] and how do they benefit from using a dark pool as opposed to just going through a broker and trading on the exchange?

A: Our clients are mutual funds, pension funds, hedge funds and some other large broker–dealers, so it is always institutional clients . . .

All the large high-frequency trading firms, Schwall knew, were "broker-dealers." They had to be, to gain the special access they had to the public stock exchanges. So Mathisson had not ruled out dealing with them. The only reason he would not explicitly rule out dealing with them, Schwall assumed, was that he was dealing with them.

The LinkedIn searches became a new obsession. The former Madoff employee's profile led him to the people who worked for the former Madoff employee, who led him to the people who worked for them, and so on. Even as Credit Suisse tried to appear as if it had nothing to do with high-frequency trading, its employees begged to differ. Schwall dug out dozens of examples of Credit Suisse's computer programmers boasting on their résumés about "building high-frequency trading platforms" and "implementing high-frequency trading strategy," or of experience as a "quantitative trader on equity and equity derivatives: high-frequency trading." One guy explained that he had "managed on-boarding of all high-frequency clients to Crossfinder." Another said he had built the Credit Suisse Crossfinder dark pool and now worked in high-frequency trading market making. Credit Suisse claimed that its dark pool had nothing to do with high-frequency trading, and yet it somehow employed, in and around its dark pool, a mother lode of high-frequency trading talent.

By the time he'd finished, Schwall had built the entire Credit Suisse dark pool organization chart. "He's got these people charts," said Brad incredulously. "It's like one of those FBI boards, with the drug kingpins." Looking over Schwall's charts on Credit Suisse, the bank that went to the most trouble to sell itself as safe to investors, Brad decided that the game was probably over inside all the big Wall Street banks. All of them, one way or another, were probably using the unequal speeds in the market to claim their share of the prey. He further assumed that the big Wall Street banks must have stumbled upon his solution to high-frequency front-running, and must have chosen not to use it, because they had too great a stake in the profits generated by that front-running. "It became very obvious to me why we were the first to discover Thor, because we weren't," he said. "What that meant to me was that the problem was going to be much, much harder to solve. It also told me why the clients were so in the dark, because the clients rely on brokers for information." Creating an exchange designed to protect the prey from the predator would mean starting a war on Wall Street— between the banks and the investors they claimed to represent.

Schwall's private investigations also revealed to Brad just how little the technical people understood of their role in the financial world. "It's not like you are building a bridge connecting two pieces of land," he said. "You can't see the effects of what you are doing." The openness with which the Credit Suisse technologists described their activities made him aware of a larger, almost charming obliviousness. "I was totally shocked when John started to pull out these résumés," he recalled. "The banks had adopted a policy of saying as little as possible about what they were actually doing. They'd fire people for being quoted in the newspaper, but in their LinkedIn pages those same people said whatever they wanted." From the way the engineers described their roles in the new financial system, he could see that they had no clue about the injustices of that system. "It told me that these tech guys were completely oblivious to what they were working on," he said. "They were tying these things they were working on—helping the bank to make markets in their dark pools; building automated systems for the bank to use with its customers—in a way you never would if you understood what the banks were doing. It's like saying on your LinkedIn profile, 'I have all the skills of a robber and I know this one house intimately.'"

Schwall had started out looking for the villains who were committing crimes against the life savings of ordinary Americans, fully aware of their own villainy. He wound up finding, mainly, a bunch of people who had no idea of the meaning of their own lives. In his searches, Schwall noticed something else, though at first he didn't know what to make of it: A surprisingly large number of the people pulled in by the big Wall Street banks to build the technology for high-frequency trading were Russians. "If you went to LinkedIn and looked at one of these Russian guys, you would see he was linked to all the other Russians," said Schwall. "I'd go to find Dmitri and I'd also find Misha and Vladimir and Tolstoy or whatever." The Russians came not from finance but from telecom, physics, medical research, university math departments, and a lot of other useful fields. The big Wall Street firms had become machines for turning analytically minded Russians into high-frequency traders. Schwall filed that fact away for later, as something perhaps worth thinking about.

CHAPTER FIVE

PUTTING A FACE ON HFT

Sergey Aleynikov wasn't the world's most eager immigrant to America, or, for that matter, to Wall Street. He'd left Russia in 1990, the year after the fall of the Berlin Wall, but more in sadness than in hope. "When I was nineteen I haven't imagined leaving it," he says. "I was very patriotic about Russia. I cried when Brezhnev died. And I always hated English. I thought I was completely incapable of learning languages." His problem with Russia was that its government wouldn't allow him to study what he wanted to study. He wasn't religious in any conventional sense, but he'd been born a Jew, which had been noted on his Russian passport to remind everyone of the fact. As a Jew he expected to be given especially difficult entrance exams to university, which, if he passed them, would grant him access to just one of two Moscow universities that were more accepting of Jews, where he would study whatever the authorities permitted Jews to study. Math, in Serge's case. He'd been willing to tolerate this state of affairs; however, as it happened, he'd also been born to program computers. He hadn't laid hands on a computer until 1986, when he was already sixteen. The first thing he'd done was to write a program: He instructed the computer to draw a picture of a sine wave. When the computer actually followed his instructions, he was hooked. What hooked him, he said, was "its detailed orientation. The way it requires an ability to see the problem and tackle it from different angles. It's not just like chess, but like solving a particular problem in chess. The more challenging problem is not to play chess but to write the code that will play chess." He found that coding engaged him not just intellectually but also emotionally. "Writing a program is like giving birth to a child," he said. "It is a creation. Even though it is technical, it is a work of art. You get this level of satisfaction."

He applied to switch his major from mathematics to computer science, but the authorities forbade it. "That is what tipped me to accept the idea that perhaps Russia is not the best place for me," he says. "When they wouldn't allow me to study computer science."

He arrived in New York City in 1990 and moved into a dorm room at the 92nd Street Young Men's and Young Women's Hebrew Association, a sort of Jewish YMCA. Two things shocked him about his new home: the diversity of the people on the streets and the fantastic range of foods in the grocery stores. He took photographs of the rows and rows of sausages in Manhattan and mailed them to his mother in Moscow. "I'd never seen so many sausages," he says. But once he'd marveled at the American cornucopia, he stepped back from it all and wondered just how necessary all of this food was. He read books about fasting and the effects of various highly restrictive diets. "I decided to look at it a little bit further and ask what is beneficial and what is not," he said. In the end he became a finicky vegetarian. "I don't think all the energy you gain comes from food," he says. "I think it comes from your environment."

He'd come to America with no money at all, and no real idea how to get it. He took a course on how to apply for a job. "It was quite frightening," he says. "I didn't speak English, really, and a résumé was a totally alien concept." His first interviewer asked Serge to tell him about himself. "To a Russian mentality," said Serge, "that question means 'Where are you born?' 'Who are your siblings?'" Serge described for the man at great length how he had come from a long line of Jewish scholars and academics—and nothing else. "He tells me I will hear from him again. I never do." But he had an obvious talent for programming computers and soon found a job doing it, for $8.75 an hour, in a New Jersey medical center. From the medical center he landed a better job, in the Rutgers University computer science department, where, through some complicated combination of jobs and grants, he was able to pursue a master's degree. After Rutgers he spent a few years working at Internet start-ups until, in 1998, he received a job offer from a big New Jersey telecom company called IDT. For the next decade he designed computer systems and wrote the code to route millions of phone calls each day to the cheapest available phone lines. When he joined the company it had five hundred employees; by 2006 it had five thousand, and he was its star technologist. That year a headhunter called him and told him that there was fierce new demand on Wall Street for his particular skill: writing code that parsed huge amounts of information at great speed.

Serge knew nothing about Wall Street and was in no particular rush to learn about it. His singular talent was for making computers go fast, but his own movements were slow and deliberate. The headhunter pressed upon him a bunch of books about writing software on Wall Street, plus a primer on how to make it through a Wall Street job interview, and told him that, on Wall Street, he could make a lot more than the $220,000 a year he was making at the telecom company. Serge felt flattered, and liked the headhunter, but he read the books and decided Wall Street wasn't for him. He enjoyed the technical challenges at the giant telecom and didn't really feel the need to earn more money. A year later, in early 2007, the headhunter called him again. By this time IDT was in serious financial trouble; Serge was beginning to worry that the management was running the company into the ground. He had no savings to speak of. His wife, Elina, was carrying their third child, and they'd need to buy a bigger house. Serge agreed to interview with the Wall Street firm that especially wanted to meet him: Goldman Sachs.

At least on the surface, Serge Aleynikov had the sort of life people are said to come to America for. He'd married a pretty fellow Russian immigrant and started a family with her. They'd sold their two-bedroom Cape-style house in Clifton, New Jersey, and bought a bigger colonial-style one in Little Falls. They had a nanny. They had a circle of Russians they called their friends. On the other hand, all Serge did was work, and his wife had no real clue what that work involved; they weren't actually all that close to each other. He didn't encourage people to get to know him well or exhibit a great deal of interest in getting to know them. He was acquiring a lot of possessions in which he had very little interest. The lawn in Clifton was a fair example of the general problem. When he'd gone hunting for his first house, he'd been enchanted by the idea of having his very own lawn. In Moscow such a thing was unheard of. The moment he owned a lawn, he regretted it. ("A pain in the butt to mow.") A

Russian writer named Masha Leder, who knew the Aleynikovs as well as anyone, thought of Serge as an exceptionally intellectually gifted but otherwise typical Russian Jewish computer programmer, for whom technical problems became an excuse not to engage with the messy world around him. "All of Serge's life was some kind of mirage," she said. "Or a dream. He was not aware of things. He liked slender girls who loved to dance. He married a girl and managed to have three kids with her before he figures out he doesn't really know her. He was working his ass off and she would spend the money he was making. He would come home and she would cook him vegetarian dishes. He was serviced, basically."

And then Wall Street called. Goldman Sachs put Serge through a series of telephone interviews, then brought him in for a long day of face-to-face interviews. These he found extremely tense, even a bit weird. "I was not used to seeing people put so much energy into evaluating other people," he said. One after another, a dozen Goldman employees tried to stump him with brain teasers, computer puzzles, math problems, and even some light physics. It must have become clear to Goldman (it was to Serge) that he knew more about most of the things he was being asked than his interviewers did. At the end of the first day, Goldman invited him back for a second day. He went home and thought it over: He wasn't all that sure he wanted to work at Goldman Sachs. "But the next morning I had a competitive feeling," he says. "I should conclude it and try to pass it because it's a big challenge."

He'd been surprised to find that in at least one way he fit in: More than half the programmers at Goldman were Russians. Russians had a reputation for being the best programmers on Wall Street, and Serge thought he knew why: They had been forced to learn to program computers without the luxury of endless computer time. Many years later, when he had plenty of computer time, Serge still wrote out new programs on paper before typing them into the machine. "In Russia, time on the computer was measured in minutes," he said. "When you write a program, you are given a tiny time slot to make it work. Consequently we learned to write the code in ways that minimized the amount of debugging. And so you had to think about it a lot before you committed it to paper. . . . The ready availability of computer time creates this mode of working where you just have an idea and type it and maybe erase it ten times. Good Russian programmers, they tend to have had that one experience at some time in the past—the experience of limited access to computer time."

He returned for another round of Goldman's grilling, which ended in the office of a senior high-frequency trader—another Russian, Alexander Davidovich. The Goldman managing director had just two final questions for Serge, both designed to test his ability to solve problems. The first: Is 3,599 a prime number?

Serge quickly saw that there was something strange about 3,599: It was very close to 3,600. He jotted down the following equations:

$$3599 = (3600 - 1) = (60^2 - 1^2) = (60 - 1)(60 + 1) = 59 \times 61$$

$$3599 = 59 \times 61$$

Not a prime number.

The problem wasn't that difficult, but, as he put it, "it was harder to solve the problem when you are anticipated to solve it quickly." It might have taken him as long as two minutes to finish. The second question the Goldman managing director asked him was more involved, and involving. He described for Serge a room, a rectangular box, and gave him its three dimensions. "He says there is a spider on the floor, and he gives me its coordinates. There is also a fly on the ceiling, and he gives me its coordinates as well. Then he asked the question: Calculate the shortest distance the spider can take to reach the fly." The spider can't fly or swing; it can only walk on surfaces. The shortest path between two points was a straight line, and so, Serge figured, it was a matter of unfolding the box, turning a three-dimensional object into a two-dimensional surface, then using the Pythagorean theorem to calculate the distances. This took him several minutes to work out; when he was done, Davidovich offered him a job at Goldman Sachs. His starting salary plus bonus came to $270,000.

HE'D JOINED GOLDMAN at an interesting moment in the history of both the firm and Wall Street. By mid-2007 Goldman's bond trading department was aiding and abetting a global financial crisis, most infamously by helping the Greek government to rig its books and disguise its debt, and by designing subprime mortgage securities to fail, so that they might make money by betting against them. At the same time, Goldman's equities department was adapting to radical changes in the U.S. stock market—just as that market was about to crash. A once sleepy oligopoly dominated by Nasdaq and the New York Stock Exchange was rapidly turning into something else. The thirteen public stock exchanges in New Jersey were all trading the same stocks. Within a few years there would be more than forty dark pools, two of them owned by Goldman Sachs, also trading the same stocks.

The fragmentation of the American stock market was fueled, in part, by Reg NMS, which had also stimulated a huge amount of stock market trading. Much of the new volume was generated not by old-fashioned investors but by the extremely fast computers controlled by the high-frequency trading firms. Essentially, the more places there were to trade stocks, the greater the opportunity there was for high-frequency traders to interpose themselves between buyers on one exchange and sellers on another. This was perverse. The initial promise of computer technology was to remove the intermediary from the financial market, or at least reduce the amount he could scalp from that market. The reality turned out to be a windfall for financial intermediaries—of somewhere between $10 billion and $22 billion a year, depending on whose estimates you wanted to believe. For Goldman Sachs, a financial intermediary, that was only good news.

The bad news was that Goldman Sachs wasn't yet making much of the new money. At the end of 2008, they told their high-frequency trading computer programmers that their trading unit had netted roughly $300 million. That same year, the high-frequency trading division of a single hedge fund, Citadel, made $1.2 billion. The HFT guys were already known for hiding their profits, but a lawsuit between one of them, a Russian named Misha Malyshev, and his former employer, Citadel, revealed that, in 2008, Malyshev had been paid $75 million in cash. Rumors circulated—they turned out to be true—of two guys who had left Knight for Citadel and guarantees of $20 million a year each. A headhunter who sat in the middle of the market and saw what firms were paying for geek talent says, "Goldman had started to figure it out, but they really hadn't figured it out. They weren't top ten."

The simple reason Goldman wasn't making much of the big

money now being made in the stock market was that the stock market had become a war of robots, and Goldman's robots were slow. A lot of the moneymaking strategies were of the winner-take-all variety. When every player is trying to do the same thing, the player who gets all the money is the one whose computers can take in data and spit out the obvious response to it first. In the various races being run, Goldman was seldom first. That is why they had sought out Serge Aleynikov in the first place: to improve the speed of their system. There were many problems with that system, in Serge's view. It wasn't so much a system as an amalgamation. "The code development practices at IDT were much more organized and up-to-date than at Goldman," he says. Goldman had bought the core of its system fifteen years earlier in the acquisition of one of the early electronic trading firms, Hull Trading. The massive amounts of old software (Serge guessed that the entire platform had as many as 60 million lines of code in it) and fifteen years of fixes to it had created the computer equivalent of a giant rubber-band ball. When one of the rubber bands popped, Serge was expected to find it and fix it.

Goldman Sachs often used complexity to advantage. The firm designed complex subprime mortgage securities that others did not understand, for instance, and then took advantage of the ignorance they had introduced into the marketplace. The automation of the stock market created a different sort of complexity, with lots of unintended consequences. One small example: Goldman's trading on the Nasdaq exchange. In 2007, Goldman owned the (unmarked) building closest to Nasdaq. The building housed Goldman's dark pool. When Serge arrived, tens of thousands of messages per second were flying back and forth between computers inside the two buildings. Proximity, he assumed, must offer Goldman Sachs some advantage—after all, why else buy the building closest to the exchange? But when he looked into it he found that, to cross the street from Goldman to Nasdaq, a signal took 5 milliseconds, or nearly as much time as it would take, a couple of years later, for a signal to travel on the fastest network from Chicago to New York. "The theoretical limit [of sending a signal] from Chicago to New York and back is something like seven milliseconds," said Serge. "Everything more than that is the friction caused by man." The friction could be caused by physical distance—say, if the signal moving across a street in Carteret traveled in something less direct than a straight line. It could be caused by computer hardware. But it could also be caused by slow, clunky software—and that was Goldman's problem. Their high-frequency trading platform was designed, in typical Goldman style, as a centralized hub-and-spoke system. Every signal sent was required to pass through the mother ship in Manhattan before it went back out into the marketplace. "But the latency [the 5 milliseconds] wasn't mainly due to the physical distance," says Serge. "It was because the traffic was going through layers and layers of corporate switching equipment."

Broadly speaking, there were three problems Serge had been hired to solve. They corresponded to the three stages of an electronic trade. The first was to create the so-called ticker plant, or the software that translated the data from the thirteen public exchanges so that it could be viewed as a single stream. Reg NMS had imposed on the big banks a new obligation: to take in the information from all the exchanges in order to ensure that they were executing customers' orders at the official best market price—the NBBO. If Goldman Sachs purchased 500 shares of IBM at $20 a share on the New York Stock Exchange on behalf of a customer without first taking the 100 shares of IBM offered

at $19.99 on the BATS exchange, they'd have violated the regu-
lation. The easiest and cheapest solution for the big banks to this
problem was to use the combined data stream created by public
exchanges—the SIP. Some of them did just that. But to assuage
the concerns of their customers that the SIP was too slow and
offered them a dated view of the market, a few banks promised
to create a faster data stream—but nothing they created for customers' orders was as fast as what they created for themselves.

Serge had nothing to do with anything used by Goldman's
customers. His job was to build the system that Goldman Sachs's
own proprietary traders would use in their activities—and it
went without saying that it needed to be faster than anything
used by the customers. The first and most obvious thing he did
to make Goldman's robots faster was exactly what he had done
at IDT to enable millions of phone calls to find their cheapest
route: He decentralized Goldman's system. Rather than have
signals travel from the various exchanges back to the Goldman
hub, he set up separate mini–Goldman hubs inside each of the
exchanges. To acquire the information for its private ticker plant,
Goldman needed to place its computers as close as possible to the
exchange's matching engine. The software that took the out-
put from the ticker plant and used it to figure out smart trades
in the stock market was the second stage of the process: Serge
rewrote a lot of that code to make it run faster. The third stage
was called "order entry." As it sounds, this was the software that
sent those trades back out into the market to be executed. Serge
worked on that, too. He didn't think of it this way, but in effect
he was building a high-frequency trading firm within Goldman
Sachs. The speed he created for Goldman Sachs could be used
for many purposes, of course. It could be used simply to execute
Goldman's prop traders' smart strategies as quickly as possible.

It could also be used by Goldman's prop traders to trade the slow-moving customer orders in their own dark pool against the wider market. The speed Serge gave them could be used, for example, to sell Chipotle Mexican Grill to Rich Gates at a high price in the dark pool while buying it from him at a lower price on a public exchange.

Serge actually didn't know what the speed was being used for by Goldman's prop traders. As he worked, he became aware of a gulf in understanding between himself and his employer. The people at Goldman with whom he dealt understood the effects of what he did but not their deep causes. No one at Goldman had a global view of the firm's computer software, for instance: He figured that out on the first day, when they asked him to look into the code base and figure out how the different components talked to each other. In doing so, he saw that there was shockingly little documentation left behind by the people who had written that code, and that no one at Goldman could explain it to him. He, in turn, was not privy to the commercial effects of his actions—in part, he sensed, because his superiors did not want him to know them. "I think it is done intentionally," he said. "The less you know about how they make the money, the better it is for them."

But even if they had wanted him to know how the money was made, it is unclear Serge would have cared to know. "I think the engineering problems are much more interesting than the business problems," he says. "Finance is just who gets money. Does it wind up in the right pocket or the left pocket? It just so happens that the companies that make money are the companies like Goldman Sachs. You can't really win in that game unless you are one of these people." He understood that Goldman's quants were forever dreaming up new trading strategies, in the form of

algorithms, for his robots to execute, and that these traders were
meant to be extremely shrewd. He grasped further that "all their
algorithms are premised on some sort of prediction—predicting
something one second into the future." But you needed only
to observe the 2008 stock market crash from inside of Goldman Sachs, as Serge had, to see that what seemed predictable
often was not. Day after volatile day in September 2008, Goldman's supposedly brilliant traders were losing tens of millions
of dollars. "All of the expectations didn't work," recalls Serge.
"They thought they controlled the market, but it was an illusion. Everyone would come into work and were blown away by
the fact that they couldn't control anything at all. . . . Finance
is a gambling game for people who enjoy gambling." He wasn't
a gambler by nature. He preferred the deterministic world of
programming to the pseudo-deterministic world of speculation,
and he never fully grasped the connection between his work and
the Goldman traders'.

What Serge did know about Goldman's business was that the
firm's position in the world of high-frequency trading was inse-
cure. "The traders were always afraid of the small HFT shops,"
as he put it. He was making Goldman's bulky, inefficient system faster, but he could never make it as fast as a system built
from scratch, without the burden of 60 million lines of old code
underneath it. Or a system that, to change it in any major way,
did not require six meetings and signed documents from informational security officers. Goldman hunted in the same jungle
as the small HFT firms, but it could never be as quick or as
nimble as those firms: No big Wall Street bank could. The only
advantage a big bank enjoyed was its special relationship to the
prey: its customers. (As the head of one high-frequency trading
firm put it, "When one of these people from the banks inter-

views with us for a job, he always talks about how smart his algos are, but sooner or later he'll tell you that without his customer he can't make any money.")

After a few months working on the forty-second floor at One New York Plaza, Serge came to the conclusion that the best thing they could do with Goldman's high-frequency trading platform was to scrap it and build a new one from scratch. His bosses weren't interested. "The business model of Goldman Sachs was, if there is an opportunity to make money right away, let's do that," he says. "But if there was something long-term, they weren't that interested." Something would change in the stock market—an exchange would introduce a new, complicated rule, for instance—and that change would create an immediate opportunity to make money. "They'd want to do it immediately," says Serge. "But if you think about it, it's just patching the existing system constantly. The existing code base becomes an elephant that's difficult to maintain."

That is how he spent the vast majority of his two years at Goldman, patching the elephant. For their patching material he and the other Goldman programmers resorted, every day, to open source software—software developed by collectives of programmers and made freely available on the Internet. The tools and components they used were not specifically designed for financial markets, but they could be adapted to repair Goldman's plumbing. He discovered, to his surprise, that Goldman had a one-way relationship with open source. They took huge amounts of free software off the Web, but they did not return it after he had modified it, even when his modifications were very slight and of general, rather than financial, use. "Once I took some open source components, repackaged them to come up with a component that was not even used at Goldman Sachs," he says. "It was basically a way to make two computers look like one, so if one went down the other could jump in and perform the task." He'd created a neat way for one computer to behave as the stand-in for another. He described the pleasure of his innovation this way: "It created something out of chaos. When you create something out of chaos, essentially, you reduce the entropy in the world." He went to his boss, a fellow named Adam Schlesinger, and asked if he could release it back into open source, as was his inclination. "He said it was now Goldman's property," recalls Serge. "He was quite tense."

Open source was an idea that depended on collaboration and sharing, and Serge had a long history of contributing to it. He didn't fully understand how Goldman could think it was okay to benefit so greatly from the work of others and then behave so selfishly toward them. "You don't create intellectual property," he said. "You create a program that does something." But from then on, on instructions from Adam Schlesinger, he treated everything on Goldman Sachs's servers, even if it had just been transferred there from open source, as Goldman Sachs's property. (Later, at his trial, his lawyer flashed two pages of computer code: the original, with its open source license on top, and a replica, with the open source license stripped off and replaced by the Goldman Sachs license.)

The funny thing was that Serge actually liked Adam Schlesinger, and most of the other people he worked with at Goldman. He liked less the environment the firm created for them to work in. "Everyone lived for the year-end number," he said. "You get satisfied when the bonus is sizable and you get not satisfied when the number is not. Everything there is very possessive." It made no sense to him the way people were paid individually for achievements that were essentially collective achievements. "It was quite competitive. Everyone's trying to show how good their individual contribution to the team is. Because the team doesn't get the bonus, the individual does."

More to the point, he felt that the environment Goldman created for its employees did not encourage good programming, because good programming required collaboration. "Essentially there was very minimal connections between people," he says. "In telecom you usually have some synergies between people. Meetings when people exchange ideas. They aren't under stress in the same way. At Goldman it was always, 'Some component is broken and we're losing money because of it. Fix it now.'" The programmers assigned to fix the code sat in cubicles and hardly spoke to one another. "When two people wanted to talk they wouldn't just do it out on the floor," says Serge. "They would go to one of the offices around the floor and close the door. I never had that experience in telecom or academia."

By the time the financial crisis hit, Serge had a reputation of which he himself was unaware: He was known to corporate recruiters outside Goldman as the best programmer in the firm. "There were twenty guys on Wall Street who could do what Serge could do," says a headhunter who recruits often for high-frequency trading firms. "And he was one of the best, if not the best." Goldman also had a reputation in the market for programming talent—for keeping its programmers in the dark about their value to the firm's trading activities. The programmer types were different from the trader types. The trader types were far more alive to the bigger picture, to their context. They knew their worth in the marketplace down to the last penny. They understood the connection between what they did and how much money was made, and they were good at exaggerating the importance of the link. Serge wasn't like that. He was a little-picture person, a narrow problem solver. "I think he didn't know his own value," says the recruiter. "He compensated for being narrow by being good. He was that good."

Given his character and his situation, it's hardly surprising that the market kept finding Serge Aleynikov and telling him what he was worth, rather than the other way around. A few months into his new job, headhunters were calling him every other week. A year into his new job, he had an offer from UBS, the Swiss bank, and a promise to bump up his salary to $400,000 a year. Serge didn't particularly want to leave Goldman Sachs just to go and work at another big Wall Street firm, and so when Goldman offered to match the offer, he stayed. But in early 2009 he had another call, with a very different kind of offer: to create a trading platform from scratch for a new hedge fund run by Misha Malyshev.

The prospect of creating a new platform, rather than constantly patching an old one, excited him. Plus Malyshev was willing to pay him more than a million dollars a year to do it, and he suggested that they might even open an office for Serge near his home in New Jersey. Serge accepted the job offer and then told Goldman he was leaving. "When I put in the resignation letter," he said, "everyone comes to me one by one. The common perception was that if they had the right opportunity to quit Goldman they would do that in no time." Several hinted to him how much they would like to join him at his new firm. His bosses asked him what they could do to persuade him to stay. "They were trying to pursue me into this monetary discussion," says Serge. "I told them it wasn't the money. It was the chance to build a new system from the ground up." He missed his telecom work environment. "Whereas at IDT I was really

seeing the results of my work, here you had this monstrous system and you are patching it right and left. No one is giving you
the whole picture. I had a feeling no one at Goldman really
knows how it works as a whole, and they are just uncomfortable
admitting that."

He agreed to hang around for six weeks and teach other Goldman people everything he knew, so that they could continue
to find and fix the broken bands in their gigantic rubber ball.
Four times in the course of that last month he mailed himself
source code he was working on. The files contained a lot of
open source code he had worked with, and modified, over the
past two years, mingled with code that wasn't open source but
was obviously proprietary to Goldman Sachs. He hoped to dis-
entangle one from the other in case he needed to remind himself how he had done what he had done with the open source
code; he might need to do it again. He sent these files the same
way he had sent himself files nearly every week since his first
month on the job at Goldman. "No one had ever said a word
to me about it," he says. He pulled up his browser and typed
into it the words: "free subversion repository." Up popped a list
of places that stored code for free and in a convenient fashion.
He clicked the first link on the list. To find a place to send the
code took about eight seconds. And then he did what he had
always done since he'd first started programming computers: He
deleted his bash history—the commands he had typed into his
own Goldman computer keyboard. To access the computer, he
was required to type his password. If he didn't delete his bash
history, his password would be there to see, for anyone who had
access to the system.

It wasn't an entirely innocent act. "I knew that they wouldn't
be happy about it," he said, because he knew their attitude was

that anything that happened to be on Goldman's servers was the wholly owned property of Goldman Sachs—even when Serge himself had taken that code from open source. When asked how he felt when he did it, he says, "It felt like speeding. Speeding in the car."

FOR MUCH OF the flight from Chicago he'd slept. Leaving the plane, he noticed three men in dark suits waiting in the alcove of the Jetway reserved for baby strollers and wheelchairs. They confirmed his identity, explained that they were from the FBI, handcuffed him, searched his pockets, removed his backpack, told him to remain calm, and then walled him off from the other passengers. This last act was no great feat. Serge was six feet tall but weighed roughly 140 pounds: To hide him you needed only to turn him sideways. He resisted none of these actions, but he was genuinely bewildered. The men in black refused to tell him his crime. He tried to guess it. His first guess was that they'd gotten him mixed up with some other Sergey Aleynikov. Next it occurred to him that his new employer, Misha Malyshev, then being sued by Citadel, might have done something shady. Wrong on both counts. It wasn't until the plane had emptied and they'd escorted him into Newark Airport that they told him his crime: stealing computer code owned by Goldman Sachs.

The agent in charge of the case, Michael McSwain, was new to law enforcement. Oddly enough, he'd spent twelve years, until 2007, working as a currency trader on the Chicago Mercantile Exchange. He and others like him had been put out of business by Serge and people like him—or, more exactly, by the computers that had replaced the traders on the floors of every

U.S. exchange. It wasn't an accident that McSwain's career on Wall Street ended the same year that Serge's began.

McSwain marched Serge into a black town car and drove him to the FBI building in lower Manhattan. After making a show of stashing his gun, McSwain led him into a tiny interrogation room, handcuffed him to a rod on the wall, and, finally, read him his Miranda rights. Then he explained what he knew, or thought he knew: In April 2009 Serge had accepted a job at a new high-frequency trading shop, Teza Technologies, but had remained at Goldman for the next six weeks. Between early April and June 5, when Serge left Goldman for good, he sent himself, through the so-called subversion repository, 32 megabytes of source code from Goldman's high-frequency stock trading system. McSwain clearly found it damning that the website Serge used was called a subversion repository, and that it was in Germany. He also seemed to think it significant that Serge had used a site not blocked by Goldman Sachs, even after Serge tried to explain to him that Goldman did not block any sites used by its programmers but merely blocked its employees from porn sites and social media sites and suchlike. Finally, the FBI agent wanted him to admit that he had erased his bash history. Serge tried to explain why he always erased his bash history, but McSwain had no interest in his story. "The way he did it seemed nefarious," the FBI agent would later testify.

All of which was true, as far as it went, but, to Serge, that didn't seem very far. "I thought it was like, crazy, really," he says. "He was stringing these computer terms together in ways that made no sense. He didn't seem to know anything about high-frequency trading or source code." For instance, Serge had no idea where the subversion repository was physically located. It was just a place on the Internet used by developers to store the code they were working on. "The whole point of the Internet is to abstract the physical location of the server from its logical address," he said. To Serge, McSwain sounded like a man repeating phrases that he'd heard from others but that to him actually meant nothing. "There is a game in Russia called Broken Phone," he said—a variation on the American game Telephone. "It felt like he was playing that."

What Serge did not yet know was that Goldman had discovered his downloads—of what appeared to be the code they used for their proprietary high-speed stock market trading—just a few days earlier, even though Serge had sent himself the first batch of code months ago. They'd called the FBI in haste and had put McSwain through what amounted to a crash course in high-frequency trading and computer programming. McSwain later conceded that he didn't seek out independent expert advice to study the code Serge Aleynikov had taken, or seek to find out why he might have taken it. "I relied on statements from Goldman employees," he said. He had no idea himself of the value of the stolen code ("representatives from Goldman told me it was worth a lot of money"), or if any of it was actually all that special ("representatives of Goldman Sachs told us there were trade secrets in the code"). The agent noted that the Goldman files were on both the personal computer and the thumb drive that he'd taken from Serge at Newark Airport, but he failed to note that the files remained unopened. (If they were so important, why hadn't Serge looked at them in the month since he'd left Goldman?) The FBI's investigation before the arrest consisted of Goldman explaining some extremely complicated stuff to McSwain that he admitted he did not fully understand—but trusted that Goldman did. Forty-eight hours after Goldman called the FBI, McSwain arrested Serge. Thus the only Goldman Sachs employee arrested by the FBI in the aftermath of a financial crisis Goldman had done so much to fuel was the employee Goldman asked the FBI to arrest.

On the night of his arrest, Serge waived his right to call a lawyer. He called his wife, told her what had happened, and said that a bunch of FBI agents were on the way to their home to seize their computers, and to please let them in, although they had no search warrant. Then he sat down and politely tried to clear up the confusion of this FBI agent who had arrested him without an arrest warrant. "How could he figure out if this was a theft if he didn't understand what was taken?" he recalls having asked himself. What he'd done, in his view, was trivial; what he stood accused of—violating both the Economic Espionage Act and the National Stolen Property Act—did not sound trivial at all. Still, he thought that if the agent understood how computers and the high-frequency trading business actually worked, he'd apologize and drop the case. "The reason I was explaining it to him was to show that there was nothing there," he said. "He was completely not interested in the content of what I am saying. He just kept saying to me, 'If you tell me everything, I'll talk to the judge and he'll go easy on you.' It appeared they had a very strong bias from the very beginning. They had goals they wanted to fulfill. One was to obtain an immediate confession."

The chief obstacle to the FBI's ability to extract his confession, oddly, wasn't Serge's willingness to provide it but its own agent's ignorance of the behavior to which Serge was attempting to confess. "In the written statement he was making some very obvious mistakes, computer terms and so on," recalled Serge. "I was saying, 'You know, this is not correct.'" Serge patiently walked the agent through his actions. At 1:43 in the morning on July 4, after five hours of discussion, McSwain sent a giddy one-line email to the U.S. Attorney's office: "Holy crap he signed a confession."

Two minutes later, he dispatched Serge to a cell in the Metropolitan Detention Center. The prosecutor, Assistant U.S. Attorney Joseph Facciponti, argued that Serge Aleynikov should be denied bail. The Russian computer programmer had in his possession computer code that could be used "to manipulate markets in unfair ways." The confession Serge had signed, scarred by phrases crossed out and rewritten by the FBI agent, later would be presented by prosecutors to a jury as the work of a thief who was being cautious, even tricky, with his words. "That's not what happened," said Serge. "The document was being crafted by someone with no previous expertise in the matter."

Sergey Aleynikov's signed confession was the last anyone heard from him, at least directly. He declined to speak to reporters or testify at his trial. He had a halting manner, a funny accent, a beard, and a physique that looked as if it had been painted by El Greco: In a lineup of people chosen randomly from the streets, he was the guy most likely to be identified as the Russian spy, or a character from the original episodes of *Star Trek*. In technical discussions he had a tendency to speak with extreme precision, which was great when he was dealing with fellow experts but mind-numbing to a lay audience. In the court of U.S. public opinion, he wasn't well suited to defend himself, and so, on the advice of his attorney, he didn't. He kept his long silence even after he was sentenced, without the possibility of parole, to eight years in a federal prison.

CHAPTER SIX

HOW TO TAKE BILLIONS FROM WALL STREET

R onan didn't intend to tell his father exactly how much money he made, or anything else that sounded like boasting, but he wanted him to know he needn't worry about his son any longer. For Christmas, in 2011, he'd fly back to Ireland, as he did every year, only this year he'd travel toward a conversation. He felt no particular attachment to the place. "I don't belong there at all," he said. "There's fucking fat kids everywhere. When I was growing up there was no fat kids. It's lost its charm." He missed his family, nothing more. When he arrived at their house in the Dublin suburbs, his parents would be waiting with a list of their stuff that needed to be repaired or reprogrammed. After he'd rebooted their computer, or recaptured their satellite signal, he'd sit down with them and have this talk. "American parents get into their fucking kids' business," said Ronan. "In Ireland they don't. They mind their own fucking business." His father still had no clear idea what he did for a living, or, for that matter, why a big Wall Street bank would find him useful. "He didn't think I was a fucking teller or something. But if I said to my dad, 'I'm a trader,' he'd say, 'What the fuck do you know about trading?'" His life was his life, theirs was theirs. "My mom and dad, I know they love me. It's just Irish love. And I just kinda wanted him to know I was legit in this business. It was semi to set him at ease. I didn't want him to think I was putting the family in jeopardy."

Ireland's economy had collapsed three years earlier, under the weight of a lot of American-style financial machinations and bad advice from American financiers. Many of Ronan's childhood friends were still out of work. It didn't seem like the best time to be taking a risk. Just days before Ronan was to fly back to Ireland, however, Brad Katsuyama had pulled him into a meeting with John Schwall and Rob Park. Brad had wanted to know, if he left RBC to create a new stock exchange, who might leave with him. They'd taken turns answering the same question: *You in?* On some level, Ronan could not believe what he was hearing as he listened to the sound of his own voice: He'd spent his entire career trying to get a job on Wall Street, and now that he finally had one, the guy who had given it to him was asking him to throw it away. On another level, the question answered itself. "Too much was riding on me," he said. "And I felt like I owed Brad. He was the one who gave me a chance. I trusted him: He's not a fucking idiot."

By the end of 2011, there was something else on Ronan's mind, too. He'd now seen Wall Street from the inside. It wasn't as persuasive to him as he had expected it to be. "It's like if I stay here I'll become full of shit," he said.

They were all very much in; what they were in for was less clear. Until they found someone willing to pay for the building of a new stock exchange, they couldn't very well quit their jobs to do it. Ronan's commitment to Brad was less a promise of immediate action than a promissory note to be cashed at some point in the indefinite future. But they did have a goal: to restore fairness to the U.S. stock market—for the first time in Wall Street history, perhaps, to institutionalize fairness. And they had a rough idea: to deploy Thor as the backbone of a strange new kind of stock exchange, to which brokers could send stock market orders so that Thor might route them to all the other exchanges. And yet none of them, least of all Ronan, believed that Thor alone could change the stock market, mainly because they doubted that the big brokerage firms would hand over their most valuable commodity (their customers' stock market orders) to any third party to execute. They also suspected that other forms of unfairness plagued the market, problems that Thor didn't begin to address. "I give what we have right now a ten percent chance of working," Ronan told his colleagues. "But with the four of us I give us a seventy percent chance of figuring it out."

After he left Brad's office, Ronan realized that the talk he wanted to have with his father had changed: He needed his father's advice. He'd already taken one big risk, when he had quit a telecom job in which he'd made nearly half a million a year for a Wall Street job that paid him a third of that. It had panned out: RBC had just handed him a bonus of nearly a million bucks and was asking him if he would like to run the more lucrative half of their stock market trading operation. ("They told me I could name my price.") As his plane dipped toward the Irish coast, he wanted to know if he was out of his mind to quit his $910,000-a-year job for one that paid $2,000 a month— money that would quite possibly be paid to him out of funds he himself invested in the new company. His father might not care to know the details, but he'd grasp the gist of his predicament.

"I wanted to ask him: 'Is there a time when you stop rolling the dice?' I didn't know if RBC was that time." But when he finally sat his father down, Ronan realized he couldn't explain even the gist of his predicament unless he confessed the size of his bonus. "When I was telling him I'd made nine hundred and ten thousand dollars he about had a fucking heart attack," said Ronan. "I mean, he doubled over in his chair."

At length his father recovered, then looked up at his son and said, "You know what, Ro, your risks seem to have paid off so far. Why the fuck not?"

Ronan landed back in New York on Tuesday, January 3, 2012, turned on his BlackBerry, and watched the new messages flood in. The first was from Brad, announcing his resignation from the Royal Bank of Canada. As Ronan later recalled the moment, "The next ten messages said, 'Holy shit, Brad Katsuyama just fucking resigned.'" Ronan knew that RBC's bosses up in Canada had been refusing, artfully, to deal with Brad's insistence that it would be better for all concerned if he not only quit the bank to pursue an idea he had conceived while working for the bank but also took several of the bank's most valuable employees with him. The bosses in Canada clearly didn't like the sound of any part of this. They assumed that if they stalled for time, Brad would come to his senses. What kind of Wall Street trader quits a secure $2-million-plus-a-year job to start a risky business—a business for which he doesn't have even the financial backing?

At baggage claim, Ronan reached Brad by phone. "I just wanted to ask him: 'What the fuck is going on?'" Brad told him, in surprisingly few words: He was tired of all these supposedly important people who ran this supposedly important bank nodding politely when he tried to speak to them about something that was far, far more important than any one person or any one bank. "They were thinking he'd never do it," said Ronan. "And he was like, 'Oh yeah, motherfucker?' And he did it!" When Ronan rang off, he thought: *Well, he's pushed me all in.*

BRAD GOT TO work around 6:30 every morning. That first morning after the Christmas break, he went to his immediate superior and told him that he was done. Then he went to his desk and wrote one email to Ronan, Rob Park, and John Schwall, and another to three senior guys in Canada. Five minutes later his phone rang. It was Canada, outraged. *What the hell are you doing?* asked the senior manager on the other end of the line. *You can't do this.* To which Brad said: *I just did.*

He left the bank with nothing—no paper, no code, no certainty that anyone would actually follow him out, and not even, as it turned out, a clear idea for a business. Like everyone else in the stock market, Brad had received a jolt when he read that a Goldman Sachs high-frequency programmer had gone to jail for mailing himself computer code. Goldman's sensitivity confirmed his suspicion that, around 2009, the big Wall Street banks, previously distracted by the financial crisis, had finally woken up to the value of the customer orders inside their own dark pools. They were using fear and intimidation to control the technologists who, ultimately, could exploit that value; and the culture of finance suddenly was becoming more closed and secretive—which was saying something. The people who now did what Ronan had once done for the big banks and HFT firms, for instance, would not be allowed to see and hear all that Ronan had been allowed to see and hear. And the banks were now using the legal system to make it harder for their more technical employees to leave. "I said to Rob, 'No fucking around,'" recalled Brad. "He said, 'Don't worry. There's nothing I'd want to take from here anyway.'"

They'd be starting fresh. They could use the insights about the stock market gained from Thor, but Thor itself belonged to the Royal Bank of Canada. Their main advantage—their only sustainable advantage—was that investors trusted them. The investors on the receiving end of Wall Street's sales pitches were not, by nature, trusting; or, if they were trusting by nature, their natures were reshaped by their environment. People on Wall Street were simply paid too much to lie and dissemble and obfuscate, and so every trusting feeling in the financial markets simply had to be followed by a trailing doubt. Something about Brad had led investors to lower their guard and to trust him. Whatever that was, it was sufficiently powerful that a group of people who ran some of the world's biggest mutual funds and hedge funds, and who controlled roughly one third of the entire United States stock market, petitioned his superiors at RBC, after he had quit, to allow him to leave, so that he might restore trust to the financial markets on a grander scale.

And yet—even as he walked away from millions of Wall Street dollars—some of these very people raised questions about his motives. He needed $10 million or so to hire the people who could help him to design his new stock market, and to write the computer code that would be the basis for that market. He'd hoped—assumed, even—that these big investors would supply him with the capital to build the new stock exchange, but eight of every ten pitch meetings began with some version of the same question: "Why are you doing this? Why are you attacking a system that has made you rich and will make you even richer if you just go along with it?" As one investor put it, behind Brad's

back, "I have a question about Brad: Have you figured out why
he's playing Robin Hood?"

Brad's first answer to that question was the thing he'd told
himself: The stock market had become grotesquely unjust, and
badly needed to be changed, and he'd come to see that, if he
didn't do it, no one else would. "That didn't sit well," he recalled.
"They'd just say, 'That sounds like complete bullshit.' The first
couple of times it happened, it really bothered me." Then he got
over it. If this new stock exchange flourished, its founders stood
to make money—maybe a lot of money. He wasn't a monk; he
simply didn't feel any need to make great sums of money. But
he noticed, weirdly, that when he stressed how much money
he himself might make from the new stock exchange, potential
investors in his new business warmed to him—and so he started
to stress how much money he might make. "We had a saying
that seemed to appease everyone when they asked why we are
doing this," he said. "*We are long-term greedy.* That worked very
well. . . . It always got a better response out of them than my
first answer."

He spent six months running around New York faking greed
he didn't really feel, to put money people at ease. It was mad-
dening: He couldn't get the people who should give him money
to do so, and he couldn't take the money from the people who
wanted to give it to him. Just about all of the big Wall Street
banks either asked him outright if they might buy a stake in his
exchange or wanted at least to be considered as possible investors. But if he took their money, his stock exchange would lose
both its independence and its credibility with investors. His
friends and family in Toronto also all wanted to invest in his
new company. They presented a different issue. Two hours after
Brad had let them know, via email, that he was pounding the

pavement to raise money for a new stock market, they ponied up, collectively, $1.5 million. Some of these people could afford to take risks with their money, but some had no more than a few thousand dollars in savings. Before he allowed them to invest, Brad insisted that they send him bank statements to prove that they could afford to lose whatever they invested. "Your brother has never failed at anything he has ever done," one old friend wrote to Brad's older brother, Craig, to explain why the new business wasn't at all risky, and to ask him to intercede on his behalf and overrule Brad's decision not to take his money.

What he needed was for the big stock market investors who had said they wanted him to quit RBC to fix the stock market— that is, the mutual funds, pension funds, and hedge funds—to put their money where their mouth was. They offered all sorts of excuses why they couldn't help: They weren't designed to invest in start-ups; the investment managers thought it was a great idea, but the compliance arm simply wasn't equipped to evaluate Brad; and so on. "The amount of money we were asking for was so small that it was too much of a pain in the ass for them to figure out how to give it to us," said Brad. They all wanted him to build his exchange; they all hoped to benefit from that exchange; but they all also assumed that someone else would supply the capital to do it. Many had good excuses— it was indeed outside the mission of a giant pension fund to invest in start-ups. Still, it was disappointing. "They're like one of those fucking friends who say he'll back you up in a fight and they don't do anything," said Ronan, after one long and frustrating day of begging for capital. "You're on the ground, bloody, and only then do they jump in and throw a punch."

Some of them were like that; but not all of them. The giant mutual fund manager Capital Group pledged to invest—on the

condition that they weren't the lone investor but part of a con-
sortium; so did another, Brandes Investment Partners. And there
were several that voiced a sound objection: The business Brad
was pitching to them was a foggy proposition—a stock exchange
that existed mainly to route their stock market orders to all the
other exchanges. How would that work? Thor had worked great,
but why did Brad imagine that the predators who operated with
such abandon on America's public and private exchanges would
not adapt to it? And why did he think Wall Street's biggest banks
would subcontract the routing of their stock market orders to his
new exchange? Because it was "fair"? The banks' salesmen ran
around every day selling the banks' own routers. They weren't
going to turn on a dime and say, "Oh yeah, we've been paid
huge sums of money to sell you out to high-frequency traders,
but now we're going to give all the stock market orders to Brad,
so we can't sell you out any longer."

Brad didn't fully understand the enterprise he needed to create until the market forced him to, by not giving him the capital
for the enterprise he thought he wanted to create. Fuller understanding arrived in August 2012, in a meeting with David Einhorn, who ran the hedge fund Greenlight Capital. After listening
to Brad's pitch, Einhorn asked him a simple question: *Why aren't
we all just picking the same exchange?* Why didn't investors organize
themselves to sponsor a single stock exchange entrusted with
guarding their interests and protecting them from Wall Street
predators? There'd never been any collective pressure brought
by investors on the big banks to route their stock market orders
to any one exchange, but that was only because there was no
good reason to prefer one exchange over another: The fifty or so
places on which stocks were traded were all designed by financial intermediaries, for financial intermediaries. "It was so obvi-

ous it was almost embarrassing," said Brad. "That should have been our pitch: not that we should route the orders using Thor but [that] we should create the one place investors would choose to go." That is, they shouldn't simply seek to defend investors on the existing stock exchanges. They should seek to put all the other exchanges out of business.

By mid-December he'd sewn up $9.4 million from nine different big money managers.* Six months later he'd raise $15 million from four new investors. The money Brad needed that he didn't get he kicked in himself: By January 1, 2013, he'd put his life savings on the line.

At the same time, he went looking for people: software developers and hardware engineers and network engineers to build the system, the operations people to run it, and the salespeople to explain it to Wall Street. He had no trouble attracting people who knew him—just the opposite. A shockingly large number of people he'd worked with at RBC apparently felt the urge to entrust him with their careers. Several dozen people had hinted that they'd like to join him and do whatever he was doing. He found himself in a series of bizarre conversations, in which he tried to explain why they were better off being paid hundreds of thousands of dollars a year to work at a big Wall Street bank than taking a flier on a new business that had neither a clear plan nor a penny of financing. Still, people followed. Allen Zhang, the Golden Goose himself, got fired for sending RBC's computer code to himself and instantly turned up at Brad's front door. Billy Zhao was made redundant after he automated a compli-

---

* The first round of investors included Greenlight Capital, Capital Group, Brandes Investment Partners, Senator Investment Group, Scoggin Capital Management, Belfer Management, Pershing Square, and Third Point Partners.

cated task so well that the bank no longer needed his help to do it: He came on board, too. But Brad needed people who didn't know him, and who knew things he did not know. He needed, especially, people with a deep understanding of high-frequency trading and stock exchanges. And the first person he found was Don Bollerman.

WHAT EVERYONE NOTICED about Don Bollerman—even if they didn't quite put it this way—was how badly he wanted not to be surprised by his own life. On top of that, he'd grown up in the Bronx and carried with him a resistance to sentiment. He ripped the filters off cigarettes before he smoked them. He weighed a hundred pounds more than he should and ignored entreaties from his colleagues to exercise or take care of himself. "I'm gonna die young anyway," he'd say. His finer feelings he treated much the way he treated his body, with something approaching disdain. "Much is made of a kind heart," he said. "I'm more of a feed-yourself-or-die kind of guy."

To eliminate the possibility of surprise required not that Don's life be especially unsurprising but that he control his feelings about whatever surprise it produced. How much he wished to manage these emotions could be seen when they were at their least manageable. On September 11, 2001, Don worked at a small new electronic stock exchange on the twelfth floor of 100 Broadway, five hundred yards from the World Trade Center. He'd arrived at seven that morning. Before the stock market opened, he heard a bump, which sounded as if it had come from upstairs. "What we thought is that it was guys moving heavy equipment," he said. "Five minutes later it's snowing office memos." He and his colleagues went to the window and heard the news on the office TV about the plane hitting one of the towers. "I thought it was an attack right away," he said, and so he was less shocked than his colleagues by what happened next. They had a direct view of the Twin Towers, across the Trinity Church graveyard, over the top of the American Stock Exchange. The second plane hit. "I felt the heat on my face through the window. You open the barbecue and your face feels like it pulls back—that feeling," he said. They discussed whether the towers were tall enough to reach them if one fell over. Then the first tower fell. "That's when we ran for the staircase." By the time they got to the sixth floor, Don couldn't see his hands in front of his face. Once outside, in the blizzard, he headed east. He walked alone and matter-of-factly up Third Avenue and then across the bridge over the Harlem River to his apartment in the Bronx, sixteen miles in all. What stuck out in his mind from the day was how, when he arrived in Harlem, some women were waiting outside their homes with fruit juice for him to drink. "That one caught in my throat," he said. He added quickly, "Actually, I feel like a bit of a pussy, that it got to me that way."

The attack, and the ensuing market convulsions, killed off the new electronic stock exchange that employed him. Don, who had thought that the business was probably going to die anyway, went back to NYU to finish his college degree, and then on to a career at the Nasdaq stock exchange. Seven years in, his job was to deal with everything that happened after a trade occurred, but his specific role was less important than his general understanding—both Ronan and Schwall thought that Don Bollerman knew breathtakingly more about the inner workings of the stock exchanges than anyone they had ever met. He'd been privy to just about everything that happened inside

Nasdaq, and brought an understanding not just of what had gone wrong but how it might be set right.

What had gone wrong, in Don's view, wasn't all that surprising or complicated. It had to do with human nature, and the power of incentives. The rise of high-frequency trading—and its ability to gain an edge on the rest of the market—had created an opportunity for new exchanges, like BATS and Direct Edge. By giving HFT what it wanted (speed, in relation to the rest of the market; complexity only HFT understood; and payment to brokers for their customers' orders, so that HFT had something to trade against), the new stock exchanges had stolen market share from the old stock exchanges. Don couldn't speak for NYSE, but he had watched Nasdaq respond by giving HFT firms what they asked for—and then figuring out how to charge them for it. "It was almost like you couldn't do anything about it," he said. "We did all this speed, and I don't think we fully understood what it was being used for. We just thought, The new rules caused people to have a new experience and then new wants and needs." Nasdaq had become a public company in 2005, a year after Don had joined it. It had earnings targets to hit; it was incentivized to make decisions, and to make changes in the nature of the exchange, with a focus on their short-term consequences. "It's hard to be forward-thinking when the whole of corporate America is about the next quarter's earnings," said Don. "It went from 'Is this good for the market?' to 'Is this bad for the market?' And then it slides to: 'Can we get this through the SEC?' The demon in this part of the story is expediency." By late 2011, when Bollerman quit his job ("I felt there was a lack of leadership"), more than two-thirds of Nasdaq's revenues derived, one way or another, from high-frequency trading firms.

Don wasn't shocked or even all that disturbed by what had

happened, or, if he was, he disguised his feelings. The facts of Wall Street life were inherently brutal, in his view. There was nothing that he couldn't imagine someone on Wall Street doing. He was fully aware that the high-frequency traders were preying on investors, and that the exchanges and brokers were being paid to help them to do it. He refused to feel morally outraged or self-righteous about any of it. "I would ask the question, 'On the savannah, are the hyenas and the vultures the bad guys?'" he said. "We have a boom in carcasses on the savannah. So what? It's not their fault. The opportunity is there." To Don's way of thinking, you were never going to change human nature—though you might alter the environment in which it expressed itself. Or maybe that's just what Don wanted to believe. "He's kind of like the mob guy who cries every now and then after a hit," said Brad, who thought that Don was exactly the sort of person he needed. Brad wasn't in the market for self-righteousness, or for people who defined themselves by their fine moral sentiment. "Disillusion isn't a useful emotion," he said. "I need soldiers." Don was a soldier.

THEIR NEW EXCHANGE needed a name. They called it the Investors Exchange, which wound up being shortened to IEX.* Its goal was not to exterminate the hyenas and the vultures but, more subtly, to eliminate the opportunity for the kill. To do that, they needed to figure out the ways that the financial ecosystem favored predators over their prey. Enter the Puzzle Masters.

---

* In the interest of clarity, they'd hoped to preserve the full name, but they discovered a problem doing so when they set out to create an Internet address: investorsexchange. com. To avoid that confusion, they created another.

Back in 2008, when it had first occurred to Brad that the stock market had become a black box whose inner workings eluded ordinary human understanding, he'd gone looking for technologically gifted people who might help him open the box and understand its contents. He'd started with Rob Park; with less precision, he gathered others. One was a twenty-year-old Stanford junior named Dan Aisen, whose résumé Brad discovered in a pile at RBC. The line that leapt out at him was "Winner of the Microsoft College Puzzle Challenge." Every year, Microsoft sponsored this one-day, ten-hour national brain-twisting marathon. It attracted thousands of young math and computer science types. Aisen and three friends had competed, in 2007, against one thousand other teams and had won the whole thing. "It's kind of a mix of cryptography, ciphers, and Sudoku," explained Aisen. The solution to each puzzle offered clues to the other puzzles; to be really good at it, a person needed not only technical skill but exceptional pattern recognition. "There's some element of mechanical work, and some element of 'aha!'" said Aisen. Brad had given Aisen both a job and a nickname, the Puzzle Master, soon shortened, by RBC's traders, to Puz. Puz was one of the people who had helped him create Thor.

Puz's peculiar ability to solve puzzles was suddenly even more relevant. Creating a new stock exchange is a bit like creating a casino: Its creator needs to ensure that the casino cannot in some way be exploitable by the patrons. Or, at worst, he needs to know exactly how his system might be exploited, so that he might monitor the exploitation—as a casino monitors card counting at the blackjack tables. "You are designing a system," said Puz, "and you don't want the system to be gameable." The trouble with the stock market—with all of the public and private exchanges—was that they were fantastically gameable, and had been gamed: first by clever guys in small shops and then by prop traders at the big Wall Street banks. That was the problem, Puz thought. From the point of view of the most sophisticated traders, the stock market wasn't a mechanism for channeling capital to productive enterprise but a puzzle to be solved. "Investing shouldn't be about gaming a system," he said. "It should be about something else."

The simplest way to design a stock exchange that could not be gamed was to hire the very people best able to game it, and encourage them to take their best shots. Brad didn't know any other national puzzle champions, but Puz did. The first person he mentioned was his former Stanford teammate Francis Chung. Francis worked as a trader at a high-frequency trading firm but didn't like his job. Brad invited him in for a job interview. Francis turned up—and just sat there.

Brad gazed across a table: The young man was round-faced and shy and sweet-natured but essentially noninteractive.

"Why are you good at solving puzzles?" Brad asked him. Francis thought about it a moment.

"I'm not sure how good I am," said Francis.

"You just won the national puzzle-solving championship!"

Francis thought about that some more.

"Yeah, I guess," he said.

Brad had done a lot of these interviews with technologists whose skills he could not judge. He left it to Rob to figure out if they could actually write code. He just wanted to know what kind of people they were. "I'm just looking for the type of people who won't get along here," said Brad. "Typically, it's because the way they describe their experience, and the things they say, are very self-serving. 'I don't get enough credit for what I do,' or 'I'm overlooked.' It's all about me. They're obsessed with titles and other things that don't matter. I try to find out how they work with other people. If they don't know something, what do they do? I look for sponges, learners." With Francis he had no idea. Every question elicited some choked reply. Desperate to get something, anything, out of him, Brad finally asked, "All right, just tell me: What do you like to do?" Francis thought about it.

"I like to dance," he said. Then he went completely silent.

After Francis had left, Brad hunted down Puz. "Are you sure this is the guy?" he asked.

"Trust me," said Puz.

It took roughly six weeks for Francis to get comfortable enough to speak up. Once he did, he wouldn't shut up. It was Francis who would eventually take all the rules they created for the exchange and translate them into step-by-step instructions for a computer to follow. Francis alone had the entire logic of the new exchange in his head. Francis fought more than anyone for, as he put it, "making the system so simple there is nothing to game." And it was Francis whom Bollerman dubbed The Spoiler, because every time the other guys thought they had figured something out, Francis would step in and show them some loophole in their logic. "The level to which the kid will worry a problem is what really separates him," said Don Bollerman, "without any prior concern for whose theory he's going to upset—including his own."

The only problem with the Puzzle Masters was that neither of them had ever worked inside a stock exchange. Bollerman brought in a guy from Nasdaq, Constantine Sokoloff, who had helped to build the exchange's matching engine. "The Puzzle Masters needed a guide, and Constantine was that guide," said Brad. Constantine was also Russian, born and raised in a small town on the Volga River. He had a theory about why so many

Russians had wound up inside high-frequency trading. The old Soviet educational system channeled people away from the humanities and into math and science. The old Soviet culture also left its former citizens oddly prepared for Wall Street in the early twenty-first century. The Soviet-controlled economy was horrible and complicated but riddled with loopholes. Everything was scarce; everything was also gettable, if you knew how to get it. "We had this system for seventy years," said Constantine. "People learn to work around the system. The more you cultivate a class of people who know how to work around the system, the more people you will have who know how to do it well. All of the Soviet Union for seventy years were people who are skilled at working around the system." The population was thus well suited to exploit megatrends in both computers and the United States financial markets. After the fall of the Berlin Wall, a lot of Russians fled to the United States without a lot of English; one way to make a living without having to converse with the locals was to program their computers. "I know people who never programmed computers but when they get here they say they are computer programmers," said Constantine. A Russian also tended to be quicker than most to see holes built into the U.S. stock exchanges, even if those holes were unintentional, because he had been raised by parents, in turn raised by their own parents, to game a flawed system.

The role of the Puzzle Masters was to ensure that the new stock exchange did not contain aspects of a puzzle. That it had no problem inside its gears that could be "solved." To begin, they listed the features of the existing stock exchanges and picked them apart. Aspects of the existing stock exchanges obviously incentivized bad behavior. Rebates, for instance: The maker-taker system of fees and kickbacks used by all of the exchanges was simply a method for paying the big Wall Street banks to screw the investors whose interests they were meant to guard. The rebates were the bait in the high-frequency traders' flash traps. The moving parts of the traps were order types. Order types—like "market" and "limit"—exist so that the person who submits the order to buy or sell stock retains some control over his order after it has entered the marketplace.* They are an acknowledgment that the investor cannot be physically present on the exchange to micromanage his situation. Order types also exist, less obviously, so that the person who is buying or selling stock can embed, in a single simple instruction, a lot of other, smaller instructions.

The old order types were simple and straightforward and mainly sensible. The new order types that accompanied the explosion of high-frequency trading were nothing like them, either in detail or spirit. When, in the summer of 2012, the Puzzle Masters gathered with Brad and Don and Ronan and Rob and Schwall in a room to think about them, there were maybe one hundred fifty

---

* The market order is the first and simplest type. Say, for instance, an investor wishes to buy 100 shares of Procter & Gamble. When he submits his order, the market for the shares in P&G is, say, 80–80.02. If he submits a market order, he will pay the offering price—in this case, $80.02 per share. But a market order comes with a risk: that the market will move between the time the order is submitted and the time it reaches the market. The flash crash was a dramatic illustration of that risk: Investors who submitted market orders wound up paying $100,000 a share for P&G and selling those same shares for a penny apiece. To control the risk of a market order, a second order type was invented, the limit order. The buyer of P&G shares might say, for instance: "I'll buy a hundred shares, with a limit of eighty dollars and three cents a share." By doing so, he will ensure that he does not pay $100,000 a share; but this may lead to a missed opportunity—he may not buy the shares at all, because he never gets the price he wanted. Another simple, and long-used, order type is "good 'til canceled." The investor who says he wants to buy 100 shares of P&G at $80 a share, "good 'til canceled," will never have to think about it again until he buys them, or does not.

different order types. What purpose did each serve? How might each be used? The New York Stock Exchange had created an order type that ensured that the trader who used it would trade only if the order on the other side of his was smaller than his own order; the purpose seemed to be to prevent a high-frequency trader from buying a small number of shares from an investor who was about to crush the market with a huge sale. Direct Edge created an order type that, for even more complicated reasons, allowed the high-frequency trading firm to withdraw 50 percent of its order the instant someone tried to act on it. All of the exchanges offered something called a Post-Only order. A Post-Only order to buy 100 shares of Procter & Gamble at $80 a share says, "I want to buy a hundred shares of Procter & Gamble at eighty dollars a share, but only if I am on the passive side of the trade, where I can collect a rebate from the exchange." As if that weren't squirrely enough, the Post-Only order type now had many even more dubious permutations. The Hide Not Slide order, for instance. With a Hide Not Slide order, a high-frequency trader—for who else could or would use such a thing?—would say, for example, "I want to buy a hundred shares of P&G at a limit of eighty dollars and three cents a share, Post-Only, Hide Not Slide."

One of the joys of the Puzzle Masters was their ability to figure out what on earth that meant. The descriptions of single order types filed with the SEC often went on for twenty pages, and were in themselves puzzles—written in a language barely resembling English and seemingly designed to bewilder anyone who dared to read them. "I considered myself a somewhat expert on market structure," said Brad. "But I needed a Puzzle Master with me to fully understand what the fuck any of it means."

A Hide Not Slide order—it was just one of maybe fifty such problems the Puzzle Masters solved—worked as follows: The trader said he was willing to buy the shares at a price ($80.03) *above* the current offering price ($80.02), but only if he was on the passive side of the trade, where he would be paid a rebate. He did this not because he wanted to buy the shares. He did this in case an actual buyer of stock—a real investor, channeling capital to productive enterprise—came along and bought all the shares offered at $80.02. The high-frequency trader's Hide Not Slide order then established him as first in line to purchase P&G shares if a subsequent investor came into the market to sell those shares. This was the case even if the investor who had bought the shares at $80.02 expressed further demand for them at the higher price. A Hide Not Slide order was a way for a high-frequency trader to cut in line, ahead of the people who'd created the line in the first place, and take the kickbacks paid to whoever happened to be at the front of the line.

The Puzzle Masters spent days working through the many order types. All of them had one thing in common: They were designed to create an edge for HFT at the expense of investors. "We'd always ask, 'What is the point of that order, if you want to trade?'" said Brad. "Most of the order types were designed to *not* trade, or at least to discourage trading. [With] every rock we turned over, we found a disadvantage for the person who was actually there to trade." Their purpose was to hardwire into the exchange's brain the interests of high-frequency traders—at the expense of everyone who wasn't a high-frequency trader. And the high-frequency traders wanted to obtain information, as cheaply and risklessly as possible, about the behavior and intentions of stock market investors. That is why, though they made only half of all trades in the U.S. stock market, they submitted more than 99 percent of the orders: Their orders were a tool for divining information about ordinary investors. "The Puzzle

Masters showed me the length the exchanges were willing to go to—to satisfy a goal that wasn't theirs," said Brad.

The Puzzle Masters might not have thought of it this way at first, but in trying to design their exchange so that investors who came to it would remain safe from high-frequency traders, they were also divining the ways in which high-frequency traders stalked their prey. As they worked through the order types, they created a taxonomy of predatory behavior in the stock market. Broadly speaking, it appeared as if there were three activities that led to a vast amount of grotesquely unfair trading. The first they called "electronic front-running"—seeing an investor trying to do something in one place and racing him to the next. (What had happened to Brad, when he traded at RBC.) The second they called "rebate arbitrage"—using the new complexity to game the seizing of whatever kickbacks the exchange offered without actually providing the liquidity that the kickback was presumably meant to entice. The third, and probably by far the most widespread, they called "slow market arbitrage." This occurred when a high-frequency trader was able to see the price of a stock change on one exchange, and pick off orders sitting on other exchanges, before the exchanges were able to react. Say, for instance, the market for P&G shares is 80–80.01, and buyers and sellers sit on both sides on all of the exchanges. A big seller comes in on the NYSE and knocks the price down to 79.98–79.99. High-frequency traders buy on NYSE at $79.99 and sell on all the other exchanges at $80, before the market officially changes. This happened all day, every day, and generated more billions of dollars a year than the other strategies combined.

All three predatory strategies depended on speed, and to speed the Puzzle Masters turned their attention, once they were done with the order types. They were trying to create a safe place, where every dollar stood the same chance. How to do that, when a handful of people in the market would always be faster than everyone else? They couldn't very well prohibit high-frequency traders from trading on the exchange—an exchange needed to offer fair access to all broker-dealers. And, anyway, it wasn't high-frequency trading in itself that was pernicious; it was its predations. It wasn't necessary to eliminate high-frequency traders; all that was needed was to eliminate the unfair advantages they had, gained by speed and complexity. Rob Park put it best: "Let's say you know something before everyone else. You are in a privileged state. Eliminating the position of privilege is impossible—some people always will get the information first. Some people will always get it last. You can't stop it. What you can control is how many moves they can make to monetize it."

The obvious starting point was to prohibit high-frequency traders from doing what they had done on all the other exchanges—co-locating inside them, and getting the information about whatever happened on those exchanges before everyone else.* That helped, but it did not entirely solve the problem: High-frequency traders would always be faster at processing the information they acquired from any exchange, and they would always be faster than anyone else to exploit that information on

---

* The value of the microseconds saved by proximity to the exchanges explained why the exchanges expanded, bizarrely, after the people inside them had vanished. You might have thought that, when the whole of the stock market moved from a floor that needed to accommodate thousands of human traders into a single black box, the building that housed the exchange might shrink. Think again. The old New York Stock Exchange building on the corner of Wall and Broad streets was 46,000 square feet. The NYSE data center in Mahwah, which housed the exchange, was 400,000 square feet. Because the value of the space around the black box was so great, the exchanges expanded to enclose greater amounts of that space so that they might sell it. IEX could function happily inside a space roughly the size of a playhouse.

other exchanges. This new exchange would be required both to execute trades on itself and to route, to the other exchanges, the orders it was unable to execute. The Puzzle Masters wanted to encourage big orders, and larger-sized trades, so that honest investors with a lot of stock to sell might collide with honest investors who had a lot of stock to buy, without the intercession of HFT. If some big pension fund came to IEX to buy a million shares of P&G and found only 100,000 for sale there, it would be exposed to some high-frequency trader figuring out that its demand for P&G shares was unsatisfied. The Puzzle Masters wanted to be sure that they could beat any HFT firm to the supply of P&G stock on the other exchanges.

They entertained all sorts of ideas about how to solve the speed problem. "We had professors coming through here constantly," said Brad. For instance, one professor suggested a "randomized delay." Every order submitted to the new stock exchange would be assigned, at random, some time lag before it entered the market. The market information some high-frequency trader obtained with his 100-share sell order, the sole intention of which was to uncover the existence of a big buyer, might thus move so slowly that it would prove of no use to him. An order would become, like a lottery ticket, a matter of chance. The Puzzle Masters instantly spotted the problem: Any decent HFT firm would simply buy huge numbers of lottery tickets— to increase its chances of being the 100-share sell order that collided with the massive buy order. "Someone will just flood the market with orders," said Francis. "You end up massively increasing quote traffic for every move."

It was Brad who had the crude first idea: *Everyone is fighting to get in as close to the exchange as possible. Why not push them as far away as possible? Put ourselves at a distance, but don't let anyone else be there*. In designing the exchange, they needed to consider what the regulators would tolerate; they couldn't just do whatever they wanted. Brad kept a close eye on what the regulators already had approved, and paid special attention when the New York Stock Exchange won the SEC's approval for the strange thing they had done in Mahwah. They'd built this 400,000-square-foot fortress in the middle of nowhere, and they planned to sell, to high-frequency traders, access to their matching engine. But the moment they announced their plans, high-frequency trading firms began to buy up land surrounding the fort—so that they might be near the NYSE matching engine, without paying the NYSE for the privilege. In response, the NYSE somehow persuaded the SEC to let them make a rule for themselves: Any banks or brokers or HFT firms that did not buy (expensive) space inside the fort would be allowed to connect to the NYSE in one of two places: Newark, New Jersey, or Manhattan. The time required to move a signal from those places to Mahwah undermined HFT strategies; and so the banks and brokers and HFT firms were all forced to buy space inside the fort from the NYSE. Brad thought: *Why not create the distance that undermines HFT's strategies, without selling high-frequency traders the right to put their computers in the same building?* "There was a precedent: They'd let NYSE do it," Brad said. "Unless the regulators said, 'You must allow co-location,'" they'd have to let IEX forbid it.

The idea was to establish the IEX computer that matched buyers and sellers (the matching engine) at some meaningful distance from the place traders connected to IEX (called the "point of presence"), and to require anyone who wanted to trade to connect to the exchange at that point of presence. If you placed every participant in the market far enough away from the exchange, you could eliminate most, and maybe all, of the advantages created by speed. Their matching engine, they already knew, would be located in Weehawken, New Jersey (they'd been offered cheap space in a data center). The only question was: Where to put the point of presence? "Let's put it in Nebraska," someone said, but they all knew it would be harder to get the already reluctant Wall Street banks to connect to their market if the banks had to send people to Omaha to do it. Actually, though, it wasn't necessary for anyone to move to Nebraska. The delay needed only to be long enough for IEX, once it had executed some part of a customer's buy order, to beat HFT in a race to any other shares available in the marketplace at the same price—that is, to prevent electronic front-running. It needed to be long enough, also, for IEX, each time a share price moved on any exchange, to process the change, and to move the prices of any orders resting on it, so that they didn't get picked off—in the way, say, that Rich Gates had been picked off, when he ran his tests to determine if he was being ripped off inside the dark pools run by the big Wall Street banks. (That is, to prevent "slow market arbitrage.") The necessary delay turned out to be 320 microseconds; that was the time it took them, in the worst case, to send a signal to the exchange farthest from them, the NYSE in Mahwah. Just to be sure, they rounded it up to 350 microseconds.

The new stock exchange also cut off the food source for all identifiable predators. Brad, when he was a trader, had been cheated because his orders had arrived first at BATS, where HFT guys had picked up his signal and raced him to the other exchanges. The fiber routes through New Jersey that Ronan handpicked were chosen so that an order sent from IEX to the other exchanges arrived at them all at precisely the same time. (He thus achieved with hardware what Thor had achieved with software.) Rich Gates had gotten himself picked off in the Wall Street dark pools because the dark pools had not moved fast enough to re-price his order. The slow movement of the dark pools' prices had made it possible for a high-frequency trader (or the Wall Street banks' own traders) to exploit the orders inside it—legally. To prevent the same thing from happening on their new exchange, IEX needed to be extremely fast—much faster than any other exchange. (At the same time that they were slowing down everyone who traded on their exchange, they were speeding themselves up.) To "see" the prices on the other stock exchanges, IEX didn't use the SIP or some phony improvement on the SIP but instead created their own private, HFT-like pictures of the entire stock market. Ronan had scoured New Jersey for paths from their computers in Weehawken to all the other exchanges; there turned out to be thousands of them. "We used the fastest subterranean routes," said Ronan. "All the fiber we used was created by HFT for HFT. One hundred percent of it." The 350-microsecond delay worked like a head start in a foot-race. It ensured that IEX would be faster to see and react to the wider market than even the fastest high-frequency trader, thus preventing investors' orders from being abused by changes in that market. In the bargain, it prevented high-frequency traders—who would inevitably try to put their computers nearer than everyone else's to IEX's in Weehawken—from submitting their orders onto IEX more quickly than everyone else.

To create the 350-microsecond delay, they needed to keep the new exchange roughly thirty-eight miles from the place the brokers were allowed to connect to the exchange. That was a problem. Having cut one very good deal to put the exchange in Weehawken, they were offered another: to establish the point of presence in a data center in Secaucus, New Jersey. The two data

centers were less than ten miles apart, and already populated
by other stock exchanges and all the high-frequency traders.
("We're going into the lion's den," said Ronan.) A bright idea
came from a new employee, James Cape, who had just joined
them from an HFT firm: *Coil the fiber.* Instead of running straight
fiber between the two places, coil thirty-eight miles of fiber
and stick it in a compartment the size of a shoebox to simulate
the effects of the distance. And that's what they did. The information flowing between IEX and all the players on it would
thus go round and round, in thousands of tiny circles, inside the
magic shoebox. From the high-frequency traders' point of view,
it was as if they'd been banished to West Babylon, New York.

Creating fairness was remarkably simple. They would not sell
to any one trader or investor the right to put his computers next
to the exchange, or special access to data from the exchange.
They would pay no kickbacks to brokers or banks that sent orders;
instead, they'd charge both sides of any trade the same amount:
nine one-hundredths of a cent per share (known as 9 "mils").
They'd allow just three order types: market, limit, and Mid-Point
Peg, which meant that the investor's order rested in between the
current bid and offer of any stock. If the shares of Procter & Gamble were quoted in the wider market at 80–80.02 (you can buy at
$80.02 or sell at $80), a Mid-Point Peg order would trade only at
$80.01. "It's kind of like the fair price," said Brad.

Finally, to ensure that their own incentives remained as closely
aligned as they could be with those of stock market investors, the
new exchange did not allow anyone who could trade directly on
it to own any piece of it: Its owners were all ordinary investors
who needed first to hand their orders to brokers.

The design of the new stock exchange was such that it would
yield all sorts of new information about the inner workings of

the U.S. stock market—and, indeed, the entire financial system. For instance, it did not ban but welcomed high-frequency traders who wished to trade on it. If high-frequency traders performed a valuable service in the financial markets, they should still do so, after their unfair advantages had been eliminated. Once the new stock exchange opened for business, IEX would be able to see how much of what HFT did was useful simply by watching what, if anything, high-frequency traders did on the new exchange, where predation was not possible. The Puzzle Masters' only question was whether, in their design, they had accounted for every possible form of market predation. That was the one thing even they did not know: whether they had missed something.

THE HIDDEN PASSAGES and trapdoors that riddled the exchanges enabled a handful of players to exploit everyone else; the latter didn't understand that the game had been designed precisely for the former. As Brad put it, "It's like you run this casino, and you need to get players in to attract other players. You invite a few players in to start a game of Texas Hold'em by telling them that the deck doesn't have any jacks or queens in it, and that you won't tell the other people who come to play with them. How do you get people into the casino? You pay the brokers to bring them there." By the summer of 2013, the world's financial markets were designed to maximize the number of collisions between ordinary investors and high-frequency traders—at the expense of ordinary investors, and for the benefit of high-frequency traders, exchanges, Wall Street banks, and online brokerage firms. Around those collisions an entire ecosystem had arisen.

Brad had heard many firsthand accounts about the nature

of that ecosystem. One came from a man named Chris Nagy, who, until 2012, had been responsible for selling the order flow for TD Ameritrade. Every year, people from banks and high-frequency trading firms would fly to Omaha, where TD Ameritrade was based, and negotiate with Nagy. "Most of the deals tend to be handshake deals," Nagy said. "You go out to a steak dinner. 'We'll pay you two cents a share. Everything is good.'" The negotiations were always done face-to-face, because no one involved wanted to leave a paper trail. "The payment for the order flow is as off-the-record as possible," said Nagy. "They never have an email or even a phone call. You had to fly down to meet with us." For its part, TD Ameritrade was required to publish how much per share they were making from the practice but not the total amounts, which were buried on its income statements on a line labeled "Other Revenue." "So you can see the income, but you can't see the deals."

In his years selling order flow, Nagy noticed a couple of things—and he related them both to Brad and his team when he came to visit them to find out why he kept hearing about this strange new thing called IEX. The first was that the market complexity created by Reg NMS—the rapid growth in the number of stock markets, and in high-frequency trading—raised the value of a stock market customer's order. "It caused the value of our flow to triple, a least," Nagy said. The other thing he couldn't help but notice was that not all of the online brokers appreciated the value of what they were selling. TD Ameritrade was able to sell the right to execute its customers' orders to high-frequency trading firms for hundreds of millions a year. The bigger Charles Schwab, whose order flow was even more valuable than TD Ameritrade's, had sold its flow to UBS back in 2005, in an eight-year deal, for only $285 million. (UBS charged the high-frequency trading firm Citadel some undisclosed sum to execute Schwab's trades.) "Schwab left at least a billion dollars on the table," Nagy said. A lot of the people selling their customers' orders, it seemed to Nagy, had no idea of the value of the information the orders contained. Even he was unsure; the only way to know would be to find out how much money high-frequency traders were making by trading against slow-footed individual investors. "I've tried over the years [to find out how much money was being made by high-frequency trading]," Nagy said. "The market makers are always reluctant to share their performance." What Nagy did know was that the simple retail stock market order was, from the point of view of high-frequency traders, easy kill. "Whose order flow is the most valuable?" he said. "Yours and mine. We don't have black boxes. We don't have algos. Our quotes are late to the market—a full second behind."*

High-frequency traders sought to trade as often as possible with ordinary investors, who had slower connections. They were able to do so because the investors themselves had only the faintest clue of what was happening to them, and also because the investors, even big, sophisticated ones, had no ability to control their own orders. When, say, Fidelity Investments sent a big stock market order to Bank of America, Bank of America treated that order as its own—and behaved as if it, not Fidelity, owned the information associated with that order. The same was true

---

* In 2008, Citadel bought a stake in the online broker E★Trade, which was floundering in the credit crisis. The deal stipulated that E★Trade route some percentage of its customers' orders to Citadel. At the same time, E★Trade created its own high-frequency trading division, eventually called G1 Execution Services, to exploit the value of those orders for itself. Citadel's founder and CEO, Kenneth Griffin, pitched a fit, and called out E★Trade publicly for failing to execute its customers' orders properly.

when an individual investor bought stock through an online broker. The moment he pressed the Buy icon on his screen, the business was out of his hands, and the information about his intentions belonged, in effect, to E★Trade, or TD Ameritrade or Schwab.

But the role in this of the nine big Wall Street banks that controlled 70 percent of all stock market orders was more complicated than the role played by TD Ameritrade. The Wall Street banks controlled not only the orders, and the informational value of those orders, but dark pools in which those orders might be executed. The banks took different approaches to milking the value of their customers' orders. All of them tended to send the orders first to their own dark pools before routing them out to the wider market. Inside the dark pool, the bank could trade against the orders themselves; or they could sell special access to the dark pool to high-frequency traders. Either way, the value of the customers' orders was monetized—by the big Wall Street bank, for the big Wall Street bank. If the bank was unable to execute a stock market order in its own dark pool, the bank directed that order first to the exchange that paid the biggest kickback for it—when the kickback was simply the bait for some flash trap.

If the Puzzle Masters were right, and the design of IEX eliminated the advantage of speed, IEX would reduce the value of investors' stock market orders to zero. If the orders couldn't be exploited on this new exchange—if the information they contained was worthless—who would pay for the right to execute them? The big Wall Street banks and online brokers charged by investors with routing stock market orders to IEX would surrender billions of dollars in revenues in the process. And that, as everyone involved understood, wouldn't happen without a fight.

One afternoon during the summer of 2013, a few months before the exchange planned to open for business, Brad called a meeting to figure out how to make the big Wall Street banks feel watched. IEX had raised more capital and hired more people and moved to a bigger room, on the thirtieth floor of 7 World Trade Center. There still was no separate place to meet, however, so they gathered in a corner of the big room, where a whiteboard met a window that offered a spectacular view of the 9/11 memorial. Don leaned with his back against the window, along with Ronan, Schwall, and Rob Park, while Brad stood in front of the whiteboard and took a whiteboard marker out of a bin. The twenty or so other employees of IEX remained at their desks in the room, pretending that nothing was happening.

Then Matt Trudeau appeared and joined in. Matt was the only person in the room who had ever opened a brand-new stock exchange, and so he tended to be included in every business discussion. Oddly enough, among them he was least, by nature, a businessman. He'd entered college to major in painting and then, deciding he lacked the talent to make it as a painter, and thinking he might make it as an academic, had moved into the anthropology department. He didn't become an anthropologist, either. After college he'd found work adjusting auto insurance claims—a job he judged to be among the world's most soul-sucking. One day on a lunch break, he noticed a television switched on to CNBC and wondered, "Why are there two separate ticker tapes?" He began to study the stock market. Five years later, in the mid-2000s, he was opening new, American-style stock exchanges in foreign countries for a company with the mystifying name Chi-X Global. ("It was marketing gone awry," he said. "We spent the first fifteen minutes of every meeting trying to explain our name.") He'd been one part businessman and

one part missionary: He met with officials of various govern-
ments, wrote white papers, and sat on panels to extol the virtues
of American financial markets. After opening Chi-X Canada,
he'd advised firms trying to open stock exchanges in Singapore,
Tokyo, Australia, Hong Kong, and London. "Did I think I was
doing God's work?" he said later. "No. But I did think market
efficiency was something important for the economy."

As he spread the American financial gospel, he couldn't help
but notice a pattern: A new exchange would open, and nothing
would happen on it—until the high-frequency traders showed
up, stuck their computers beside the exchange's matching
engine, and turned the exchange around. Then he began to hear
things—that some of the HFT guys might be shady, that stock
exchanges had glitches built into them that HFT could use to
exploit ordinary investors. He couldn't point to specific wrongdoing, but he felt less and less easy about his role in the universe.
In 2010, Chi-X promoted him to a big new job, Global Head of
Product; but before he took the job he came across an Internet
post by Sal Arnuk and Joseph Saluzzi.* The post showed, in
fine detail, how data about investors' orders provided to high-
frequency traders by two of the public exchanges, BATS and
Nasdaq, helped HFT discern investors' trading intentions. Most
investors, Arnuk and Saluzzi wrote, "have no idea that the private trade information they are entrusting to the market centers
is being made public by the exchanges. The exchanges are not
making this clear to their clients, but instead are actively broad-

---

* Arnuk and Saluzzi, the principals of Themis Trading, have done more than anyone to
explain and publicize the predation in the new stock market. They deserve more lines
in this book than they receive but have written their own book on the subject, *Broken
Markets*.

casting the information to the HFTs in order to court their order flow." "It was the first credible evidence of Big Foot," said Matt. He dug around on his own and saw that the glitches at BATS and Nasdaq that queered the market for the benefit of HFT weren't flukes but symptoms of a systemic problem, and that "many other little market quirks were there that were potentially being exploited."

He was then in an awkward position: that of a public spokesman for the new American-style stock market who doubted the integrity of that market. "I'm at the point where I no longer feel I can authentically defend high-frequency trading," he said. "I look at us exporting our business model to all these different countries and I think, *It's like exporting a disease.*" He was thirty-four years old, and married, with a one-year-old child. Chi-X was paying him more than $400,000 a year. And yet, with no idea what he was going to do to earn a living, he up and quit. "I don't want to say I'm an idealist," he said. "But you have a limited amount of time on this planet. I don't want to be twenty years from now and thinking I hadn't lived my life in a way I could be proud of." He kicked around for the better part of a year before he thought to call Ronan, whom he'd met when Ronan came through to run cables for HFT inside his Canadian exchange. In October 2012 they met for coffee at the McDonald's near Liberty Plaza, and Ronan explained he'd just left RBC to open a new stock exchange. "My first reaction was, *I feel so bad for the guy,*" said Matt. "*He's just destroyed his future. They're just doomed.* Then, afterwards, I asked myself, 'What causes a bunch of people making a million a year to quit?'" He came back in November and asked Ronan some more questions about this new exchange. In December, Brad hired him.

Standing in front of the whiteboard, Brad now reviewed the

problem at hand: It was unusual for an investor to direct his broker to send his order to one exchange, but that is what investors
were preparing to do with IEX. But these investors had no way of
determining if the Wall Street brokers followed their instructions
and actually sent the orders to IEX. The report investors typically received from their brokers—the Transaction Cost Analysis, or TCA—was useless, so sloppily and inconsistently compiled
as to be beyond analysis. Some of it came time-stamped to the
second; some, time-stamped in tenths of microseconds. None of
it told you which exchange you traded on. As a result, there was
no way to determine the context of any transaction, the event
immediately before it and the one immediately after. If you didn't
even know the order of the trades in the stock market, you could
hardly determine if you had traded at a fair price. "It's a Pandora's
box of ridiculousness," said Brad. "Just getting an answer to the
question: 'Where did I trade?' It isn't really possible."

"What if they [investors] send us their trade orders and we
check them to see if they ever got here?" asked Rob Park sensibly.

"We can't," said Don. "It violates our confidentiality agreement with brokers."

True. An investor might hand Bank of America an order and
ask the Bank of America broker to route it to IEX. The investor might also ask that IEX be permitted to inform him of the
outcome. And yet Bank of America might refuse, on principle,
to allow IEX to inform the investor that they had followed his
instructions—on the grounds that doing so would reveal Bank
of America's secrets!

"Why can't we just publish what happened?" asked Ronan.

"It's the banks' information," said Don.

"We can't publish what happened to an investor's trade because
what happened to the investor is Goldman Sachs's information?"

Ronan was incredulous—but then he knew less about this than the others.

"Correct."

"What can they do to us if we do it—shut us down?"

"Probably just a slap on the wrist the first time," said Don.

Brad wondered aloud if it was possible to create a mechanism through which investors might be informed, in real time, where their brokers sent their stock market orders. "Like a security camera," he said. "You don't care if it's even turned on. Just the fact that it's there might alter behavior."

"It's a finger in the eye of the brokerage community," said Don. He wore a t-shirt that said I Love Aquatic Life, and tossed a rugby ball to himself, but he didn't feel as comfortable as he wished to appear. All these other guys had worked at big Wall Street banks; none of them had ever had to deal with those banks as a customer. They didn't know their market power. As Don later put it, "The brokers, if they all decide to hate us, we're fucked. End of story." He didn't put it so bluntly to the others, maybe because he sensed that they all knew it.

"It's like saying, 'I think people are stealing in this office,'" said Brad, with growing enthusiasm. "I can run in and run out and run in and run out and keep checking and try to catch someone. Or I can install a camera. It may be plugged in—or not. But there's still this camera. And whoever is fucking stealing my coffee pots won't know if it's on."

"We don't really give a fuck if the investors use it," added Ronan. "We just want the brokers scared they'll check."

Somewhere in the big room a phone rang, and the sound was as jolting as a car honking in a small town in the middle of the night. The room was an open pit, with no barriers between the people in it, but the young men inside it behaved as if they worked with walls around them. They were, all but one, young men. The exception, Tara McKee, had been a research associate at RBC until Brad found her, in 2009, and asked her to be his personal assistant. ("The first time I met him, I said, 'I don't care what I do—I just want to work for him.'") She'd followed him out when he left the bank, even after he tried to talk her out of it, as he couldn't pay her properly and didn't think she could tolerate the risk. The cast of technologists Brad had assembled at this new place Tara found even more peculiar than the one he'd put together at RBC. "For geniuses, they are really dumb," she said. "Some of them are really pampered: They can't even put together a cardboard box. They don't think you do something. They think you call somebody."

They were also amazingly self-contained. This meeting concerned them all—compelling the big Wall Street banks' cooperation might mean the difference between success and failure—but they all at least feigned indifference. The etiquette here was a kind of willed incuriosity—even about each other. "Communication with a lot of the guys is not that great," said Brad. "It's something we need to work on." It was funny. To a man, they were puzzle solvers, and yet, to each other, they remained unsolved puzzles.

Schwall looked over the desks and shouted, "Whose phone is that?"

"Sorry," someone said, and the ringing stopped.

"It's a *nanny*," said Don, of Brad's security camera idea. "It's demeaning. It could be a strain on the relationship."

"When you get patted down in the airport, do you hate the people who pat you down?" asked Brad.

"I fuckin' hate them," said Don.

"I say, 'I'm glad you're checking my bags, because that means you're checking other people's,'" said Brad.

"The problem is that everyone is carrying marijuana through the checkpoint," said Schwall.

"If anyone gets fucking angry it's because they're guilty," said Brad hotly.

"I'm sorry," said Don. "I'm fat and white and I'm not gonna bomb this airplane. I shouldn't get extra swabbing." He'd stopped tossing the rugby ball.

"Is there some use for this other than policing brokers?" asked Schwall. He was asking, "Can we police them without their realizing it?" The person among them most adept at uncovering the secrets of others believed it was possible for IEX to keep its own affairs secret.

"No," said Brad.

"So it's a nanny," said Schwall with a sigh.

"*Broker Nanny*," said Don. "It's a great name. Shame we can't patent it."

The meeting went quiet. This was just one of a thousand arguments they'd had in designing the exchange. The group was roughly split—between people (Ronan and, to a lesser extent, Brad) who wanted to pick a fight with the biggest Wall Street banks, and people who thought it was insane to pick that fight (Don and, to a lesser extent, Schwall). Rob and Matt hadn't yet come clean, but for different reasons. After his initial suggestion had been swatted away, Rob had gone silent. "Rob is farthest from the chaos," said Brad. "He doesn't meet with brokers. The solutions to the problems they [the Wall Street brokers] create are illogical because they solve a problem that is illogical."

Matt Trudeau, also quiet, often tended to step back and observe. "I've always felt a little outside the groups of people I hung around with," he said. He was a natural conciliator as well. He may have quit his job on principle, but he didn't enjoy conflict, even the internal kind. "I might not be jaded enough," Matt now said carefully. "But let's say we launch and we're wildly successful and we never have to roll this out."

That thought was dead on arrival: No one believed they would be wildly successful the moment they launched—least of all Matt. He knew firsthand what happened when a new exchange opened: nothing. Chi-X Canada was now a huge success—20 percent of the Canadian market—but in its first month it had traded 700 shares total. Entire days passed without a single trade on that exchange; and the next few months weren't much better. And that was what success looked like. IEX didn't have the luxury of going months without activity. Their new stock exchange didn't need to be an instant sensation, but it had to host enough trading to illustrate the positive effects of honesty. They needed to be able to prove to investors that an explicitly fair exchange yielded better outcomes for investors than all the other exchanges. To prove the case, they needed data; to generate that data, they needed trades. If the big Wall Street banks colluded to keep trades off IEX, the new exchange would be stillborn. And they all knew it.

"They're gonna be pissed," said Schwall finally.

"We're in a fight," said Brad. "If every client felt like their instructions were being followed, we wouldn't be having this discussion. It's not about IEX wanting to go punch some broker in the face for no reason. It's not about saying, 'Who is our enemy?' It's about saying who we are aligned with. We're aligned with the investor."

"They're still gonna be pissed," said Schwall.

"Are we really in the police business?" asked Don.

"Maybe we don't have to have it at all," added Schwall. "Maybe we just have to create the illusion we have it. We talk to

the buy side about having it, and they whisper to their brokers—
that might be enough."

"But they'll all know," said Don. "They know we have to
keep the brokers' junk private. And the broker has to keep the
clients' junk private. And the client can't opt out."

Brad offered one last idea: a chat room in which investors
could converse with their brokers as the trade was happening.
"Or they can always get their broker on the phone and say, 'Tell
me what the fuck is going on,'" he said. "It's always been a
solution."

"They've never done it," said Ronan.

"They've never been motivated to do it," said Matt. True:
Investors had never been given a compelling reason to favor one
stock exchange over another.

"You get Danny Moses in a chat room with Goldman," said
Brad, referring to the head trader at Seawolf. "He'll ask them."

"But Danny's a bit argy-bargy," said Ronan.

"*Argy-bargy,* I like that," said Don.

Ronan had been teaching Don Irish epithets, one at a time.
"You got *wanker. Tosser.* Now you got *argy-bargy,*" said Ronan.

"You do nothing, and everyone does what they want," said
Brad. "You do something and you can influence behavior. But,
by creating the tool, do we incentivize behavior we want to
eliminate? By shining the light, do we create a gray zone, just
outside the light? Is it like Reg NMS, where you create the very
thing you're trying to get rid of?"

"Shining a light creates shadows," said Don. "If you try to
create this bright line, you are going to create gray zones on
either side."

"If we sincerely believe it creates too many blind spots, we
might not want to do it," said Brad.

"If we bill it as a nanny and she's drunk on the couch, are we gonna look like assholes?" added Don. "Better not to have a nanny at all. Just leave the kids home alone."

"If you can think of any other possible use for this fucker, that would help," said Schwall, who clung to his hope that they might disguise their actions. That they might be secret cops.

"I'm less bullish on this than I was before," said Brad. "I'll be honest. Because a drunk nanny might not be better than no nanny at all."

"How drunk can a nanny get?" asked Ronan idly.

Brad tossed the marker back into the whiteboard bin. "You can see why the client has been left in the dust," he said. "The system is designed to leave the client in the dust." Then he turned to Don. "At Nasdaq did they talk about this?"

"No," said Don, leaning back against the window.

For a moment, Brad looked at Don, and at the view that he only partly concealed. In that moment, he might as well have been, not on the inside of his new exchange looking out, but on the outside looking in. How did they seem to others? To the people *out there*? Out there, where the twin symbols of American capitalism once loomed, reduced in a few hours to a blizzard of office memos and a ruin. Out there, where idealism was either a ruse or a species of stupidity, and where the people who badly needed them to succeed hadn't the faintest idea of their existence. But out there a lot of things happened. People built new towers to replace the old ones. People found strength they didn't know they had. And people were already coming to their aid, and bracing for the war. Out there, anything was possible.

CHAPTER SEVEN

AN ARMY OF ONE

On the morning of September 11, 2001, Zoran Perkov took the subway from his home in Queens to Wall Street, as he did every day. As usual, he wore headphones and listened to music, and pretended that the other people on the train didn't exist. The difference between that morning and all the others was that he was running late, and the people on the train were harder than usual to ignore. *They were talking to each other.* "Nobody talks to each other," said Zoran. "It was a weird feeling, when you feel something is off." He was twenty-six years old, tall and broad, with hooded eyes that saw everything in one shade of gray or another. Born in Croatia, into long lines of fishermen and stonemasons, he'd moved with his parents to the United States when he was a small child. He'd grown up in Queens, and he worked on a tech help desk for the cryptically named Wall Street Systems, at 30 Broad Street, immediately next door to the New York Stock Exchange. His job bored him. What precisely he did on Wall Street Systems' tech help desk didn't matter. He wouldn't be doing it much longer. In the next few hours, he'd discover a reason for doing something else. This discovery—and the clear sense of purpose that came with it—would put him on a course to be of serious use to Brad Katsuyama.

The subway car was a silent movie. Zoran watched the people in it talking to each other all the way to Wall Street. Ascending from the hole in the ground in front of Trinity Church and into the morning light, he noticed the necks tilted back and the eyes gazing upward. He, too, looked up, just as the second plane hit the South Tower. "You couldn't see the plane," he said. "You just saw this explosion."

He took off his headphones and heard the sounds. "All around people crying, people screaming, people puking." He saw people running up Broadway. He crossed the street and went to work. "Work isn't work for me," he said. "I got friends there. I went to find out what is going on." Outside the front door, he spotted the same pretty woman with a cigarette he always saw on his way in. ("You know, the one hot chick in the building.") She was smoking but also crying. He went upstairs, checked in with his friends, and called some guys he'd grown up with who worked on or around Wall Street. One of them worked in the Twin Towers—which tower Zoran couldn't recall. A couple more worked in the buildings around the towers. He reached them and they agreed to use his office as their meeting point. When his friend from the Twin Tower arrived, he said that on his way out he'd heard the bodies hitting the ground.

The small group of five friends set out to escape. They discussed strategy. Zoran argued for walking out, up Broadway; the others voted to leave on the subway. "Democracy won," said Zoran, and back down into the Wall Street station they went. It turned out that this was not an original idea. The crowds forced them apart; three of them squeezed into one car, while Zoran and another pushed into the next car. "It was such a mixed crowd," said Zoran, "not your usual subway crowd." There were all these Wall Street people: guys from the stock exchange in their colored jackets; people you just never saw there. The car lurched out of the station and into the dark tunnel, then stopped. "That's when my ears popped," said Zoran. "Like when you go swimming under water."

The tunnel filled with smoke. Zoran had no idea what had happened—why his ears had popped, why the tunnel was full of smoke—but he noticed a guy trying to open a window, and he hollered at him to stop. *Who gave you the authority?* the guy screamed back at Zoran. "It's *smoke*," Zoran shouted. "Breathe it. Die. It's that fucking simple." The window stayed shut, but the car remained fractious and unsettled. The car holding his other friends was tranquil. People bent over, praying.

The conductor came on and announced that the train needed to return to the Wall Street station. To general concern, the guy who drove the train walked from the front car to the back car, did whatever needed to be done to allow the train to go the wrong way inside a tunnel, and jolted it back from whence it had come. But not completely: Only the front two cars gained access to the platform. The people in what was now the rear of the train needed to file out through the cars to reach the exit.

That's when Zoran noticed the old man—his neighbor, in a crowd trying to form a line to exit the train. "He's got a cane," said Zoran. "He's in an old suit—he's gotten thinner and smaller, so it doesn't fit him very well. I remember thinking: *I should probably make sure this guy doesn't get crushed.* So I just kind of kept him in front of me. I felt responsible for him." Half-guiding the

old man, he nudged his way back up the steps of the subway station and onto Wall Street. Then everything went totally black.
"We get to street level, and I had to realize it *was* street level,"
said Zoran. "And I lost the old guy. From that moment I was just
paying attention to everything around me."

He now couldn't see, but he could hear people shouting.
"Over here! Over here!" he heard someone scream. He and
the friend who'd been in the subway car with him followed
the sound of the voices, walking into what turned out to be
the American Express building—though Zoran didn't realize it
until they'd been inside for a minute. What he noticed was the
pregnant woman, sitting on the floor with her back against a
wall. He went to her, made sure she wasn't about to give birth,
then gave her his phone, which still worked. The black air outside began to acquire a color. "For some reason everything had
this beige-like tone," he recalled. He could now see more or less
where they were, and which direction was which. A cop inside
the building said, "You need to stay in here." Zoran grabbed his
friend and left. They walked east and north until they arrived at
some faceless apartment buildings on the Lower East Side. "It's
the projects," said Zoran, "and people are coming out with cups
of water and all of their cordless phones. To help. That's when I
started to cry."

Eventually they reached the FDR Drive and continued due
north. That might have been the oddest feeling of the entire
morning: that walk along a stretch of the FDR. They were
alone. It was quiet. For an amazingly long time, the only human
being they encountered was a half-dressed cop who roared past
them on a motorbike toward the catastrophe. Then the papers
began to flutter down from above. On them Zoran could read
the address of the World Trade Center.

To say that Zoran found the whole experience exhilarating—well, that wouldn't be quite right, though, as he told his story, he said that "somehow I feel guilty about telling it." It was more that there hadn't been even a moment when he had felt he didn't know what he should do next. He'd been jarred into a new kind of awareness, and interest in the people around him, and he liked the feeling. His reactions had surprised him into an observation about himself. "I was impressed that I did not fall apart," he said. "I didn't use it as an excuse for anything. What it tells me is that I wasn't afraid of those situations. I like being front and center. I like being in a drama." He could even pinpoint the moment he realized he was better suited to a crisis than he expected himself to be. "It was when I realized I've started to give a shit about other people," he said.

Two days later he returned to work, but he'd been biffed from an ill-defined career path onto another, clearer one. He wanted to be in a job that required him to perform in a crisis. If you worked on the technology end of Wall Street and were looking for pressure, you ran an electronic stock market. By early 2006, that's what Zoran was doing—at Nasdaq. "They just sat me in front of four machines with buttons that could, like, destroy everything," he said. "It was the best thing in the world. Every day was the Super Bowl. The value of what you were doing felt so high." The feeling of the job was hard to get across to anyone who wasn't a technologist, but there was definitely a feeling to it. "Put it this way," said Zoran. "If I fuck up, I'm going to be in the news. I'm the only one who can break it, and if it breaks I'm the only one who can fix it."

He'd learned this the hard way, of course. Not long after he started at Nasdaq, he'd broken one of the markets. (Nasdaq has owned several markets—Nasdaq OMX, Nasdaq BX, INET,

PSX.) It happened when he was making changes to the system during trading hours. He entered a command, then heard the people around him panicking; but he failed to immediately connect one event to the other. A former Nasdaq colleague recalled the ensuing bedlam. "I remember seeing people running around and screaming while it was happening," he said. Zoran looked up at the stock market on his computer screen: It was frozen. It took him a few seconds to realize that, even though the thing he'd been working on should have had no connection to the market in real time, he had somehow shut his entire market down. It took him another few seconds to see exactly how he had done it. Then he fixed it, and the market resumed trading. From start to finish the crisis had lasted twenty-two seconds. Twenty-two seconds, during which all trading had simply ceased. "I remember sitting there and thinking: *I'm done*," said Zoran. "The CTO [chief technology officer] saved me. He said, 'How can you get rid of a guy who makes a mistake, stops it, and fixes it?'"

Still, the event shaped him. "I said, 'How do I never do that again?'" said Zoran. "I started really jumping into how to control large-scale complex systems. I became a student of complexity— defined as something you cannot predict. How do you have stability in a system that is by its nature unpredictable?" He read everything he could find on the subject. One of his favorite books was actually called *Complexity,* by M. Mitchell Waldrop. His favorite paper to pass out was "How Complex Systems Fail," an eighteen-bullet-point summary by Richard I. Cook, now a professor of health care systems safety in Sweden. *(Bullet Point #6: Catastrophe is always just around the corner.)* "People think that complex is an advanced state of complicated," said Zoran. "It's not. A car key is simple. A car is complicated. A car in traffic is complex."

A stock market was a complex system. One definition of a complex system was a place where, as Zoran put it, "Shit will break and there is nothing you can do about it." The person whose job it was to make sure shit didn't break ran two kinds of career risks: the risk of shit breaking that was within his control, and the risk of shit breaking over which he had no control. Zoran continued to run one of the Nasdaq markets. Eventually, the company handed him bigger markets to run; and the risk of running them grew. By the end of 2011, he was overseeing all of Nasdaq's market running. (Head of Global Operations, he was called.) He had spent the better part of six years adding complexity to those markets, for reasons he did not always understand. The business people would just decide to make some change, which it was his job to implement. "The Post-Only order type was the first thing that got me," said Zoran, of the order designed to be executed only if the trader received a kickback from the exchange. "What the fuck is the point of a Post-Only order?" He was somehow expected to cope with the demands made on Nasdaq's markets by Nasdaq's biggest customers (high-frequency traders) and, at the same time, keep those markets safe and stable. It was as if a pit crew had been asked to strip down the race car, rip out the seat harnesses, and do whatever else they might to make the car go faster than it ever had before—and at the same time reduce the likelihood that the driver would die. Only in this case, if the driver was killed, blame for his death would be assigned, arbitrarily, to one member of the pit crew. Him.

This state of affairs led to a certain skittishness in the pit crew. It wasn't just that the high-frequency traders were demanding changes to the market that would benefit only them: The mere act of changing the system increased the risks to everyone who

depended on it. Adding code and features to a trading system
was like adding traffic to a highway: You couldn't predict the
consequences of what you had done; all you knew was that you
had made the situation more difficult to understand. "No one is
trying to control what they don't know," said Zoran. "And what
they don't know is growing." He thought of himself as good in
a crisis, but he didn't see the point of manufacturing crises so
that he might demonstrate his virtuosity. He was also far less
suited to managing a bunch of market runners than he was to
running a market himself. He had no gift for corporate politics.
Every day, he liked his job less and less—until, in March 2012, he
was fired, whereupon he got a phone call from Don Bollerman.
Don wanted Zoran to run the market for IEX. "I'm not going
to pitch you just now, mainly because we have no money and we
don't even know what we're going to do," said Don. "But I may
pitch you later." Don knew that Zoran had been a casualty of an
office political battle, and, more to the point, that he was maybe
the best exchange runner he'd ever seen. "He has all the qualities," said Don. "Poise under pressure. The ability to understand
a complex and vast system. And be able to think into it—imagine
into it—accurately. To diagnose and foresee problems."

It was a little unsettling that the geeks who now ran the
financial markets were also expected to have the nerves of a test
pilot. But by the time Don approached Zoran, it had grown
clear that the investing public had lost faith in the U.S. stock
market. Since the flash crash back in May 2010, the S&P index
had risen by 65 percent, and yet trading volume was down 50
percent: For the first time in history, investors' desire to trade
had not risen with market prices. Before the flash crash, 67
percent of U.S. households owned stocks; by the end of 2013,
only 52 percent did: The fantastic post-crisis bull market was

noteworthy for how many Americans elected not to participate in it. It wasn't hard to see why their confidence in financial markets had collapsed. As the U.S. stock market had grown less comprehensible, it had also become more sensationally erratic. It wasn't just market prices that were unpredictable but the market itself—and the uncertainty it created was bound to extend, sooner or later, to the many foreign stock markets, bond markets, options markets, and currency markets that had aped the U.S stock market's structure.

In March 2012 the BATS exchange had to pull its own initial public offering because of "technical errors." The next month, the New York Stock Exchange canceled a bunch of trades by mistake because of a "technical glitch." In May, Nasdaq bungled the initial public offering of shares in Facebook Inc. because, in essence, some investors who submitted orders to buy those shares changed their minds before the price was agreed upon—and certain Nasdaq computers couldn't deal with the faster speeds at which other Nasdaq computers allowed the investors to change their minds. In August 2012, the computers of the big HFT firm Knight Capital went berserk and made stock market trades that cost Knight $440 million and triggered the company's fire sale. In November, the NYSE suffered what was termed a "matching engine outage" and was forced to halt trading in 216 stocks. Three weeks later, a Nasdaq employee clicked the wrong icon on his computer screen and stopped the public offering of shares in a company called WhiteHorse Finance. In early January 2013, BATS announced that, because of some unspecified computer error, it had, since 2008, inadvertently allowed trades to occur, illegally, at prices worse (for the investor) than the National Best Bid and Offer.

That was just a sampling from a single year of what were usually described as "technical glitches" in the new, automated U.S. stock markets: Collectively, they had experienced twice as many outages in the two years after the flash crash as in the previous ten. The technical glitches were accompanied by equally bewildering irregularities in stock prices. In April 2013, the price of Google's shares fell from $796 to $775 in three-quarters of a second, for instance, and then rebounded to $793 in the next second. In May the U.S. utilities sector experienced a mini–flash crash, with stocks falling by 50 percent or more for a few seconds before bouncing back to their previous prices. These mini–flash crashes in individual stocks that now occurred routinely went largely unnoticed and unremarked upon.*

Zoran liked to argue that there were actually fewer, not more, "technical glitches" in 2012 than there had been in 2006—it was only the financial consequences of system breakdowns that had grown. He also took issue with the word "glitch." ("It's the worst word in the world.") When some machine malfunctioned and a stock market came under scrutiny, the head of that market usually had no clue either what had happened or how to fix it: He was at the mercy of his technologists. But he had to say something, and so he said that there had been a "technical glitch." It was as if there was no way to explain how the financial market actually worked—or didn't—without resorting to fuzzy

---

* Eric Hunsader, the founder of Nanex, a stock market data company, is a fantastic exception to the general silence on this subject. After the flash crash, it occurred to him to use his data to investigate what had gone wrong, and the search never really ended. "Almost every rock I overturn, something nefarious crawls out from under it," he said. Hunsader has brilliantly and relentlessly described market dysfunction and pointed out many strange micro-movements in stock prices. When the last history of high-frequency trading is written, Hunsader, like Joe Saluzzi and Sal Arnuk of Themis Trading, deserves a prominent place in it.

metaphors and meaningless words.* If stock market computer–related problems were to be reduced to a single phrase, Zoran preferred it to be "normal accidents."†

When Bollerman called him again, late in the summer of 2012, IEX had an idea, and the first glimmer of hope that they would find money. That the idea was also idealistic made Zoran skeptical; he wasn't sure it was possible ever to make a financial market fair. But he absolutely loved the idea of running a market he helped to design—to limit the number of things in it he could not control. He came in to IEX to meet Brad and Rob and John Schwall and Ronan. Brad and Schwall and Rob liked him, Ronan not so much. "What put me off is that he wouldn't shut the fuck up," said Ronan.

His first few months on the job, Zoran drove everyone nuts. Lacking a market crisis, he proceeded to create a social one. They'd tell him about some new feature they had thought to introduce into the system and ask, "Will this make the system harder to manage?" To which Zoran would reply, "It depends on your definition of 'harder.'" Or they would ask him if some small change in the system would cause the system to become less stable—to which Zoran would reply, "It depends on your definition of 'stable.'" Every question he answered with an uneasy chuckle, followed by some other question. A rare exception came when he was asked, "Why do you always answer a question with another question?" "Clarity," he said.

Zoran also seemed to assume that his new colleagues would

---

* "Glitch" belongs in the same category as "liquidity" or, for that matter, "high-frequency trading." All terms used to obscure rather than to clarify, and to put minds to early rest.

† From a book of that name by Charles Perrow.

fail to understand the difference between what he could control and what he couldn't. In one thirty-day span after he joined IEX, he shot out fifteen emails on this one subject—to hammer home the mystery inherent in any stock market technological failure. He even invited a speaker to come in to reinforce the point. "It was one the few times that the people in the room wound up at each other's throats," said Brad. "The tech people were all agreeing with him, and the business people were saying, 'If something melts down, how could it not be someone's fault?'" Brad's breaking point came after the guest speaker had left and Zoran circulated a blog post called "A Short Story on Human Error." The gist of it was that when complex systems broke, it was never the fault of any one person. The post described some computer catastrophe and then concluded, ". . . you'll notice that it wasn't just one little thing that caused it. It wasn't the developer who just so happened to delete the wrong table. It was a number of causes that came together to strike hard, all of them very likely to be bigger issues inside the organization rather than a problem with the individual." At which point Brad finally walked the ten yards from his desk to Zoran's desk and shouted, "Stop sending these fucking emails!"

And he did, finally. "I know what to do when things are exploding around me," he later said. "But when nothing is exploding, the overthinking comes into play."

Initially Brad was mystified: How could a guy who thrived under pressure also have such a fear of being blamed if things went wrong? "He's so good in a crisis," said Brad later. "In game-time situations. Under pressure. I've seen it. But it's like a quarterback who is great in the game, then spends the other six days explaining how it isn't his fault if he throws an interception. *Dude, your passer rating is 110. Stop it.*" Brad realized something: "It comes from a sense of insecurity that comes from the fact that he will be more recognized when things go wrong than when things go right." Brad further realized that the problem was not peculiar to Zoran but general to Wall Street technologists. The markets were now run by technology, but the technologists were still treated like tools. Nobody bothered to explain the business to them, but they were forced to adapt to its demands and exposed to its failures—which was, perhaps, why there had been so many more conspicuous failures. (The exception was the high-frequency trading firms, where the technologists were kings. But then, the HFT firms didn't have clients.) Nasdaq's famously talented engineers were an extreme Wall Street case. The constant pressure on Nasdaq's tech guys to adapt the stock markets' code to the needs of high-frequency traders had created a miserable, politicized workplace. The Nasdaq business guys foisted all these unreasonable demands on the tech guys and then, when the demands busted the system, blamed the tech guys for the failure. The tech guys all wound up with this abused animal quality to them. "You just have to unabuse them," Brad explained, "and let them know they aren't going to be blamed just because something goes wrong." *We all know that things will go wrong and it isn't necessarily anyone's fault.*

Rob and John Schwall seemed to agree that this was the correct approach to take with the people they hired from Nasdaq: to tell them over and over that they weren't to blame for whatever had just happened, to include them in every business discussion so that they could see why they could be a part of it, and so on. Ronan had no patience for any of it. "C'mon, they came from a corporate American job," he said. "They didn't come from Auschwitz." On the other hand, in time, even Ronan saw that Zoran possessed useful qualities he hadn't at first perceived. "Someone who will be good at running the market—you need to be the most paranoid fuck in the world," said Ronan. "And he's the most paranoid fuck in the world. He thinks ten steps down the road of what could go wrong— because he's thinking of what could happen to him if it goes wrong. He's really good at it."

On the morning of October 25, 2013, Zoran Perkov took the subway from his home to Wall Street, as he always did. As usual, he read some book or white paper, and tried to pretend that the people around him didn't exist. The difference between that morning and the others was that he was running early and had a stock market to open—and it was unlike any market he'd ever run. Spare, clean, single-minded, and built from the ground up by people he not only admired but now trusted. "Every single morning, the system is stateless," he said, of exchange matching engines generally. "It doesn't know what it's supposed to do. Ninety-nine percent of the time, it's the same thing it did the day before." On this day, that could not possibly have been true, as the IEX matching engine had never actually done anything. Zoran sat down at his desk in IEX's office and punched a few buttons and watched code scroll down his screen. He pulled out an old, battered computer mouse—then noticed it was dead. He frowned. "It's my war mouse," he said. "Every single market I have opened in the past ten years has been with this mouse." He knocked it against the desk, realized that its battery had probably died, and wondered, briefly, how to replace it. "My wife mocks me because I can't work the microwave oven but I can run a market," he said. He switched out his war mouse for another, and checked his computer screens. The seconds ticked down; it was approaching nine thirty in the morning, when the U.S. stock market would open and, with it, this new market inside of it that aimed to transform it. He waited and watched for something to go wrong. It didn't.

A minute before nine thirty, Brad walked over to Zoran's desk: By popular agreement, Brad was to open the market that first day. He looked down at the keyboard, perplexed.

"What do I do?" he asked.

"Just hit Enter," said Zoran.

The entire room counted down the final seconds before the opening.

"Five . . . four . . . three . . . two . . . one."

Six and a half hours later, the market closed. Zoran had no idea whether the market as a whole had finished up or down for the day. Ten minutes after that he could be found, alone, pacing outside the 9/11 memorial, smoking a cigarette. "This is like the first day of the battle against complacency," he said.

TWO AND A half months later, sixteen people—the chief executives or the head traders of some of the world's biggest stock market money managers—gathered in a conference room on top of a Manhattan skyscraper. They'd flown in from around the country to hear Brad describe what he'd learned about the U.S. stock market since IEX had opened for trading. From that trading, he'd gotten new information. To afford people interested in the truth even a glimpse of it was now considered faintly seditious.* "This is the perfect seat to figure all this out," said Brad.

---

* In March 2013, the Commodity Futures Trading Commission, a derivatives regulator, ended its nascent program to give outside researchers access to market data after one of those researchers, Adam Clark-Joseph, of Harvard University, used the data to study the tactics of high-frequency traders. The commission shut down the research after lawyers for the Chicago Mercantile Exchange wrote the regulators a letter arguing that the data

"It's not like you can stand outside and watch. We had to be in the game to see it."

The sixteen investors controlled roughly $2.6 trillion in stock market investments among them, or roughly 20 percent of the entire U.S. market. Collectively, they paid to the big Wall Street banks roughly $2.2 billion of the $11 billion a year the Street earned from stock market commissions.* They weren't exactly of one mind or spirit. A few of them were also investors in IEX, but most were not. A couple held the knowing, seemingly grown-up view that it was naïve to think that idealism could have any effect on Wall Street. A few thought it was important to remember that technology had lowered their trading costs from what they had been decades earlier—and half-turned a half-blind eye to the stunts Wall Street intermediaries had pulled to prevent technology from lowering those costs even further. But whatever their predispositions, they were all at least a little bit angry, because they all had spent the past few years listening to Brad's descriptions of the inner workings of the U.S. stock market. They now thought of him less as a guy trying to sell them something than as a partner, in a possibly quixotic attempt to fix a financial system that had become deeply screwed up. "You kind of know what's going on, but you don't have a good explanation for it," said one. "He gave us the explanation." A second said, "This isn't about execution. It's about a movement.

Clark-Joseph had collected belonged to the high-frequency traders, and that sharing it was illegal. Before he was booted out of the place, Clark-Joseph showed how HFT firms were able to predict price moves by using small loss-making stock market orders to glean information from other investors. They then used that information to place much bigger orders, the gains from which more than compensated for the losses.

* Estimates of commission paid to Wall Street banks for stock market trades in 2013 range from $9.3 billion (Greenwich Associates) to $13 billion (the Tabb Group).

I'm sick and tired of getting fucked. When I go into the market I want to know it's clean." A third added, "All of a sudden the market is all about algos and routers. It's hard to figure this stuff out. There's no book you can read. It's just calling up people and talking to them. From the people at the banks you can't get a straight answer to any question. You say, 'The sky is blue.' They say, 'The sky is green.' And you're like, 'What are you talking about?' And after half an hour it comes out that they have changed the definition of 'sky.' You know what you're asking. They know what you're asking. But they don't want to answer it. The first time I talked to Brad and he was telling me how it all actually worked, my jaw must have hit the floor."

Another investor had a question about Brad. "Why does a person take the harder path? It's a different situation from what you typically see. If it works, he will make money. But he'll make less" than if he had stayed at RBC.

The sixteen were all men. Most wore suits, with deep creases on the backs of their jackets that looked as if they'd been made with a bullwhip. They were different from the people who worked at the big Wall Street banks, and from the HFT guys. They were a lot less likely to bounce from firm to firm—a lot more likely to have a career in one place. They were more isolated, too: They didn't know each other well and didn't, until Brad suggested it, have any reason to organize themselves into any kind of fighting force. Many had just landed in New York City, and a few of them were obviously weary. Their tone was informal and familiar, with none of the usual jockeying for status. They might not all have been capable of outrage, but they were all still capable of curiosity.

At some level, they all now realized that this thirty-five-year-old Canadian guy somehow had put himself in a position to

understand the United States stock market in a way that the
system, possibly, had never been understood. "The game is
now clear to me," Brad said. "There's not a press release I don't
understand." On August 22, Nasdaq had experienced a two-
hour outage caused by what they said was a technical glitch
in the SIP. Brad thought he understood why it had happened:
Nasdaq threw vast resources into the cool new technology used
by HFT to speed up its trading and little into the basic plumbing
of the market used by the ordinary investor. "Nasdaq's got this
state-of-the-art facility for HFT," he said. "Seventeen-kilowatt
liquid-cooled cabinets and cross-connects everywhere and all
this shit, and then they have this single choke point in the entire
market—the SIP—and they don't care about it. The B team is
servicing it." Four days later, two of the public exchanges, BATS
and Direct Edge, revealed their intention to merge. In a normal
industry, the point of a merger of two companies that performed
identical functions would be to consolidate—to reduce costs.
But, as a subsequent press release explained, both exchanges
intended to remain open after the merger. To Brad the reason
was obvious: The exchanges were both at least partially owned
by high-frequency trading firms, and, from the HFT point of
view, the more exchanges the better.

A few weeks later, both Nasdaq and the New York Stock
Exchange announced that they had widened the pipe that carried
information between the HFT computers and each exchange's
matching engine. The price for the new pipe was $40,000 a
month, up from the $25,000 a month the HFT firms had been
paying for the old, smaller pipe. The increase in speed was *two
microseconds*. Brad understood that the reason for this was not that
the market was better off if HFT had information two microseconds faster than before, but that the high-frequency traders were

all terrified of being slower than their peers, and the exchanges had figured out how to milk this anxiety. In a stock market now defined by its technology accidents, nothing actually happened by accident: There was a reason for even the oddest events. For instance, one day, investors woke up to discover that they'd bought shares in some company for $30.0001. Why? How was it possible to pay ten-thousandths of a penny for anything? Easy: High-frequency traders had asked for an order type that enabled them to tack digits on the right side of the decimal, so that they might jump the queue in front of people trying to pay $30.00. The reason for change was seldom explained; change just happened. "The fact that it is such an opaque industry should be alarming," Brad said. "The fact that the people who make the most money want the least clarity possible—that should be alarming, too."

Everything he had done with his new exchange was aimed at making it more transparent, and forcing Wall Street to follow. The sixteen investors understood IEX's basic commercial strategy: to open as a private stock market and convert to a public exchange once their trading volume justified incurring the millions of dollars in regulatory fees they would have to pay. Although technically a dark pool, IEX had done something no Wall Street dark pool had ever done: It had published its rules. Investors could see, for the first time, what order types were allowed on the exchange, and if any traders had been given special access. IEX, as a dark pool, would thus try to set a new standard of transparency—and perhaps shame others into following its example. Or perhaps not. "I would have thought one dark pool would have come forward after us and published their own rules," Brad now told the investors. "*Someone* must have nothing to hide. My prediction was six or seven out of the forty-four would have done it. None. Zero. There are now forty-five markets. On forty-four of them no one has any idea how they trade. Has it not dawned on anyone that it might actually be a good idea to tell people how the market works? People can look back on the financial crisis and say, 'How can you give a mortgage loan with no documentation? It's preposterous.' But banks did it. And now trillions of dollars of trades are being executed on markets where no one has any idea of how it works, because there is no documentation. Does that sound familiar?"

Now he explained just how badly the market wanted to remain in the shadows—and just how badly the people at the heart of it wanted IEX to fail. Even before IEX opened, brokers from the big Wall Street banks went to work trying to undermine them. One investor called to inform Brad that a representative of Bank of America had just told him that IEX was owned by high-frequency trading firms. On the morning IEX opened, a manager at an investment firm called ING sent out a mass email that looked as if it had been written on her behalf by someone inside one of the big Wall Street banks: "With the pending launch of IEX, we request that all ING Equity Trading executions be excluded from executing on the IEX venue. . . . I am still challenged by the conflict of interest inherent in their business model. As a result I request to opt out of trading with the IEX venue."

The employees of IEX had risked their careers to attack the conflicts of interest in the stock market. They had refused the easy capital from the big Wall Street banks—to avoid conflicts of interest. To avoid conflicts of interest, the investors who had backed IEX had structured their investments so that they themselves did not personally profit from sending trades onto the exchange: Profits from their investment flowed through to the people whose money they managed. These investors had further insisted on having a stake of less than 5 percent in the exchange, to avoid having even the appearance of control over it. Before IEX launched, Brad had rebuffed an overture from IntercontinentalExchange (known as ICE), the new owners of the New York Stock Exchange, to buy IEX for hundreds of millions of dollars—and walked away from the chance to get rich quick. To align their interests with the broader market's, IEX planned to lower their fees as their volumes rose—for everyone who used the exchange. And on the day IEX opened for trading, this manager at ING—who had earlier refused to meet with them so that they might explain the exchange to her—was spreading a rumor that IEX had a conflict of interest.*

But then all sorts of bizarre behavior had attended IEX's arrival in the U.S. stock market. Ronan had gone to a private trade conference—no media, lots of Wall Street big shots. It was the first time he had been invited to the exclusive event, and he intended to lie low. He was outside in the hallway on his way to the bathroom when someone said, "You know, they're in there talking about IEX." Ronan returned to the conference room and listened to the heads of several big public U.S. stock exchanges on a panel. All agreed that IEX would only contribute to the biggest problem in the U.S. stock market: its fragmentation. The market already had thirteen public exchanges and forty-four private ones: Who needed another? When it came time for audience participation, Ronan found a microphone. "Hi, I'm

---

* ING, oddly enough, managed IEX's then thirty-person 401(k) plan. Seeing this, John Schwall returned to his side career in private investigation. After some digging, he developed the opinion that any money manager who arbitrarily denied his clients access to markets might have violated his fiduciary responsibility. On those grounds, Schwall pulled the company's 401(k) from ING.

Ronan, and I think I went to go take a piss at the wrong time," he said, and then gave a little speech. "We're not like you guys," he concluded. "Or anyone else in the market. We're an army of one." He thought he was being calm and measured, but the crowd, by its standards, went wild—which is to say they actually clapped. "Jesus, I thought you were about to throw a punch," some guy said afterward.

The stock exchanges didn't like IEX for obvious reasons, the big Wall Street banks for less obvious ones. But the more the big banks sensed that Brad was being regarded by big investors as an arbiter of Wall Street behavior, the more carefully they confronted him. Instead of voicing their own objections to him directly, they would voice objections they claimed to have heard from other big banks. The guy from Deutsche Bank would say that the guy from Citigroup was upset that IEX was telling investors how to tell the banks to route to IEX—that sort of thing. "When I visited, they were all cordial," said Brad. "It made me feel that the plan was to starve us out." But without seeming to do so. The day before they'd opened for trading, a guy from Bank of America called Brad and said, *Hey, buddy, what's going on? I'd appreciate it if you'd say we're being supportive.* Bank of America had been the first to receive the documents they needed to connect to the exchange and, on opening day, were still dragging their feet in establishing a connection. Brad declined to help Bank of America out of its jam. "Shame is a huge tactic we have to deploy," he said.

Nine weeks after IEX launched, it was already pretty clear that the banks were not following their customers' instructions to send their orders to the new exchange. A few of the investors in the room knew this; the rest now learned. "When we told them we wanted to route to IEX," one said, "they said, 'Why would you want that? We can't do that!' The phrase 'squealing pigs' comes to mind." After the first six weeks of IEX's life, UBS, the big Swiss bank, inadvertently disclosed to one big investor that it hadn't routed a single order onto IEX—despite explicit instructions from the investor to do so. Another big mutual fund manager estimated that, when he told the big banks to route to IEX, they had followed his instructions "at most ten percent of the time." A fourth investor was told, by three different banks, that they didn't want to connect to IEX because they didn't want to pay the $300-a-month connection fee.

Of all the banks that dragged their feet after their customers asked them to send their stock market orders to IEX, Goldman Sachs had offered the best excuse: They were afraid to tell their computer system to do anything it hadn't done before. In August 2013, the Goldman automated trading system generated a bunch of crazy and embarrassing trades that lost Goldman hundreds of millions of dollars (until the public exchanges agreed, amazingly, to cancel them). Goldman wanted to avoid giving new instructions to its trading machines until it figured out why they had ceased to follow the old ones. There was something about the way Goldman had treated Brad when he visited their offices—listening to what he had to say, bouncing him up the chain of command rather than out the door—that led him to believe their excuse. He sensed that they were taking him seriously. After his first meeting with their stock market people, for instance, Goldman's analysts had told the firm's clients that they should be more wary of investing in Nasdaq Inc.

The other banks—Morgan Stanley and J.P. Morgan were the exceptions—were mostly passive-aggressive, but there were occasions when they became simply aggressive. Employees of Credit Suisse spread rumors that IEX wasn't actually independent but owned by the Royal Bank of Canada—and so just a tool of a big bank. One night, in a Manhattan bar, an IEX employee bumped into a senior manager at Credit Suisse. "After you guys fail, come to me and I'll give you a job," he said. "Wait, no, everyone hates your fucking guts, so I won't." In the middle of their first day of trading, one of IEX's employees got a call from a senior executive of Bank of America, who said that one of his colleagues had "ties to the Irish Mafia," and "you don't want to piss those guys off." The IEX employee went to Brad, who just said, "He's full of shit." The IEX employee was less sure, and followed the call with a text.

> IEX employee: Should I be concerned?
> Bank of America employee: Yes.
> IEX employee: Are you serious?
> Bank of America employee: Jk [Just kidding].
> IEX employee: Haven't noticed any Irish guys following me.
> Bank of America employee: Be careful next time you get in your car.
> IEX employee: Good thing I don't own a car.
> Bank of America employee: Well, maybe your gf's car.

Brad also heard what the big Wall Street banks were already saying to investors to dissuade them from sending orders to IEX: *It's too slow.* For years, the banks had been selling the speed and aggression of their trading algos, along with the idea that, for an investor, slower always meant worse. They seemed to have persuaded themselves that the new speed of the markets actually helped their clients. They'd even dreamed up a technical-sounding name for an absence of speed: "duration risk." ("If you make it sound official, people will believe that it's something you really need to care about," Brad explained.) The 350-microsecond delay IEX had introduced to foil the stock market predator was roughly one-thousandth of the blink of an eye. But investors for years had been led to believe that one-thousandth of the blink of an eye might matter to them, and that it was extremely important for their orders to move as fast and aggressively as possible. *Guerrilla! Raider!* This emphasis on speed was absurd: No matter how fast the investor moved, he would never outrun the high-frequency traders. Speeding up his stock market order merely reduced the time it took for him to arrive in HFT's various traps. "But how do you prove that a millisecond is irrelevant?" Brad asked.

He threw the problem to the Puzzle Masters. The team had expanded to include Larry Yu, whom Brad thought of as the guy with the box of Rubik's cubes under his desk. (The standard 3x3-inch cube he could solve in under thirty seconds, and so he kept it oiled with WD-40 to make it spin faster. His cube box held more challenging ones: a 4x4-incher, a 5x5-incher, a giant irregularly shaped one, and so on.) Yu generated two charts, which Brad projected onto the screen for the investors.

To *see* anything in the stock market, you have to stop trying to see it with your eyes and instead attempt to imagine it as it might appear to a computer, if a computer had eyes. The first chart showed the investors how trading on all public U.S. stock exchanges in the most actively traded stock of a single company (Bank of America Corp) appeared to the human eye over a period of ten minutes, in one-second increments. The activity appears constant, even frantic. In virtually every second, something occurs: a trade or, more commonly, a new buy or sell order. The second chart illustrated the same activity on all public U.S. stock exchanges as it appeared to a computer, over the

course of a single *second*, in millisecond increments. All the market activity within a single second was so concentrated—within
a mere 1.78 milliseconds—that on the graph it resembled an
obelisk rising from a desert. In 98.22 percent of all milliseconds,
nothing at all happened in the U.S. stock market. To a computer,
the market in even the world's most actively traded stock was an
uneventful, almost sleepy place. "Yes, your eyeballs think the
markets are going fast," Brad said. "They aren't really going that
fast." The likelihood an investor would miss out on something
important in a third of a millisecond was close to zero, even in
the world's most actively traded stock. "I knew it was bullshit to
worry about milliseconds," said Brad, "because if milliseconds
were relevant, every investor would be in New Jersey."

"What's the spike represent?" asked one of the investors,
pointing to the obelisk.

"That's one of your orders touching down," said Brad.

A few investors shifted in their seats. It was growing clear to
them, if it wasn't already so, that, if the stock market was the
party, they were the punch bowl. They were unlikely to miss
any action as the result of a delay of one-third of a millisecond.
They were the reason for all the action! "Every time a trade
happens at the exchange, it creates a signal," said Brad. "In the
fifty milliseconds running up to it—total silence. Then there is
an event. Then there is this massive reaction. Then a reaction to
that reaction. The HFT algos on the other side are predicting
what you'll do next based on what you just did." The activity
peaked roughly 350 microseconds after an investor's order triggered the feeding frenzy, or the time it took for HFT to send
its orders from the stock exchange on which the investor had
touched down to all of the others. "Your eye will never pick up
what is really happening," said Brad. "You don't see shit. Even

if you're a fucking cyborg you don't see it. But if there was no value to reacting, why would anyone react at all?" The arrival of the prey awakened the predator, who deployed his strategies—rebate arbitrage, latency arbitrage, slow market arbitrage. Brad didn't need to dwell on these; he'd already walked each of the investors through his earlier discoveries. It was his new findings that he wanted them to focus on.*

On IEX's opening day—when it had traded just half a million shares—the flow of orders through its computers had been too rapid for the human eye to make sense of it. Brad had spent the first week or so glued to his terminal, trying to see whatever he could see. Even that first week, he was trying to make sense of lines scrolling down his computer screen at a rate of fifty per second. It felt like speed-reading *War and Peace* in under a minute. All he could see was that a shocking number of the orders being sent by the Wall Street banks to IEX came in small 100-share lots. The HFT guys used 100-share lots as bait on the exchanges, to tease information out of the market while taking as little risk as possible. But these weren't HFT orders; these were from the big banks. At the end of one day, he asked for a count of one bank's orders: 87 percent of them were in these tiny 100-share lots. Why?

The week after Brad had quit his job at the Royal Bank of Canada, his doctor noted that his blood pressure had collapsed to virtually normal levels, and he'd cut his medication in half. Now, in response to this new situation he couldn't make sense

---

* Sixty percent of the time that this feeding frenzy occurs on a public stock exchange, no trade is recorded. The frenzy comes in response to a trade that has occurred in some dark pool. The dark pools are not required to report their trades in real time; and so, on the official tape, the frenzy appears unprovoked. It isn't.

of, Brad had migraines, and his blood pressure was again spik-
ing. "I'm straining to see patterns," he said. "The patterns are
being shown to me, but my eyes can't pick them up."

One afternoon, an IEX employee named Josh Blackburn
overheard Brad mention his problem. Josh was quiet—not just
reserved, but intensely so—and didn't say anything at first. But
he thought he knew how to solve the problem. With pictures.

Josh, like Zoran, traced his career back to September 11,
2001. He'd just started college when a friend messaged him to
turn on the TV, and he'd watched the Twin Towers collapse.
"When that happened it was kind of a *what can I do* moment?" A
couple of months later, he'd gone to the local air force recruit-
ing center and attempted to enlist. They'd told him to wait
until the end of his freshman year. At the end of the school year
he'd returned. The air force sent him to Qatar, where a colonel
figured out that he had a special talent for writing computer
code; one thing led to another, and two years later he was in
Baghdad. There he created a system for getting messages to
all remote units, and another system for creating a Google-
like map, before the existence of Google maps. From Baghdad
he'd gone to Afghanistan, where he wound up being in charge
of taking the data from all the branches of the U.S. military
across all battlefields and turning it into a single picture the
generals could use to make decisions. "It told them everything
that was going on, real-time, on a twenty-foot wall map," Josh
said. "You could see trends. You could see origins of rocket
attacks. You could see patterns in when they occurred—the
attacks on [U.S. Army base] Camp Victory would come after
afternoon prayer. You could see what the projections were [of
where and when the attacks might occur] and how they compared to where attacks actually happened." The trick was not

simply to write the code that turned information into pictures but to find the best pictures to draw—shapes and colors that led the mind to meaning. "Once you got all that stuff together and showed it in the best way possible, you could find patterns," Josh said.

The job was hard to do, but, as it turned out, harder to stop doing. When his first tour of duty was up, Josh reenlisted, and when that tour ended, he re-upped again. When his third tour was over, he saw the war winding down and his usefulness diminish. "You find it very difficult to come home from," said Josh. "Because you see the impact of your work. After that, I couldn't find any passion in anything I did, any meaning." Coming home, he looked for a place to deploy his skill—and a friend in finance told him about an opening in a new high-frequency trading firm. "In the war, you're trying to use the picture you create to take advantage of the enemy," said Josh. "In this case, you're trying to take advantage of the market." He worked for the HFT firm for six weeks before it failed, but he found the job unsatisfying.

He'd come to IEX in the usual way: John Schwall had found him while trolling on LinkedIn and asked him to come for an interview. At that point, Josh was being inundated with offers from other high-frequency trading firms. "There was a lot of 'we are elite,'" he said. "They kept hitting the elite thing." He didn't care all that much about being elite; he just wanted his work to mean something. "I came in for an interview on Friday. Saturday they made me an offer. Brad said, we're going to change the way things work. But I didn't really know what Brad was talking about." Since joining, he'd been quiet and had put himself where he liked to be, in the background. "I just try to take in what people are saying, and listen to what everyone is complaining about," he said. "*I wish this* or *I wish that*, and then bring it together and find the solution."

Brad knew little of Josh's past—only that whatever Josh had done for the U.S. military sounded like the sort of thing he couldn't talk about. "All I knew was that he was in a trailer in Afghanistan, working with generals," said Brad. "When I tell him my problem—that I couldn't *see* the data—he just says, 'Hit Refresh.'"

Quietly, Josh had gone off and created for Brad pictures of the activity on IEX. Brad hit Refresh; the screen was now organized in different shapes and colors. The strange 100-lot trades were suddenly bunched together and highlighted in useful ways: He could see patterns. And in the patterns he could see predatory activity neither he nor the investors had yet imagined.

These new pictures showed him how the big Wall Street banks typically handled investors' stock market orders. Here's how it worked: Say you are a big investor—a mutual fund or a pension fund—and you have decided to make a big investment in Procter & Gamble. You are acting on behalf of a lot of ordinary Americans who have given you their savings to manage. You call some broker—Bank of America, say—and tell them you'd like to buy 100,000 shares of Procter & Gamble. P&G's shares are trading at, say, 82.95–82.97, with 1,000 shares listed on each side. You tell the big Wall Street bank you are willing to pay up to, say, $82.97 a share. From that point on, you basically have no clue how your order—and the information it contains—is treated. Now Brad saw: The first thing the broker did was to ping IEX with an order to buy 100 shares, to see if IEX had a seller. This made total sense: You didn't want to reveal you had a big buyer until you found a seller. What made a lot less sense was what many of the brokers did after they discovered the seller. They avoided him.

Say, for example, that IEX actually had a seller waiting on it—a seller of 100,000 shares at $82.96. Instead of coming in and trying to buy a much bigger chunk of P&G, the big bank just kept pinging IEX with tiny 100-share orders—or the bank vanished entirely. If the bank had simply sent IEX an order to buy 100,000 shares of P&G at $82.97, the investor would have purchased all the shares he wanted without driving up the price. Instead, the bank had pinged away and—by revealing its insistent, noisy demand—goosed up the price of P&G's stock, at the expense of the investor whose interests the bank was meant to represent. Adding to the injury, the bank typically wound up with only a fraction of the stock its customer wanted to buy. "It opened up this whole new realm of activity that was crazy to me," Brad told his audience. It was as if the big Wall Street banks were looking to see if IEX had a big seller to avoid trading with him. "I thought, Why the hell would anyone do this? All you do is increase the chances that an HFT will pick up your signal."

They didn't all behave this way: A couple of the big banks followed up their 100-share orders by forking over the meat of the buy order, and executed the trade their customer had asked them to execute. (The Royal Bank of Canada was by far the best behaved.) But, in general, the big Wall Street banks who had connected to IEX—a group that in the first week of trading excluded Bank of America and Goldman Sachs—connected disingenuously. It was as if they wished to appear to be interacting with the entire stock market, while actually they were trying to prevent any trades from happening outside their own dark pools.

Brad now explained to the investors, who were of course paying the price for this behavior, the reasons that the banks behaved as they did. The most obvious was to maximize the chance of executing the stock market orders given to them by investors in their own dark pools. The less honestly a bank looked for P&G stock outside of its own dark pool, the less likely it was to find it. This evasiveness explained the banks' incredible ability to find, eventually, the other side of any trade inside their own dark pools. A bank that controlled less than 10 percent of all U.S. stock market orders was somehow able to satisfy more than half of its customers' orders without ever leaving its own dark pool. Collectively, the banks had managed to move 38 percent of the entire U.S. stock market now traded inside their dark pools—and this is how they had done it. "It's a façade that the market is interconnected," said Brad.

The big Wall Street banks wanted to trade in their own dark pools not only because they made more money—on top of their commissions—by selling the right to HFT to exploit orders inside their dark pools. They wanted to trade their orders inside their dark pools to boost the volumes in those pools, for appearances' sake. The statistics used to measure the performance of the dark pools, as well as the performance of the public stock exchanges, were more than a little screwy. A stock market was judged by the volume of trading that occurred on it, and the nature of that volume. It was widely believed, for example, that the bigger the average trade size on an exchange, the better the market was for an investor. (By requiring fewer trades to complete his purchase or sale, the exchange reduced the likelihood of revealing an investor's intentions to high-frequency traders.) Every dark pool and every stock exchange found ways to cook its own flattering statistics; the art of torturing data may never have been so finely practiced. For example, to show that they were capable of hosting big trades, the exchanges published the number of "block" trades of more than 10,000 shares they facilitated. The New York Stock Exchange sent IEX a record of

26 small trades it had made after IEX had routed an order to it—and then published the result on the ticker tape as a *single* 15,000-share block. The dark pools were even worse, as no one but the banks that ran them had a clear view of what happened inside them. The banks all published their own self-generated stats on their own dark pools: Every bank ranked itself #1. "It's an entire industry that overglorifies data, because data is so easy to game, and the true data is so hard to obtain," said Brad.

The banks did not merely manipulate the relevant statistics in their own dark pools; they often sought to undermine the stats of their competitors. That was another reason the banks were sending IEX orders in tiny 100-share lots: to lower the average trade size in a market that competed with the banks' dark pools. A lower average trade size made IEX's stats look bad—as if IEX were heavily populated by high-frequency traders. "When the customer goes to his broker and says, 'What the hell happened? Why am I getting all these hundred-share fills?,' his broker could easily say, 'Well, I put the order on IEX,'" said Brad. The strategy cost their customers money, and the opportunity to buy and sell shares, but the customers wouldn't know about it: All they would see was IEX's average trade size falling.

Soon after it opened for trading, IEX published its own statistics—to describe, in a general way, what was happening in its market. "Since everyone is behaving in a particular way, you can't see if anyone is behaving particularly badly," said Brad. Now you could see. Despite the best efforts of Wall Street banks, the average size of IEX's trades was by far the biggest of any stock exchange, public or private. More importantly, the trading that occurred was more random, unlinked to activity elsewhere in the stock market: For instance, the percentage of trades on IEX that followed the change in the price of some stock was half that of the other exchanges. (Investors were being picked off—as West Chester, Pennsylvania, money manager Rich Gates had been picked off—on exchanges that failed to move their standing orders quickly enough to keep up when stock prices changed.) Trades on IEX were also four times more likely than those elsewhere to trade at the midpoint between the current market bid and offer—which is to say, the price that most would agree was fair. Despite the reluctance of the big Wall Street banks to send them orders, the new exchange was already making the dark pools and public exchanges look bad, even by their own screwed-up standards.*

Brad's biggest weakness, as a strategist, was his inability to imagine just how badly others might behave. He had expected that the big banks would resist sending orders to IEX. He hadn't imagined they would use their customers' stock market orders to actively try *at their customers' expense* to sabotage an exchange created to help their customers. "You want to create a system where behaving correctly would be rewarded," he concluded. "And the system has been doing the opposite. It's rational for a broker to behave badly."

The bad behavior played right into the hands of high-frequency traders in the most extraordinary ways. One day while watching the pictures Josh Blackburn had created for him, Brad saw a bank machine-gun IEX with 100-share lots and drive up a stock price 5 cents inside of 232 milliseconds. IEX's delay—one-third of a millisecond—was of little use in disguising an

---

* The Financial Industry Regulatory Authority (FINRA) publishes its own odd ranking of the public and private stock markets, based on how well they avoid breaking the law, presumably inadvertently, by trading outside the National Best Bid and Offer. In its first two months of trading, IEX ranked #1 on FINRA's list.

investor's stock market order if a broker insisted on broadcasting a big order he controlled over a far longer period: HFT picked up the signal and was getting out in front of it. Wondering if the broker was spreading news of his buy order elsewhere, Brad turned his attention to the consolidated tape of all the trades that occurred in the U.S. stock market. "I just wondered: Is this broker peppering the whole Street, or is it just us?" he told the room full of investors. "What we found blew our minds."

For each trade on IEX, he'd spotted a nearly identical trade that had occurred at nearly the same time in some other market. "I noticed the odd trade sizes," he said. He'd see a trade on IEX for 131 shares of, say, Procter & Gamble, and then he'd see, in some other market, exactly the same trade—131 shares of Procter & Gamble—within a few milliseconds, but at a slightly different price. It happened over and over again. He also noticed that, in each case, on one side of the trade was a broker who had rented out his pipes to a high-frequency trader.

Up till that point, most of the predation they had uncovered occurred when stock prices moved. A stock went up or down; the high-frequency guys found out before everyone else and took advantage of them. Roughly two-thirds of all stock market trades took place without moving the price of the stock—the trade happened at the seller's offering price, or the buyer's bidding price, or in between; afterwards, the bid and offering price remained the same as they had been before. What Brad now saw was how HFT, with the help of the banks, might exploit investors even when the stock price was stable. Say the market for Procter & Gamble's shares was 80.50–80.52, and the quote was stable—the price wasn't about to change. The National Best Bid was $80.50, and the National Best Offer was $80.52, and the stock was just sitting there. A seller of 10,000 Procter & Gamble shares appeared on IEX. IEX tried to price the orders that rested on it at the midpoint (the fair price), and so the 10,000 shares were being offered at $80.51. Some high-frequency trader would come into IEX—it was always a high-frequency trader—and chip away at the order: 131 shares here, 189 shares there. But elsewhere in the market, the same HFT was selling the shares—131 shares here, 189 shares there—at $80.52. On the surface, HFT was performing a useful function, building a bridge between buyer and seller. But the bridge was itself absurd. Why didn't the broker who controlled the buy order simply come to IEX on behalf of his customer and buy, more cheaply, the shares offered?

Back when Rich Gates conducted his experiments, he had managed to get himself robbed inside Wall Street's dark pools, but only after he had changed the price of the stock (because the dark pools were so slow to move the price of his order resting inside of them). These trades that Brad was now noticing had happened without the market moving at all. He knew exactly why they were happening: The Wall Street banks were failing to send their customers' orders to the rest of the marketplace. An investor had given a Wall Street bank an order, say, to buy 10,000 shares of P&G. The bank had sent it to its dark pool with instructions for the order to stay there, aggressively priced, at $80.52. The bank was boosting its dark pool stats—and also charging some HFT a fee rather than paying a fee to another exchange—but it was also ignoring whatever else was happening in the market. In a functional market, the investors would simply have met in the middle and traded with each other at a price of $80.51. The price of the stock needn't have moved a penny. The unnecessary price movement—caused by the screwed-up stock market—also played into HFT's hands. Because high-frequency traders were always the first to detect any stock price movements, they were able to exploit, with other strategies, ordinary investors' ignorance of the fact that the market price had changed. The original false note struck by the big Wall Street bank—the act of avoiding making trades outside of its own dark pool—became the prelude to a symphony of scalping.* "We're calling this 'dark pool arbitrage,'" said Brad.

IEX had built an exchange to eliminate the possibility of predatory trading—to prevent investors from being treated as prey. In the first two months of its existence, IEX had seen no activity from high-frequency traders except this. It was astonishing, when you stopped to think about it, how aggressively capitalism protected its financial middleman, even when he was totally unnecessary. Almost magically, the banks had generated the need for financial intermediation—to compensate for their own unwillingness to do the job honestly.

Brad opened the floor for questions. For the first few minutes, the investors vied with each other to see who could best control his anger and exhibit the sort of measured behavior investors are famous for.

"Do you think of HFT differently than you did before you opened?" asked one.

That question might have been better answered by Ronan, who had just returned from a tour of the big HFT firms, and now leaned against a wall on the side of the room. Brad had asked Ronan to explain to the investors the technical end of things—

---

* The reader might question the characterization of such small-time skimming as scalping. But a penny here, a penny there adds up in the most extraordinary ways in the U.S. stock market. At IEX, the Puzzle Masters made a quick-and-dirty calculation of the likely profits made annually by HFT from dark pool arbitrage. They added up all its instances over a fifteen-day period, then came up with a number: The haul for HFT from the U.S. stock market alone came to more than a billion dollars a year. And this was just a single trading strategy. "They've been in business for ten weeks and they've now found four of these strategies," said one big investor of IEX. "Who knows how many more they'll find?" A billion here, a billion there: It adds up.

how IEX had created its 350-microsecond delay, the magic shoe-box, and so on—and to relate the details of his tour. He'd done it. But on the subject of HFT he held himself back. To speak his mind, Ronan needed to feel like himself, which, imprisoned in a gray suit and addressing a semiformal audience, he clearly did not. Put another way: It was just extremely difficult for Ronan to say what he felt without using the word "fuck." Watching him string together sentences without profanity was like watch-ing someone try to swim across a river without using his arms or his legs. Curiously, he later admitted, he wasn't worried that the audience would be offended by bad language. "It was because some of them want to be the alpha male cursing in the room," he said. "When I say 'fuck,' they think I'm stealing the show—so when I'm in front of a group I go as straight as I can."

"I hate them a lot less than before we started," said Brad. "This is not their fault. I think most of them have just rational-ized that the market is creating the inefficiencies and they are just capitalizing on them. Really, it's brilliant what they have done within the bounds of the regulation. They are much less of a villain than I thought. The system has let down the investor."

A forgiving sentiment. But at that moment the investors in the conference room did not seem in a forgiving mood. "It's still shocking to me to see how the banks are colluding against us," one of the investors later said. "It shows *everyone* is a bad actor. And then when you add in that you ask them to route to IEX and they refuse, it's even worse. Even though I had heard some of it before, I was still incensed. If that was the first time I was hearing it, I think I'd have gone bonkers."

An investor raised his hand and motioned to some numbers Brad had scribbled on a whiteboard to illustrate how a particular bank had enabled dark pool arbitrage.

"Who is that?" he asked, and not calmly.

An uneasy look crossed Brad's face. He was now hearing that question more and more. Just that morning, an outraged investor listening to a dry run of his presentation had stopped him to ask: "Which bank is the worst?" "I can't tell you," he said, and explained that the agreements the big Wall Street banks signed with IEX forbade IEX from speaking about any bank without its permission.

"Do you know how frustrating it is to sit here and hear this and not know who that broker is?" said another investor.

It wasn't easy being Brad Katsuyama—to try to effect some practical change without a great deal of fuss, when the change in question was, when you got right down to it, a radical overhaul of a social order. Brad was not by nature a radical. He was simply in possession of radical truths.

"What we want to do is highlight the good brokers," said Brad. "We need the brokers who are doing the right thing to get rewarded." That was the only way around the problem. Brad had asked for the banks' permission to highlight the virtue of the ones that behaved relatively well, and they had granted it. "Speaking about someone in a positive light does not violate the terms of not speaking about someone in a negative light," he said.

The audience considered this.

"How many good brokers are there?" asked an investor at length.

"Ten," said Brad. (IEX had dealings with ninety-four.) The ten included the Royal Bank of Canada, Sanford Bernstein, and a bunch of even smaller outfits. "Three are meaningful," he added. Morgan Stanley, J.P. Morgan, and Goldman Sachs.

"Why would any broker behave well?"

"The long-term benefit is that when the shit hits the fan, it will quickly become clear who made good decisions and who made bad decisions," said Brad.

He wondered, often, what it would look like if and when the shit in question hit the fan: The stock market at bottom was rigged. The icon of global capitalism was a fraud. How would enterprising politicians and plaintiffs' lawyers and state attorneys general respond to that news? The thought of it actually didn't give him all that much pleasure. Really, he just wanted to fix the problem. At some level, he still didn't understand why Wall Street banks needed to make his task so difficult.

"Is there a concern from you that the publicity will create even more hostility?" asked another. He wanted to know if telling the world who the good brokers were would make the bad ones worse.

"The bad brokers can't try harder at being bad," said Brad. "Some of these brokers are doing everything they can not to do what the client wants them to do."

An investor wanted to return to the scribbled numbers that illustrated how one particular bank had enabled dark pool arbitrage. "So what do these guys say when you show them that?

"Some of them say, 'You're one hundred percent right,'" said Brad. "'This shit happens.' One even said, 'We used to sit around all the time talking about how to fuck up other people's dark pools.' Some of them say, 'I have no idea what you're talking about. We have heuristic data bullshit and other mumbo jumbo to determine our routing.'"

"That's a technical term—'heuristic data bullshit and other mumbo jumbo'?" an investor asked. A few guys laughed.

Technology had collided with Wall Street in a peculiar way. It had been used, as it should have been used, to increase efficiency. But it had also been used to introduce a peculiar sort of market inefficiency. This new inefficiency was not like the inefficiencies that financial markets can easily correct. After a big buyer enters the market and drives up the price of Brent crude oil, for example, it's healthy and good when speculators jump in and drive up the price of North Texas crude, too. It's healthy and good when traders see the relationship between the price of crude oil and the price of oil company stocks, and drive these stocks higher. It's even healthy and good when some clever high-frequency trader divines a necessary statistical relationship between the share prices of Chevron and Exxon, and responds when it gets out of whack. It was neither healthy nor good when public stock exchanges introduced order types and speed advantages that high-frequency traders could use to exploit everyone else. This sort of inefficiency didn't vanish the moment it was spotted and acted upon. It was like a broken slot machine in the casino that pays off every time. It would keep paying off until someone said something about it; but no one who played the slot machine had any interest in pointing out that it was broken.

Some large amount of what Wall Street had done with technology had been done simply so that someone inside the financial markets would know something that the outside world did not. The same system that once gave us subprime mortgage collateralized debt obligations no investor could possibly truly understand now gave us stock market trades that occurred at fractions of a penny at unsafe speeds using order types that no investor could possibly truly understand. That is why Brad Katsuyama's most distinctive trait—his desire to explain things not so he would be understood but so that others would understand—was so seditious. He attacked the newly automated financial system at its core: the money it made from its incomprehensibility.

Another investor, silent till that point, now raised his hand. "It seems like there's a first mover risk for someone to behave the right way," he said. He was right: Even the banks that were

behaving relatively well weren't behaving all that well. A big
Wall Street bank that gave IEX an honest shot to execute its
customers' orders would suffer a collapse in its dark pool trading, and in its profits. The bad banks would pounce on the good
bank and argue that, because its dark pool was worse than all the
others, it shouldn't be given the orders in the first place. That,
Brad told the investors, had been maybe his biggest concern.
Would any big Wall Street bank have the ability to see a few
years down the road, and summon the nerve to go first? Then
he clicked on a slide. On top it read: *December 19, 2013.*

YOU COULD NEVER say for sure exactly what was going on inside
one of the big Wall Street banks, but it was a mistake to think of
a bank as a coherent entity. They were fractious, and intensely
political. Most everyone might be thinking mainly about his
year-end bonus, but that didn't mean there wasn't one person
who wasn't, and it certainly didn't mean that everyone inside a
big bank shared the same incentives. A dollar in one guy's pocket
was, in some places, a dollar out of another's. For instance, the
guys in the prop group who traded against the firm's customers in the dark pool would naturally feel a different concern for
those customers than the guy whose job it was to sell them stuff
would—if for no other reason than that it is harder to rip off a
person when you actually need to see him, face to face. That's
why the banks kept the prop traders on different floors from the
salespeople, often in entirely different buildings. It wasn't simply
to please the regulators; all involved would prefer that there be
no conversation between the two groups. The customer guy was
better at his job—and had deniability—if he remained oblivious to whatever the prop guy was up to. The frantic stupidity

of Wall Street's stock order routers and algorithms was simply an extension into the computer of the willful ignorance of its salespeople.

Brad's job, as he saw it, was to force the argument between the salespeople and the prop people—and to arm the salespeople with a really great argument, which included the distinct possibility that investors in the stock market were about to wake up to what was being done to them, and go to war against the people who were doing it. In most cases, he had no idea if he had succeeded and, as a result, suspected he had not.

Right from the start, the view from inside Goldman Sachs had been less cluttered than the view from inside the other big Wall Street banks. Goldman was unlike the other banks; for instance, the first thing the people he met at the other banks usually did was tell him of the hostility all the other banks felt toward IEX, and of the nefariousness of the other banks' dark pools. Goldman was aloof, and didn't appear to care what its competitors were saying or thinking about IEX. In their stock market trading and perhaps in other departments as well, Goldman was undergoing some kind of transition. In February 2013, its head of electronic trading, Greg Tusar, had left to work for Getco, the big high-frequency trading firm. The two partners then assigned to figure out Goldman's role in the global stock markets—Ron Morgan and Brian Levine—were not high-frequency trading types. They didn't bear a great deal of responsibility for whatever the high-frequency trading types had done before they took over. Morgan worked in New York and was in charge of sales; Levine, responsible for trading, worked in London. Both were apparently worried about what they had found when they stepped into their new positions. Brad knew this because, oddly, Ron Morgan had called him. "He found us by talking to clients about what they wanted," said Brad. A week after they first met, Morgan invited Brad back to meet with a group of even more senior executives. "That didn't happen anywhere else," Brad said. After he left, he was told that the ensuing discussion had reached "the highest levels of the firm."

In taking over, Morgan and Levine had been tasked with answering a big question posed by the people who ran Goldman Sachs: Why was Morgan Stanley growing so fast? Their rival's market share was booming, while Goldman's was stagnant. Levine and Morgan did what everyone on Wall Street did when they wanted to find out what was going on inside a rival bank: They invited some of its employees in for job interviews. The Morgan Stanley employees explained to them that the firm was now trading 300 million shares a day—30 percent of the volume of the New York Stock Exchange—through what it called "Speedway." Speedway was a service Morgan Stanley provided to high-frequency traders. Morgan Stanley built a high-frequency trading infrastructure—co-location at various exchanges, the fastest routes between them, a straight road into the bank's dark pool and so on—and then turned around and leased their facilities to the smaller HFT firms, which couldn't afford the up-front cost of building their own systems. Morgan Stanley got credit for, and commissions from, everything the HFT guys did inside Morgan Stanley's pipes. The Morgan Stanley employees angling for jobs at Goldman Sachs told the Goldman executives that Speedway was now making Morgan Stanley $500 million a year, and that it was growing. This raised the obvious question for Goldman Sachs: Should we create our own Speedway? Should we further embrace high-frequency trading?

One of Goldman's clients handed Ronnie Morgan a list of

thirty-three big investors to whom he should speak before making this decision. This client didn't know if Morgan had spoken to people beyond this list, but he confirmed for himself that Morgan had spoken to each of the thirty-three people individually. At the same time, Morgan and Levine began to ask some obvious questions about Goldman Sachs's stock market businesses. Could Goldman ever be as fast or as smart as the more nimble high-frequency trading firms? Why, if Goldman only controlled 8 percent of all stock market orders, was it able to trade more than a third of those orders in its own dark pool? Given how little of the flow Goldman saw, what was the likelihood that the best price for an investor's order came from some other Goldman customer? How did Wall Street dark pools interact with each other and with the exchanges? How stable was this increasingly complex financial market? Was it a good thing that the U.S. stock market model had been exported to other countries and other financial markets?

They already knew or could guess most of the answers; for the questions still hanging, the investors pointed them toward an unusually forthright and knowledgeable guy they knew and trusted who was starting a new stock exchange: Brad Katsuyama.

What struck Brad about his visit to Goldman Sachs was not only that Levine and Morgan were willing to spend time with him, but that they took the ideas from their conversations to their superiors. Levine seemed particularly concerned about the stock market's instability. "Unless there are some changes, there's going to be a massive crash," he said, "a flash crash times ten." In conversation and in presentations, he impressed the point upon Goldman's top executives, and also asked, "Do you really need the only differentiator in the market to be speed? Because that's what it seems to be." It wasn't all that hard for the people who ran Goldman Sachs to see the source of the problem, or to see why no one inside the system cared to point it out. "There's no upside in it—that's why no one ever steps out on it," said Levine. "And everyone's got career risk. And no one is thinking that far ahead. They are looking at the next paycheck."

A long string of myopic decisions had created new risks in the U.S. stock market. Its complexity was just one manifestation of the problem, but in it, the Goldman partners both felt sure, lay some future calamity. The sensational technical glitches weren't anomalies but symptoms. And a stock market calamity, Ron Morgan and Brian Levine both thought, would end up being blamed generally on the big Wall Street banks, and specifically on Goldman Sachs. Goldman earned $7 billion a year from its equity business; that business would be put at risk by any crisis.

But it was more than that. At forty-eight and forty-three, respectively, Morgan and Levine were, by Wall Street standards, old guys. Morgan had been made a Goldman partner back in 2004, Levine in 2006. Both confided to friends that IEX presented them with a choice, at what might be a pivotal financial historical moment. An investor who knew Ron Morgan said, "Ronnie's saying to himself, 'You work for twenty-five years in the business, how often do you have a chance to make a difference?'" Brian Levine himself said, "I think it's a business decision. I also think it's a moral decision. I think this is the shot we have. And I think Brad is the right guy. It's the best odds we have to fix the problem."

BEFORE THEY OPENED their market, on October 25, 2013, the thirty-two employees of IEX made private guesses as to how many shares they'd trade their first day and in their first week.

The median of the estimates came in at 159,500 shares the first day and 2.5 million shares the first week. The lowest estimate came from Matt Trudeau, the only one of them who had ever built a new stock market from scratch: 2,500 shares for the first day and 100,000 for the week. Of the ninety-four stock broker-age firms in various stages of agreeing to connect to IEX, most of them small outfits, only about fifteen were ready on the first day. "Brokers are telling their clients they're connected, but we haven't even gotten their paperwork," said Brad. When asked how big the exchange might be at the end of the first year, Brad guessed, or perhaps hoped, that it would trade between 40 and 50 million shares a day.

To cover their running costs, they needed to trade about 50 million shares a day. If they failed to cover their running costs, there was a question of how long they could last. "It's binary," said Don Bollerman. "Either we are a resounding success or we are a complete flop. We're done in six to twelve months. In twelve months I know whether I need to look for a job." Brad thought that their bid to create an example of a fair financial market—and maybe change Wall Street's culture—could take longer and prove messier. He expected their first year to feel more like nineteenth-century trench warfare than a twenty-first-century drone strike. "We're just collecting data," he said. "You cannot make a case without data. And you don't have data unless you have trades." Even Brad agreed: "It's over when we run out of money."

On the first day, they traded 568,524 shares. Most of the vol-ume came from regional brokerage firms and Wall Street brokers that had no dark pools—the Royal Bank of Canada and San-ford Bernstein. Their first week, they traded a bit over 12 million shares. Each week after that, they grew slightly, until, in the third week of December, they were trading roughly 50 million shares each week. On Wednesday, December 18, they traded 11,827,232 shares. By then Goldman Sachs had connected to IEX, but its orders were arriving on the new exchange in the same untrusting spirit as those from the other big Wall Street banks: in tiny lot sizes, resting for just a few milliseconds, then leaving.

The first different-looking stock market order sent by Goldman to IEX landed on December 19, 2013, at 3:09:42 p.m. 662 milliseconds, 361 microseconds, and 406 nanoseconds. Anyone who had been in IEX's one-room office when it arrived would have known that something unusual was happening. The computer screens jitterbugged as the information flowed into the market in an entirely new way. One by one, the employees arose from their chairs; a few minutes into the surge, all but Zoran Perkov were on their feet. Then they began to shout.

"We're at fifteen million!" someone yelled, ten minutes into the surge. In the previous 331 minutes they had traded roughly 5 million shares.

"Twenty million!"

"Fucking Goldman Sachs!"

"Thirty million!"

The enthusiasm was unpracticed, almost unnatural. It was as if an oil well had gushed up through the floor during a meeting of the chess club.

"We just passed AMEX," shouted John Schwall, referring to the American Stock Exchange. "We're ahead of AMEX in market share."

"And we gave them a one-hundred-and-twenty-year head start," said Ronan, playing a little loose with history. Someone had given Ronan a $300 bottle of Champagne. He'd told Schwall that it had cost only forty bucks, because Schwall didn't want anyone inside IEX accepting gifts of more than forty bucks from anyone outside of it. Now Ronan fished the contraband from under his desk and found some paper cups.

Someone else put down a phone and said, "That was J.P. Morgan, asking, 'What just happened?' They say they may have to do something."

Don put down his phone. "That was Goldman. They say they aren't even big. They're coming big tomorrow."

"Forty million!"

At his desk Zoran sat calmly, watching traffic patterns. "Don't tell anyone, but we're still bored," he said. "This is nothing."

Fifty-one minutes after Goldman Sachs had given them their first honest shot at Wall Street customers' stock market orders, the U.S. stock market closed. Brad walked off the floor and into a small office, enclosed by glass. He thought through what had just happened. "We needed one person to buy in and say, 'You're right,'" he said. "It means that Goldman Sachs agrees with us." Then he thought some more. Goldman Sachs wasn't a single entity; it was a bunch of people who didn't always agree with each other. Two of these people had been given a new authority, and they had used it to take a different, longer-term approach than anyone imagined Goldman Sachs was capable of. These two people made all the difference. "I got lucky Brian is Brian and Ronnie is Ronnie," said Brad. "This is because of them. Now the others can't ignore this. They can't marginalize it." Then he blinked. "I could fucking cry now," he said.

He'd just been given a glimpse of the future—he felt certain of it. Goldman Sachs was insisting that the U.S. stock market needed to change, and that IEX was the place to change it. If Goldman Sachs was willing to acknowledge to investors that this new market was the best chance for fairness and stability, the other banks would be pressured to follow. The more orders that flowed onto IEX, the better the experience for investors, and the harder it would be for the banks to evade this new, fair market. At that moment, as Goldman's orders flowed onto IEX, the stock market felt a bit like a river that wanted to jump its banks. All that had been needed was for one man with a shovel to dig a trench in an existing levee, and the pressure from the water would finish the job—which was why men caught digging into the banks on certain stretches of the Mississippi River were once shot on sight. Brad Katsuyama was the man with the shovel, positioned at the river's most vulnerable bend. Goldman had arrived, with explosives, to help him.

Three weeks later, he stood before a group of investors who, if they acted together, might force change upon Wall Street. To show them that change was possible, he flashed on a big screen the data from what had happened, for fifty-one minutes, on December 19. The data showed, among other things, the power of trust. Goldman had actually sent more orders to IEX the day before, on December 18. So much more had traded on December 19 because, on that day, for just fifty-one minutes, Goldman had entrusted them with most of its orders for ten seconds or more. That trust had been rewarded: The market felt fair; 92 percent of those orders traded at the midpoint—the fair price—compared to 17 percent that traded at the midpoint in Wall Street's dark pools. (The number on the public exchanges was even lower.) Their average trade size was twice the market average, despite the efforts of other Wall Street banks to undermine them.

IEX represented a choice. IEX also made a point: that this market which had become intentionally and overly complicated might be understood. That, to function properly, a free financial market didn't need to be rigged in someone's favor. It didn't need in some sick way the kickbacks, and payment for order flow, and co-location, and all sorts of unfair advantages handed to a small handful of traders. All it needed was for the men in the room and other investors like them to take responsibility for understanding it, and then to seize its controls. "The backbone of the market is investors coming together to trade," said Brad.

When he was finished, an investor raised his hand. "They did it on December nineteenth," he asked. "And then what?"

CHAPTER EIGHT

THE SPIDER AND THE FLY

T he trial of Sergey Aleynikov ran for ten days in December of 2010 and was notable for its paucity of informed outsiders. High-frequency trading was a small world, and the people who did it, or knew anything at all about it, apparently had far less interest in testifying at trials than in making their personal fortunes. The one outside expert witness on the subject called by the government was an assistant professor of finance at Illinois Institute of Technology named Benjamin Van Vliet. Van Vliet had become an expert in response to journalists' need for one. While teaching a computer coding course, he'd cast around for something sexy for the students to program, and landed on high-frequency trading platforms. In mid-2010, *Forbes* magazine called him out of the blue to ask him what he thought about a fiber-optic cable that Spread Networks had strung from Chicago to New Jersey. Van Vliet had never heard of Spread Networks, and knew nothing about the cable, but wound up with his name in print—which, of course, led to more calls from journalists, who needed a high-frequency trading expert. Then came the flash crash, and Van Vliet's phone rang off the hook. Eventually, federal prosecutors found him and asked him to serve as their expert witness in the trial of a former Goldman Sachs high-frequency programmer. Van Vliet still had never actually done any high-frequency trading himself, and had little to add on the value or the gist of what Serge Aleynikov had taken from Goldman Sachs. About the market itself he was badly misinformed. (He described Goldman Sachs as "the New York Yankees" of high-frequency trading.) He turned out to have testified as an expert witness in an earlier trial involving the theft of high-frequency trading code, after which the judge in the case said that the idea that a high-frequency trading program was some kind of science was "utter baloney."

The jury in Sergey Aleynikov's trial consisted mainly of high school graduates; all of the jurors lacked experience programming computers. "They would bring my computer into the courtroom," recalled Serge incredulously. "They would pull out the hard drive and show it to the jury. As evidence!" Save for Misha Malyshev, Serge's onetime employer, the people who took the stand had no credible knowledge of high-frequency trading: how the money got made, what sort of computer code was valuable, and so on. Malyshev testified *as a witness for the prosecution* that Goldman's code was of no use whatsoever in the system he'd hired Serge to build—Goldman's code was written in a different programming language, it was slow and clunky, it had been designed for a firm that was trading with its own customers, and Teza, Malyshev's firm, didn't have customers, and so on—but when he looked over, he saw that half the jury appeared to be sleeping. "If I were a juror, and I wasn't a programmer," said Serge, "it would be very difficult for me to understand why I did what I did."

Goldman Sachs's role in the trial was to make genuine understanding even more difficult. Its employees, on the witness stand, behaved more like salesmen for the prosecution than citizens of the state. "It's not that they lied," said Serge. "But they told things that were not in their expertise." When his former boss, Adam Schlesinger, was asked about the code, he said that everything at Goldman was proprietary. "I wouldn't say he lied, but he was talking about stuff that he did not understand, and so he was misunderstood," said Serge.

Our system of justice is a poor tool for digging out a rich truth. What was really needed, it seemed to me, was for Serge Aleynikov to be forced to explain what he had done, and why, to people able to understand the explanation and judge it. Goldman Sachs had never asked him to explain himself, and the FBI had not sought help from anyone who actually knew anything at all about computers or the high-frequency trading business. And so over two nights, in a private room of a Wall Street restaurant, I convened a kind of second trial. To serve as both jury and prosecution, I invited half a dozen people intimately familiar with Goldman Sachs, high-frequency trading, and computer programming. All were authorities on our abstruse new stock market; several had written high-frequency code; one had actually developed software for Goldman's high-frequency traders. All were men. They'd grown up in four different countries between them, but all now lived in the United States. All of them worked on Wall Street, and so, to express themselves freely, they needed to remain anonymous. Among them were employees of IEX.

All were naturally skeptical—of both Goldman Sachs and Serge Aleynikov. They assumed that if Serge had been sentenced to eight years in jail he must have done *something* wrong. They just hadn't bothered to figure out what that was. All of them had followed the case in the newspapers and noted the shiver it had sent through the spines of Wall Street's software developers. Until Serge was sent to jail for doing it, it was common practice for Wall Street programmers to take code they had worked on when they left for new jobs. "A guy got put in jail for taking something no one understood," as one of Serge's new jurors put it. "Every tech programmer out there got the message: Take code and you could go to jail. It was huge." The arrest of Serge Aleynikov had also caused a lot of people, for the first time, to begin to use the phrase "high-frequency trading." Another new juror, who in 2009 had worked for a big Wall Street bank, said, "When he was arrested, we had a meeting for all the electronic trading personnel, to talk about a one-pager they'd drafted to be discussed with their clients around this new topic called 'high-frequency trading.'"

The restaurant was one of those old-school Wall Street places that charge you a thousand bucks for a private room and then more or less challenge you to eat your way back to even. Food and drink arrived in massive quantities: vast platters of lobster and crab, steaks the size of desktop computer screens, smoking mountains of potatoes and spinach. It was the sort of meal cooked decades ago, for traders who spent their days trusting their gut and their nights rewarding it; but this monstrous feast was now being served to a collection of weedy technologists, the people who controlled the machines that now controlled the markets, and who had, in the bargain, put the old school out of business. They sat around the table staring at the piles of food, like a conquering army of eunuchs who had stumbled into the harem of their enemy. At any rate, they made hardly a dent. Serge, for his part, ate so little, and with such disinterest, that I half expected him to lift off his chair and float up to the ceiling.

His new jurors began, interestingly, by asking him lots of personal questions. They wanted to figure out what kind of guy he was. They took an interest, for example, in his job-market history, and noted that his behavior was pretty consistently that of a geek who had more interest in his work than in the money the work generated. They established fairly quickly—how, I do not know—that he was not just smart but seriously gifted. "These guys are usually smart in one small area," one of them later explained to me. "For a technologist to be so totally dominant in so many areas is just really, really unusual."

They then began to probe his career at Goldman Sachs. They were surprised to learn that he had "super-user status" inside Goldman, which is to say he was one of a handful of people (roughly 35, in a firm that then had more than 31,000 employees) who could log onto the system as an administrator. Such privileged access would have enabled him, at any time, to buy a cheap USB flash drive, plug it into his terminal, and take all of Goldman's computer code without anyone having any idea that he had done it. That fact alone didn't prove anything to them. As one pointed out to Serge directly, lots of thieves are sloppy and careless; just because he was sloppy and careless didn't mean he was not a thief. On the other hand, they all agreed, there wasn't anything the least bit suspicious, much less nefarious, about the manner in which he had taken what he had taken. Using a subversion repository to store code and deleting one's bash history were common practices. The latter made a great deal of sense if you typed your passwords into command lines. In short, Serge had not behaved like a man trying to cover his tracks. One of his new jurors stated the obvious: "If deleting the bash history was so clever and devious, why had Goldman ever found out he'd taken anything?"

To these new jurors, the story that the FBI found so unconvincing—that Serge had taken the files because he thought he might later like to parse the open source code contained within—made a lot of sense. As Goldman hadn't permitted him to release his debugged or improved code back to the public— even though the original free license often stated that improvements must be publicly shared—the only way for him to get his hands on these files was to take the Goldman code. That he had also taken some code that wasn't open source, which happened to be in the same files as the open source code, surprised no one. Grabbing a bunch of files that contained both open source and non–open source code was an efficient way for him to collect the open source code, even if the open source code was the only code that interested him. It would have made far less sense for him to hunt around the Internet for the open source code he wanted, as it was scattered all over cyberspace. It was also entirely plausible to them that Serge's interest was confined to the open source code, because that was the general-purpose code that might be repurposed later. The Goldman proprietary code was written specifically for Goldman's platform; it would have been of little use in any new system he wished to build. (The two small pieces of code Serge had sent into Teza's computers before his arrest both came with open source licenses.) "Even if he had taken Goldman's whole platform, it would have been faster and better for him to write the new platform himself," said one juror.

Several times Serge surprised the jurors with his answers. They were all shocked, for instance, that from the day Serge first arrived at Goldman, he had been able to send Goldman's

source code to himself weekly, without anyone at Goldman saying a word to him about it. "At Citadel, if you stick a USB drive
into your work station, someone is standing next to you within
five minutes, asking you what the hell you are doing," said a
juror who had worked there. Most were surprised by how little
Serge had taken in relation to the whole: eight megabytes, in a
platform that consisted of nearly fifteen hundred megabytes of
code. The most cynical among them were surprised mostly by
what he had *not* taken.

"Did you take the strats?" asked one, referring to Goldman's
high-frequency trading strategies.

"No," said Serge. That was one thing the prosecutors hadn't
accused him of.

"But that's the secret sauce, if there is one," said the juror. "If
you're going to take something, take the strats."

"I wasn't interested in the strats," said Serge.

"But that's like stealing the jewelry box without the jewels,"
said another juror.

"You had super-user status!" said the first. "You could easily
have taken the strats. Why didn't you?"

"To me, the technology really is more interesting than the
strats," said Serge.

"You weren't interested in how they made hundreds of millions of dollars?" asked someone else.

"Not really," said Serge. "It's all one big gamble, one way or
another."

Because they had seen it before in other programmer types,
they were not totally shocked by his indifference to Goldman's
trading, or by how far Goldman had kept him from the action.
Talking to a programmer type about the trading business was a
bit like talking to the house plumber at work in the basement

about the card game the Mafia don was running upstairs. "He knew *so* little about the business context," one of the jurors said, after attending both dinners. "You'd have to try to know as little as he did." Another said, "He knew as much as they wanted him to know about how they made money, which was virtually nothing. He wasn't there for very long. He came in with no context. And he spent all of his time troubleshooting." Another said he had found Serge to be the epitome of the programmer whose value the big Wall Street banks tried to minimize—by using their skills without fully admitting them into the business. "You see two résumés from the banks," he said. "You line them up on paper and say maybe there's a ten percent difference between them. But one guy is getting paid three hundred grand and the other is getting one point five million. The difference is one guy has been given the big picture, and the other hasn't." Serge had never been shown the big picture. Still, it was obvious to the jurors—even if it wasn't to Serge—why Goldman had hired him when it had. With the introduction of Reg NMS in 2007, the speed of any financial intermediary's trading system became its most important attribute: the speed with which it took in market data and the speed with which it responded to that data. "Whether he knew it or not," said one juror, "he was hired to build Goldman's view of the market. No Reg NMS, no Serge in finance."

At least some part of the reason he remained oblivious to the nature of Goldman Sachs's trading business, all of the jurors noticed, was that his heart was elsewhere. "I think passion plays a big role," said a juror who himself had spent his entire career writing code. "The moment he started talking about coding, his eyes lit up." Another added, "The fact that he kept trying to work on open source shit even while he was at Goldman says something about the guy."

They didn't all agree that what Serge had taken had no value, either to him or to Goldman. But what value it might have had in creating a new system would have been trivial and indirect. "I can guarantee you this: He did not steal code to use it on some other system," one said, and none of the others disagreed. For my part, I didn't fully understand why some parts of Goldman's system might not be useful in some other system. "Goldman's code base is like buying a really old house," one of the jurors explained. "And you take the trouble to soup it up. But it still has the problems of a really old house. Teza was going to build a new house, on new land. Why would you take one-hundred-year-old copper pipes and put them in my new house? It isn't that they couldn't be used; it's that the amount of trouble involved in making it useful is ridiculous." A third added, "It's *way* easier to start from scratch." Their conviction that Goldman's code was not terribly useful outside of Goldman grew even stronger when they learned—later, as Serge failed to mention it at the dinners—that the new system Serge planned to create was to be written in a different computer language than the Goldman code.

The perplexing question, at least to me, was why Serge had taken anything. A full month after he'd left Goldman Sachs, he still had not touched the code he had taken. If the code was so unimportant to him that he didn't bother to open it up and study it; if most of it was either so clunky or so peculiar to Goldman's system that it was next to useless outside Goldman—why take it? Oddly, his jurors didn't find this hard to understand. One put it this way: "If Person A steals a bike from Person B, then Person A is riding a bike to school, and Person B is walking. Person A is better off at the expense of Person B. That is clear-cut, and most people's view of theft.

"In Serge's case, think of being at a company for three years, and you carry a spiral notebook and write everything down. Everything about your meetings, your ideas, products, sales, client meetings—it's all written down in that notebook. You leave for your new job and take the notebook with you—as most people do. The contents of your notebook relate to your history at the prior company but have very little relevance to your new job. You may never look at it again. Maybe there are some ideas, or templates, or thoughts you can draw on. But that notebook is related to your prior job, and you will start a new notebook at your new job which will make the old one irrelevant. . . . For programmers, their code is their spiral notebook. [It enables them] to remember what they worked on—but it has very little relevance to what they will build next. . . . He took a spiral notebook that had very little relevance outside of Goldman Sachs."

To the well-informed jury, the real mystery wasn't why Serge had done what he had done. It was why Goldman Sachs had done what it had done. Why on earth call the FBI? Why exploit the ignorance of both the general public and the legal system about complex financial matters to punish this one little guy? Why must the spider always eat the fly?

The financial insiders had many theories about this: that it was an accident; that Goldman had called the FBI in haste and then realized the truth, but lost control of the legal process; that in 2009 Goldman had been on hair-trigger alert to personnel losses in high-frequency trading, because they could see how much money would be made from it, and thought they could compete in the business. The jurors all had ideas about why what had happened had happened. One of the theories was more intriguing than the others. It had to do with the nature of a big Wall Street bank, and the way people who worked for it, at the intersection of technology and trading, got ahead. As one juror put it, "Every manager of a Wall Street tech group likes to have people believe that his guys are geniuses. Russians, whatever. His whole persona among his peers is that what he and his team do can't be replicated. When people find out that ninety-five percent of their code is open source, it kills that perception. What the guy can't say, when he gets told Serge has taken something, is 'it doesn't matter what he took because it's worse than what they'll create on their own.' So when the security people come to him and tell him about the downloads, he can't say, 'No big deal.' And he can't say, 'I don't know what he took.'"

To put it another way: The process that ended with Serge Aleynikov sitting inside two holding facilities that housed dangerous offenders and then a federal prison may have started with the concern of some Goldman Sachs manager with his bonus. "Who is going to pull the fire alarm before they smell the fire?" asked the juror who had advanced this last theory. "It's always the people who are politically motivated." As he left dinner with Serge Aleynikov and walked down Wall Street, he thought about it some more. "I'm actually nauseous," he said. "It makes me sick."

THE MYSTERY THE jury of Sergey Aleynikov's peers had more trouble solving was Serge himself. He appeared, and perhaps even was, completely at peace with the world. Had you lined up the people at those two Wall Street dinners and asked the American public to vote for the man who had just lost his marriage, his home, his job, his life savings, and his reputation, Serge would have come dead last. At one point, one of the people at the table stopped the conversation about computer code and asked, "Why aren't you angry?" Serge just smiled back at him. "No, really," said the juror. "How do you stay so calm? I'd be fucking going crazy." Serge smiled again. "But what does craziness give you?" he said. "What does negative demeanor give you as a person? It doesn't give you anything. You know that something happened. Your life happened to go in that particular route. If you know that you're innocent, know it. But at the same time you know you are in trouble and this is how it's going to be." To which he added, "To some extent I'm glad this happened to me. I think it strengthened my understanding of what living is all about." At the end of his trial, when the original jury returned with its guilty verdict, Serge had turned to his lawyer, Kevin Marino, and said, "You know, it did not turn out the way we had hoped. But I have to say, it was a pretty good experience." It was as if he were standing outside himself and taking in the situation as an observer. "I've never seen anything like it," said Marino.

In the comfort of the Wall Street cornucopia, that notion—that the hellish experience he'd been through had actually been good for him—was too weird to pursue, and the jurors had quickly returned to discussing computer code and high-frequency trading. But Serge actually believed what he had said. Before his arrest—before he lost much of what he thought important in his life—he went through his days and nights in a certain state of mind: a bit self-absorbed, prone to anxiety and worry about his status in the world. "When I was arrested, I couldn't sleep," he said. "When I saw articles in the newspaper, I would tremble at the fear of losing my reputation. Now I just smile. I no longer panic. Or have panic ideas that something could go wrong." By the time he was first sent to jail, his wife had left him, taking their three young daughters with her. He had no money and no one to turn to. "He didn't have very close friends," his fellow

Russian émigré Masha Leder recalled. "He never did. He's not a people person. He didn't even have anyone to be power of attorney." Out of a sense of Russian solidarity, and out of pity, she took the job—which meant, among other things, frequent trips to visit Serge in prison. "Every time I would come to visit him in jail, I would leave energized by him," she said. "He radiated so much energy and positive emotions that it was like therapy for me to visit him. His eyes opened to how the world really is. And he started talking to people. For the first time! He would say: People in jail have the best stories. He could have considered himself a tragedy. And he didn't."

By far the most difficult part of his experience was explaining what had happened to his children. When he was arrested, his daughters were five, three, and almost one. "I tried to put it in the most simple terms they would understand," said Serge. "But the bottom line was I was apologizing for the fact that this had happened." In jail he was allowed three hundred minutes a month on the phone—and for a long time the kids, when he called them, didn't pick up on the other end.

The holding facility in which Serge spent his first four months was violent, and essentially nonverbal, but he didn't find it hard to stay out of trouble there. He even found people he could talk to, and enjoy talking to. When they moved him to the minimum-security prison at Fort Dix, in New Jersey, he was still in a room crammed with hundreds of other roommates, but he now had space to work. He remained in some physical distress, mainly because he refused to eat meat. "His body, he had really bad times there," said Masha Leder. "He lived on beans and rice. He was always hungry. I'd buy him these yogurts and he would gulp them down one after another." His mind still worked fine, though, and a lifetime of programming in cube farms had left him with the ability to focus in prison conditions. A few months into Serge's jail term, Masha Leder received a thick envelope from him. It contained roughly a hundred pages covered on both sides in Serge's meticulous eight-point script. It was computer code—a solution to some high-frequency trading problem. Serge feared that if the prison guards found it, they wouldn't understand it, decide that it was suspicious, and confiscate it.

A year after he'd been sent away, the appeal of Serge Aleynikov was finally heard, by the Second Circuit Court of Appeals. The judgment was swift, unlike anything his lawyer, Kevin Marino, had seen in his career. Marino was by then working gratis for a client who was dead broke. The very day he made his argument, the judges ordered Serge released, on the grounds that the laws he stood accused of breaking did not actually apply to his case. At six in the morning on February 17, 2012, Serge received an email from Kevin Marino saying that he was to be freed.

A few months later, Marino noticed that the government had failed to return Serge's passport. Marino called and asked for it back. The passport never arrived; instead Serge, now staying with friends in New Jersey, was arrested again and taken to jail. Once again, he had no idea what he was being arrested for, but this time neither did the police. The New Jersey cops who picked him up didn't know the charges, only that he should be held without bail, as he was deemed a flight risk. His lawyer was just as perplexed. "When I got the call," said Marino, "I thought it might have something to do with Serge's child support." It didn't. A few days later, Manhattan district attorney Cyrus Vance sent out a press release to announce that the State of New York was charging Serge Aleynikov with "accessing and duplicating a complex proprietary and highly confidential computer source code owned by Goldman Sachs." The press release went on to say that "[t]his code is so highly confidential that it is known in the industry as the firm's 'secret sauce,'" and thanked Goldman Sachs for its cooperation. The prosecutor assigned to the case, Joanne Li, claimed that Serge was a flight risk and needed to be re-jailed immediately—which was strange, because Serge had gone to and returned from Russia between the time of his first arrest and his first jailing. (It was Li who soon fled the case—to a job at Citigroup.)

Marino recognized the phrase "secret sauce." It hadn't come from "the industry" but from his opening statement in Serge's first trial, when he mocked the prosecutors for treating Goldman's code as if it were some "secret sauce." Otherwise Serge's re-arrest made no sense to him. To avoid double jeopardy, the Manhattan DA's office had found new crimes with which to charge Serge for the same actions. But the sentencing guidelines for the new crimes meant that, even if he was convicted, it was very likely he wouldn't have to return to jail. He'd already served time, for crimes the court ultimately determined he had not committed. Marino called Vance's office. "They told me that they didn't need him to be punished anymore, but they need him to be held accountable," said Marino. "They want him to plead guilty and let him go on time served. I told them in the politest terms possible that they can go fuck themselves. They ruined his life."

Oddly enough, they hadn't. "Inside of me I was completely witnessing," said Serge, about the night of his re-arrest. "There was no fear, no panic, no negativity." His children had reattached themselves to him, and he had a new world of people to whom he felt close. He thought he was living his life as well as it had ever been lived. He'd even started a memoir, to explain what had happened to anyone who might be interested. He began:

If the incarceration experience doesn't break your spirit, it changes you in a way that you lose many fears. You begin to realize that your life is not ruled by your ego and ambition and that it can end any day at any time. So why worry? You learn that just like on the street, there is life in prison, and random people get there based on the jeopardy of the system. The prisons are filled by people who crossed the law, as well as by those who were incidentally and circumstantially picked and crushed by somebody else's agenda. On the other hand, as a vivid benefit, you become very much independent of material property and learn to appreciate very simple pleasures in life such as the sunlight and morning breeze.

RIDING THE
WALL STREET TRAIL

For at least a few members of the Women's Adventure Club of Centre County, Pennsylvania, the weather was never much of an issue. The Women's Adventure Club had been created by Lisa Wandel, an administrator at Penn State University, after she realized that many women were afraid to hike alone in the woods. The club now had more than seven hundred members, and its sense of adventure had expanded far beyond a walk in the woods. Between them the four women who met me on their bicycles beside the Pennsylvania road had: learned the flying trapeze, swum the Chesapeake Bay, and won silver at the downhill mountain biking world championships; they had finished a road bike race called the Gran Fondo "Masochistic Metric," a footrace called the Tough Mudder, and three separate twenty-four-hour-long mountain bike races; they had graduated from race car driving school and made thirteen Polar Bear Plunges in some local river in the dead of winter. After studying the Women's Adventure Club's website, Ronan had said, "It's a bunch of lunatic women who meet up and do dangerous shit; I got to get my wife into it."

In the bleak January light we pedaled onto Route 45 out of Boalsburg, Pennsylvania, heading east, along what was once the route for the stagecoach that ran from Philadelphia to Erie. It was nine in the morning, and still below freezing, with a stiff breeze lowering the windchill to eleven degrees. The views were of farms and fallow brown fields, and the road was empty except for the occasional pickup truck, roaring past us with real anger. "They hate bikers," explained one of the women adventurers mildly. "They try to see how close they can get."

The women rode this stretch of road every so often, and had noticed when the fiber-optic line was being laid beside it, back in 2010. From time to time one of the road's two lanes was closed by the line's construction crews. You'd see these motley queues of bikes, cars, pickup trucks, Amish horse-drawn carts, and farm equipment waiting for the tail end of the oncoming traffic. The crews trenched the ground between the paved road and the farms, making it difficult for the Amish in their wagons to get back to their homes—sometimes you'd see these Amish kids, the girls in their pretty purple dresses, hopping off the wagon and leaping over the trench. The members of the Women's Adventure Club had been told by a local government official that the fiber-optic line was a government project to provide high-speed Internet access to local colleges. Hearing that it was actually a private project to provide a 3-millisecond edge to high-frequency traders, they had some new questions about it. "How does a private line get access to a public right-of-way?" asked one. "I'm really curious to know that."

———

WE'RE IN A *transition here*. That's what the Goldman Sachs people said when you asked them, in so many words, how they could have gone from bringing the wrath of U.S. prosecutors down upon Serge Aleynikov for emailing their high-frequency trading computer code to himself, to helping Brad Katsuyama change the U.S. stock market in ways that would render Goldman's high-frequency trading computer code worthless.

There was a connection between Serge Aleynikov and Goldman's behavior on December 19, 2013. The trial and the publicity that attended it caused a lot of people to think more rigorously about the value of Goldman Sachs's high-frequency trading code. High-frequency trading had a winner-take-all aspect: The fastest predator took home the fattest prey. By 2013 the people charged with determining Goldman's stock market strategy had concluded that Goldman wasn't very good at this new game, and that Goldman was unlikely ever to be very good at it. The high-frequency traders would *always* be faster than Goldman Sachs—or any other big Wall Street bank. The people who ran Goldman Sachs's stock market department had come to understand that what Serge had taken wasn't worth stealing—at least not by anyone whose chief need was speed.

The trouble for any big Wall Street bank wasn't simply that a big bureaucracy was ill-suited to keeping pace with rapid technological change, but that the usual competitive advantages of a big Wall Street bank were of little use in high-frequency trading. A big Wall Street bank's biggest advantage was its access to vast amounts of cheap risk capital and, with that, its ability to survive the ups and downs of a risky business. That meant little when the business wasn't risky and didn't require much capital. High-frequency traders went home every night with no position in the stock market. They traded in the market the way card counters in a casino played blackjack: They played only when they had an edge. That's why they were able to trade for five years without losing money on a single day.

A big Wall Street bank really had only one advantage in an ever-faster financial market: first shot at its own customers' stock market trades. So long as the customers remained inside the dark pool, and in the dark, the bank might profit at their expense. But even here the bank would never do the job as efficiently or thoroughly as a really good HFT. It was hard to resist the pressure to hand the prey over to the more skilled predator, to ensure that the kill was done quickly and discreetly, and then, after the kill, to join in the feast as a kind of junior partner—though more junior than partner. In the dark pool arbitrage IEX had witnessed, for instance, HFT captured about 85 percent of the gains, leaving the bank with just 15 percent.

The new structure of the U.S. stock market had removed the big Wall Street banks from their historic, lucrative role as intermediary. At the same time it created, for any big bank, some unpleasant risks: that the customer would somehow figure out what was happening to his stock market orders. And that the technology might some-how go wrong. If the markets collapsed, or if another flash crash occurred, the high-frequency traders would not take 85 percent of the blame, or bear 85 percent of the costs of the inevitable lawsuits. The banks would bear the lion's share of the blame and the costs. The relationship of the big Wall Street banks to the high-frequency traders, when you thought about it, was a bit like the relationship of the entire society to the big Wall Street banks. When things went well, the HFT guys took most of the gains; when things went badly, the HFT guys vanished and the banks took the losses.

Goldman had figured all of this out—probably before the other big Wall Street banks, to judge from its treatment of IEX.

By December 19, 2013, the people newly installed on top of Goldman Sachs's stock market operations, Ron Morgan and Brian Levine, wanted to change the way the market worked. They were obviously sincere. They truly believed that the market at the heart of the world's largest economy had grown too complex, and was likely to experience some catastrophic failure. But they also were trying to put an end to a game they could never win—or control. And so they'd flipped a switch, and sent lots of their customers' stock market orders to IEX. When they did this they started a process that, if allowed to play out, would take billions from Wall Street and return it to investors. It would also create fairness.

A big Wall Street bank was a complex environment. There were people inside Goldman Sachs less than pleased by what Levine and Morgan had done. And after December 19 the firm had retreated, just a little bit. It was hard even for Brad Katsuyama to know why. Was it changing its collective mind? Had it underestimated the cost of being the first mover? Was it too much to ask Goldman Sachs to look up from short-term profit and study the landscape down the road? It was possible that even Goldman Sachs did not know the answers to those questions. Whatever the answers, something Brian Levine had said still made a lot of sense. "There will be a lot of resistance," he'd said. "There will be a *lot* of resistance. Because a tremendous infrastructure has been built up around this."

It's worth performing a Goldman Sachs–like cost-benefit analysis of this infrastructure, from the point of view of the economy it is meant to serve. The benefit: Stock market prices adjust to new information a few milliseconds faster than they otherwise might. The costs make for a longer list. One obvious cost is the instability introduced into the system when its primary goal is no longer stability but speed. Another is the incalculable billions collected by financial intermediaries. That money is a tax on investment, paid for by the economy; and the more that productive enterprise must pay for capital, the less productive enterprise there will be. Another cost, harder to measure, was the influence all this money exerted, not just on the political process but on people's decisions about what to do with their lives. The more money to be made gaming the financial markets, the more people would decide they were put on earth to game the financial markets—and create romantic narratives to explain to themselves why a life spent gaming the financial markets is a purposeful life. And then there is maybe the greatest cost of all: Once very smart people are paid huge sums of money to exploit the flaws in the financial system, they have the spectacularly destructive incentive to screw the system up further, or to remain silent as they watch it being screwed up by others.

The cost, in the end, is a tangled-up financial system. Untangling it requires acts of commercial heroism—and even then the fix might not work. There was simply too much more easy money to be made by elites if the system worked badly than if it worked well. The whole culture had to want to change. "We know how to cure this," as Brad had put it. "It's just a matter of whether the patient wants to be treated."

FOR A LONG stretch along the Spread Networks line, there was no happy place for a rider to stop. The road's shoulder was narrow, and the cornfields beside it were planted with No Trespassing signs. Apart from the plastic soda bottle and the carcasses of deer killed by the speeding pickup trucks, and a shop or two, the landscape looked a lot like it once did from the Philadelphia-

Erie stagecoach. The most insistent signs of modernity were the white poles with their bright orange domes, every few hundred yards, installed three and a half years earlier. After ten miles or so we found an open field without a sign and pulled over beside a white-and-orange pole. The poles stretched into the distance in both directions. An ambitious hiker or cyclist could follow them all the way to a building beside the Nasdaq stock exchange, in New Jersey; or, if he turned and headed west, to the Chicago Mercantile Exchange.

Across the road was a local landmark: the Red Round Barn. One of the women repeated a rural legend, saying that the red barn had been built in the round so that mice had no corners in which to hide. "People don't know how to live in a world that is transparent," Brad Katsuyama had said, and mice were probably no better at it. Beyond the barn was a mountain. On top of the mountain was a microwave tower—a string of them, in fact, perched on the mountains above the valley in which the line was buried.

It takes roughly 8 milliseconds to send a signal from Chicago to New York and back by microwave signal, or about 4.5 milliseconds less than to send it inside an optical fiber. When Spread Networks was laying its line, the conventional wisdom was that microwave could never replace fiber. It might be faster, but whatever was going on between New York and Chicago required huge amounts of complicated data to be sent back and forth, and a microwave signal couldn't transmit nearly as much data as a signal in a fiber-optic cable. Microwave signals needed a direct line of sight to get to wherever they were going, with nothing in between. And microwave signals didn't travel well in bad weather.

But what if microwave technology improved? And what if the

data essential for some high-frequency trader to gain an edge over investors in the market wasn't actually all that complicated? And what if the tops of mountains afforded a direct line of sight between distant financial markets?

The risks taken by high-frequency traders were not the usual risks taken by people who purport to sit in the middle of markets, buying from sellers and selling to buyers. They didn't risk buying a bunch of shares in a falling stock, or selling a bunch of shares in a rising one. They were too skittish and well informed for that—with one obvious exception. They were all exposed to the risk that the entire stock market would move, by a lot. A big high-frequency trader might "make markets" in several thousand individual stocks in New Jersey. As the purpose of these buy and sell orders was not to buy and sell stock but to tease out market information from others, the orders would typically be tiny in each stock: 100 shares bid, 100 shares offered. There was little risk in any individual case but great risk in the aggregate. If, say, some piece of bad news hit the market, and the entire stock market fell, it would take all the individual stocks with it. Any high-frequency traders who did not receive advance warning would be left owning 100 shares each of several thousand different stocks they did not want to own, with big losses in each.

But the U.S. stock market had an accidental beauty to it, from the point of view of a trader who wished to trade only when he had some edge. The big moves occurred first in the futures market in Chicago, before sweeping into the markets for individual stocks. If you were able to detect these moves, and warn your computers in New Jersey of price movements in Chicago, you could simply withdraw your bids for individual stocks before the market fully realized that it had fallen. That's why it was so important for high-frequency traders to move information faster than everyone else from the futures exchange in Chicago to the stock markets in New Jersey: to flee the market before others. This race was run not just against ordinary investors, or even Wall Street banks, but also against other high-frequency traders. The first high-frequency trader to reach New Jersey with the news could sell 100 shares each in thousands of different stocks to the others.

After some obligatory staring at the Red Round Barn, we jumped back on our bikes and continued. A few miles down the road, we turned onto the road leading to the summit of a mountain with a tower on top of it. The woman who had won the silver medal at the downhill mountain biking world championships sighed. "I like going down more than going up," she said, then took off at speed, leaving everyone else behind. Soon I was watching the backs of female riders, climbing rapidly. It could have been worse: The Appalachians are mercifully old and worn. This particular mountain, once the size of a Swiss Alp, had been shrunken by half a billion years of bad weather. It was now almost beneath the dignity of the Women's Adventure Club.

It took maybe twenty minutes to puff to the top of the road, where the women adventurers stood waiting. From there we turned onto a smaller road leading into the woods, headed in the direction of the mountaintop. We rode through the woods for a few hundred yards until the road ended—or, rather, was barricaded by a new metal gate. There we ditched our bikes, leapt over the signs warning of various dangers, and hiked onto a gravel path that continued to the mountaintop. The women didn't think twice about any of this: To them it was just another adventure. A few minutes later the microwave tower came into view.

"I climbed up one of these towers once," one of the women said a bit wistfully.

The tower was 180 feet high, with no ladder, and festooned with electrical equipment. "Why did you do that?" I asked.

"I was pregnant and it was a lot of work," she replied, as if that answered the question.

"And that's why your baby had seven toes!" hooted one of the other women, and they all laughed.

If one of the women had hopped over the fence around the tower and climbed to the top, she would have had an unobstructed view of the next tower and, from there, the tower beyond. This was just one in a chain of thirty-eight towers that carried news of the direction of the stock market from Chicago to New Jersey: up or down; buy or sell; in or out. We walked around the site. The tower showed some signs of age. It could have been erected some time ago, for some other purpose. But the ancillary equipment—the generator, a concrete bunker to hold God knows what—was all shiny and new. The repeaters that amplify financial signals resembled kettle drums, bolted onto the side of the tower: These were also new. The speed with which they transmitted signals, and with which the computers on either end of the chain of towers turned the signals into financial actions, were still as difficult to comprehend as the forces of nature once had been. Anything said about them could be believed. *People no longer are responsible for what happens in the market, because computers make all the decisions.* And in the beginning God created the heaven and the earth.

I noticed, before we left, a metal plate attached to the fence around the tower. On it was a Federal Communications Commission license number: 1215095. The number, along with an Internet connection, was enough to lead an inquisitive person to the story behind the tower. The application to use the tower to send a microwave signal had been filed in July 2012, and it had been filed by . . . well, it isn't possible to keep any of this secret anymore. A day's journey in cyberspace would lead anyone who wished to know it into another incredible but true Wall Street story, of hypocrisy and secrecy and the endless quest by human beings to gain a certain edge in an uncertain world. All that one needed to discover the truth about the tower was the desire to know it.

ACKNOWLEDGMENTS

The U.S. financial system has experienced many changes since I first entered it, and one of them is in its relationship to any writer who attempts to figure out what's going on inside of it. Wall Street firms—not just the big banks but all of them—have grown greatly more concerned than they were in the late 1980s with what some journalist might say about them. To judge only from their behavior, they have a lot more to fear. They are more likely than they once were to seek to shape any story told about them. At the same time, the people who work in these firms have grown more cynical about them, and more willing to reveal their inner workings, so long as their name is not attached to these revelations. As a result, I am unable to thank many of the people inside banks and high-frequency trading firms and stock exchanges who spoke openly about them, and helped me to comprehend the seemingly incomprehensible.

Some other people not mentioned in this book were important to its creation. Jacob Weisberg read an early draft and had shrewd things to say about it. At different times and in different ways, Dacher Keltner, Tabitha Soren, and Doug Stumpf listened to me drone on at length about what I was working on, and responded with thoughts that never would have occurred to me. Jaime Lalinde helped me, invaluably, in researching the case of Serge Aleynikov. I apologize to Ryan Harrington, at W. W. Norton, for sending him chasing around for illustrations that I thought might be useful but which turned out to be a dumb idea. He did it very well, though.

Starling Lawrence has edited my books since I first started writing them, with his peculiar combination of encouragement and detachment. He edited this one, too, and I've never benefited so much from his unwillingness to allow me to enjoy even the briefest moment of self-satisfaction. The third member of our team, Janet Byrne, is the finest copy editor I have ever worked with. Many mornings her enthusiasm got me out of my bed, and many evenings her diligence prevented me from getting back into it.

Finally, I'd like not only to thank the employees of IEX but also to list them by name, so one day people can look back and know them. They are: Lana Amer, Benjamin Aisen, Daniel Aisen, Joshua Blackburn, Donald Bollerman, James Cape, Francis Chung, Adrian Facini, Stan Feldman, Brian Foley, Ramon Gonzalez, Bradley Katsuyama, Craig Katsuyama, Joe Kondel, Gerald Lam, Frank Lennox, Tara McKee, Rick Molakala, Tom O'Brien, Robert Park, Stefan Parker, Zoran Perkov, Eric Quinlan, Ronan Ryan, Rob Salman, Prerak Sanghvi, Eric Schmid, John Schwall, Constantine Sokoloff, Beau Tateyama, Matt Trudeau, Larry Yu, Allen Zhang, and Billy Zhao.